M

M & E Handbooks are recommended reading for examination syllabuses all over the world. Because each Handbook covers its subject clearly and concisely, books in the series form a vital part of many college, university, school and home study courses.

Handbooks contain detailed information stripped of unnecessary padding, making each title a comprehensive self-tuition course. They are amplified with numerous self-testing questions in the form of Progress Tests at the end of each chapter, each text-referenced for easy checking. Every Handbook closes with an appendix which advises on examination technique. For all these reasons, Handbooks are ideal for pre-examination revision.

The handy pocket-size and competitive price make Handbooks the perfect choice for anyone who wants to grasp the essentials of a subject quickly and easily.

To P.J.S.

THE M & E HANDBOOK SERIES

Modern Economic History

British Economic and Social History 1760–1978

Edmund Seddon
MA

Senior Lecturer in Economics,
Faculty of Business and Management Studies,
Liverpool Polytechnic

THIRD EDITION

MACDONALD AND EVANS

Macdonald & Evans Ltd.
Estover, Plymouth PL6 7PZ

First published 1966
Reprinted 1966
Reprinted 1967
Reprinted 1969
Reprinted 1970
Reprinted 1972
Second edition 1974
Reprinted 1976
Third edition 1979

© Macdonald & Evans Limited 1979

7121 1286 3

This book is copyright and may not be re-
produced in whole or in part (except for
purposes of review) without the express permission of the publishers in writing.

Printed in Great Britain by
Richard Clay (The Chaucer Press) Ltd,
Bungay, Suffolk

Preface to the First Edition

This HANDBOOK aims to provide the student with material for examination but in such a way that the significance of long-term movements in history is made clear. It is hoped that it will meet the needs of candidates for the G.C.E. at Ordinary and Advanced Levels and should also prove of value to students of Modern Economic History in the Part 2 external B.Sc.(Econ.) of London University.

In so far as economic theory and economic history are complementary studies, the book may be of assistance to the general student of economics. Equally, some knowledge of economic analysis is advantageous to a full understanding of historical trends. To this end, some attention has been given in this book to theory, particularly in respect of monetary and full employment policies.

While the subject matter in each chapter is intended to be as self-supporting as possible, the student is nevertheless advised to work through the book in the sequence given and, before attempting a fresh chapter, to check his progress with the tests provided.

Examination Questions

Specimen examination questions are placed under general headings which correspond to the parts of the book. In many cases, however, it will also be necessary to draw upon information provided elsewhere in the book.

I am indebted to the following bodies for permission to reprint their examination questions:

Joint Matriculation Board of the Universities of Manchester, Liverpool, Leeds, Sheffield and Birmingham (J.M.B.); University of London.

November 1965

E.S.

v

Preface to the Third Edition

In revising the text for this edition, while some attention has been given to reinterpretation of earlier history, the main emphasis has been on more recent events, particular account being taken of the implications for society and the economy of membership of the European Community. The book's coverage of earlier history coupled with a subject-based approach remain appropriate to the needs of G.C.E. students. Since, however, it is the author's view that contemporary problems cannot be clearly understood without tracing their historical origins, it is hoped that the updating of various topics will be of particular interest to students following economics and business courses. In this respect some historical background would seem appropriate to the new Business Education Council (BEC) courses, specifically in the modules concerned with the organisation in its environment. It is in this area that history can be of great value in integrating the insights of the economist, the political scientist, the sociologist and the lawyer.

May 1979   E. S.

Contents

PART FOUR: COMMERCE

PART ONE
THE RISE OF LAISSEZ-FAIRE

CHAPTER I

The Foundations of a Capitalist Society

THE SIGNIFICANCE OF THE INDUSTRIAL REVOLUTION

1. The nature of history. In examining any branch of history, it is tempting to visualise a series of landmarks, following each of which, in a moment of time, the political, cultural or economic scene was transformed.

However, history does not unfold in this way. It is a process of gradual and almost imperceptible change, in which many threads are interwoven to produce a dominant pattern. It is the historian's task to unravel these threads and to evaluate their contribution to the over-all design.

2. A popular view of the industrial Revolution. The true significance of the Industrial Revolution is frequently misunderstood. It is popularly supposed to mark the beginning of modern economic life. It is assumed that until then England was a primitive, rural society made up of self-supporting communities and with little trade or industry.

The development of the steam engine, textile machinery, machine tools and new processes for iron smelting in the late eighteenth century are supposed in themselves to have given rise to the following phenomena which we associate with today's industrial society.

(*a*) *The capitalist system of production* on a large scale, with its central figure, the entrepreneur, i.e. the business organiser who hires labour, raises capital and accepts the risks of production in the expectation of a profit.

(b) *A wage-earning proletariat* deriving its strength from association in trade unions.

(c) *A cleavage of interest* in the system of production between labour and capital, expressing itself in open antagonism.

(d) *A market economy*, which implies a dependence upon fluctuating home and overseas demand. This in turn gives rise to the danger of unemployment and allied social problems.

(e) *Trusts and cartels.* Monopolies and price rings are commonly considered to be the product of industrialism in its most sophisticated form.

3. A balanced view. The facts do not support this popular conception. The capitalist system of production was well entrenched long before 1760, the date which traditionally marks the beginning of the Industrial Revolution. This is shown by the following.

(a) *The separation of the functions* of the capital-providing employer and the wage-earning workman (the hallmark of the capitalist system) was already clearly perceptible.

(b) *The entrepreneur* was already the mainspring of production in industry, commerce and agriculture.

(c) *National markets* had already begun to replace local markets while, overseas, English manufactures were in great demand.

(d) *Many of the problems* of a capitalist society (e.g. unemployment, depressed wages, poor working conditions, long hours of work) were apparent before the advent of machinery.

The great inventions of the eighteenth and early nineteenth centuries, which we identify with the Industrial Revolution, were not conjured up magically to give rise to a capitalist system but were the product of a society already organised on a capitalist basis.

4. The laissez-faire doctrine. The motive force of this society was an unshakeable belief in *laissez-faire.* The doctrine of the French physiocratic school of philosophers crossed the Channel in the eighteenth century to give formal expression to views which had long been developing in England. It taught that a natural law governed the affairs of the universe and that man, a creature of nature, could only develop free and unfettered if imperfect human law was kept to a minimum.

The economic implication was that if every man were allowed

to pursue his own genuine self-interest, society would benefit from a general increase in prosperity. Unrestrained private enterprise was therefore the accepted order.

5. Conclusion. The technical advances of the Industrial Revolution, although giving immeasurable impetus to England's subsequent economic growth, were themselves the climax of a long evolutionary process (*see* Fig. 1 on p. 14). In order to give perspective to events after 1760, it is therefore necessary to make some examination of these formative influences.

ORGANISATION OF AGRICULTURE IN THE MIDDLE AGES

6. The manor. The Middle Ages may be said to span the period from the eleventh to the mid-fifteenth centuries, and during that time English agriculture was based upon the manor.

The manor was a large estate centred upon a village and sometimes surrounded by a hedge which separated it from adjacent manors or from wilderness. Each manor had its lord, who was a tenant of the king. He occupied the manor house, the most substantial building in the village.

7. Manorial self-sufficiency. The economic objective of the manor was self-sufficiency, and this was widely—although never completely—achieved. Bread, ale, milk, eggs, beef and mutton were all produced from the manor's own resources. In the cottages, wool was spun and woven into a rough cloth and the hides of the cattle were made into shoes.

However, it was beyond the manor's resources to produce luxury items such as silk, muslin or certain necessities such as salt, iron implements and weapons, needles, thread and nails. These were obtained in neighbouring towns.

8. Minimal use of money. Internally, the manor had little use for money. Goods and services were paid for in kind. Money was only necessary for the limited amount of external trade.

9. Division of the land. The manor was divided into the demesne, the land tilled for the lord's benefit, and the outland which fed the serfs. Since the latter held their land only by custom and not by legal right, strictly the whole manor was demesne land save for the holdings of a few free men.

10. The open fields. The land was divided into two or more, usually three, great open fields. Each field was divided into broad belts or "shots" and each shot into strips between one and four rods (5–20 m) wide and a furlong (about 0.2 km) in length. The strips were separated by balks of unploughed earth.

(*a*) Some strips were held by the lord and others by his serfs but no one man had a consolidated holding. Everyone's strips were scattered throughout the three fields.

(*b*) Meadowland which yielded hay was also divided into strips, each man reaping his own.

(*c*) The waste comprised the common pasture and woodland to which all had certain rights.

11. Social organisation. The lord, his bailiff, the village priest and a number of liberated serfs constituted the free men.

(*a*) *Villeins.* These were serfs, not slaves. They had certain disabilities but also customary rights. They held a cottage and about thirty acres of land and had legal rights against anyone save their lord. In return, they gave labour service on the lord's strips, cartage service and special "boon" service at harvest time. However, they might not leave the manor, marry, learn to read, sell their oxen nor do many other things without their lord's consent.

(*b*) *Bordars and cottars.* These were villeins with a smaller land-holding. Since their labour service was reduced accordingly, they had time to work for wages on the strips of the lord or the more substantial villeins, or to work as carpenters, blacksmiths, etc.

12. The character of manorial life. The manor was a tightly-knit community whose life was regulated by custom and by decisions taken collectively, e.g. the routines of agriculture. There was little scope or need for individual enterprise, with the result that the principal characteristic of manorial life—as indeed of all medieval life—was stability.

This same feature pointed also to stagnation, since custom was a bar to experiment and improvement.

THE ORGANISATION OF TRADE IN THE MIDDLE AGES

13. Towns and trade. Medieval towns, with few exceptions, were small. By the fourteenth century, there were only about forty with populations in excess of 1,000.

The majority owed their existence to the stimulus of trade, since the accumulation of valuable merchandise in a village, a harbour or route junction necessitated the building of some form of protective wall, the hallmark of a town.

14. Freedom from controls. The new towns at first had obligations to the lord of the manor of which they were a part. As the wealth of the burgesses increased, so they were able to purchase charters which gave them freedom to regulate their own affairs. This they did through a borough court which was both a legal and an administrative body.

In addition, the charter normally made townsmen free men and guaranteed certain privileges to the merchant gilds.

15. The merchant gilds. Since a communal spirit pervaded every aspect of medieval life, it is not surprising that the merchants of a town tended to group together to advance their common interests. These associations were termed merchant gilds. They had the privilege of trade within the town, free of the tolls imposed upon strangers.

16. Aims of the merchant gilds. In the same way that agricultural practice was governed by custom and collective decisions, so the gilds regulated trade in order to:

(*a*) *guarantee a "just price"*, i.e. the customary price, fair both to buyer and seller;

(*b*) *guarantee standards of quality and quantity* in order to protect the consumer from dishonest practice;

(*c*) *protect their members* from the bad debts of gild members in other towns; they often did this by distraining upon the goods of other members of the debtor's gild;

(*d*) *share out the benefit* to all members of a cheap purchase of goods made by any one of them (the "right of lot").

THE ORGANISATION OF INDUSTRY IN THE MIDDLE AGES

17. The craft gilds. Associations of craftsmen existed in the towns as early as the twelfth century. Like the merchants, craftsmen were drawn together by common interests. The town authorities encouraged them, since the organisation of a craft made its regulation in the public interest easier.

When membership eventually became compulsory, the gilds were able to exercise complete control over the practice of their crafts. However, with few exceptions, they were themselves subject to the authority of the borough council.

18. Functions of the gilds. A council imposed regulations whose broad intention was to ensure justice to both buyer and producer and to develop a corporate pride and sense of responsibility.

(*a*) *Minimum standards* of workmanship and material were imposed.

(*b*) *The council insisted upon a "just price"* which would remain stable in times of scarcity or excess.

(*c*) *Wages* were regulated.

(*d*) *Apprenticeships* were regulated. Admission to a craft was controlled in the interest of efficient training and, later, to forestall an excessive supply of craftsmen. The responsibility of the master craftsman for his apprentices extended to their moral and religious instruction.

(*e*) *Philanthropic activities* might include the provision of almshouses, schools and relief in sickness or distress for members and their dependants.

(*f*) *The gilds adjudicated in disputes* between their members.

The relationship between employer and employee was not antagonistic. Journeymen (qualified workmen) and apprentices were not destined to a life as wage earners, but later in their careers would themselves assume positions as master craftsmen.

19. Relationship between merchant and craft gilds. Frequently, the merchant gildsmen were themselves the town government. In the twelfth and thirteenth centuries, therefore, the merchant gilds were dominant but in the fourteenth and fifteenth centuries, with the extension of industry and trade, the wealthier craftsmen tended to become the merchants of their own product and members of both types of gild.

The merchant gilds therefore tended to sub-divide into gilds closely associated with particular crafts.

THE GROWTH OF INDIVIDUALISM IN INDUSTRY

20. The rise of self-interest. Between the twelfth and fifteenth centuries, planning and regulation by the municipal or village authorities were the principal features of economic life. The aim was social harmony and well-being, and to this extent all forms of production were regarded as a public service rather than as a means of self-aggrandisement.

During this time, man's strong acquisitive instinct was largely contained within the framework of a corporate society. As industry and trade prospered, there began to evolve in the towns a middle class whose ambitions, drive and energy laid the foundations of England's greatness as an industrial and commercial nation.

Under these pressures, the craft gilds began to decay. Capital became more essential to production, and the wealthier master craftsmen began to emerge as an employing class. Their journeymen and apprentices, who now had little chance of advancement, became antagonistic to their employers. The gilds themselves became narrow in their outlook, insisting upon their monopolies but caring little for fair dealing.

21. The domestic system. The declining craft system was replaced by the domestic system of production which survived into the nineteenth century. The new entrepreneurial class of merchants and ex-master craftsmen co-ordinated the production of a large number of craftsmen, providing raw materials and marketing the product.

The workman now lost his independence. He remained a wage earner permanently, subject to the direction of an employer even though he still used his own tools and worked in his own home.

EXAMPLES: (1) In England's oldest industry, woollen manufacturing, the entrepreneur can be traced to the fourteenth century. By the close of the fifteenth century, the majority of woollen workers were directed by owners of capital. (2) By the seventeenth century, the entrepreneur had risen to prominence in the other great English staple industries, coal and iron.

Ambition and self-interest provided the driving force towards an individualist and capitalist system of production, but we must look further afield for the opportunities through which ambition was satisfied.

(A capitalist system is one in which labour and capital are provided by two distinct classes of people.)

22. Expansion of the market. Trade and industry prospered slowly through the Middle Ages, and by the fourteenth century a vigorous market was developing both at home and abroad.

(*a*) *Home market.* There was already trade in some commodities on a national scale, e.g. London drew woollen cloth in specialised forms from East Anglia, coal from Tyneside, agricultural produce from the Home Counties. London was not alone among the towns in its dependence upon the produce of the nation.

(*b*) *Overseas markets.* English manufactures, particularly woollen cloth, had long enjoyed a high reputation and a wide sale in Europe. With the discovery of America and a sea route to India, vast new outlets were opened.

Increasingly, it became impossible for small producers, working in isolation, to satisfy demand and it was a natural development that they should be superseded by entrepreneurs who co-ordinated their efforts. Moreover, organisation called for the outlay of large sums of money and only the wealthy merchant or master craftsman had access to such funds.

Frequently he was able to meet his capital requirements from his personal resources but, if not, financial and commercial institutions were developing which could assist him.

23. Sixteenth-century financial and commercial institutions. By the sixteenth century, the scale of enterprise was such that fresh capital was often required. This was especially true in overseas trade, in which English merchants were beginning to participate for the first time. Previously English overseas trade had been conducted by foreign merchants from the Baltic, in the north, and Italy, in the south.

Geographical discoveries in the reign of Elizabeth widened the market but overseas ventures were costly and risky. In response, there developed the following institutions.

(*a*) *Banking.* Fundamentally, the business of banking consists of accepting deposits and making loans on payment of interest. During the Middle Ages, this had not been possible, since the Church condemned the practice of usury. Later, economic pressures began to weaken the traditional morality. In the hands of wealthy merchants and goldsmiths, modern deposits banking was created.

There is ample evidence that the business world was only too anxious to avail itself of the opportunity of credit and by the end of the seventeenth century a large part of English commerce was conducted on this basis.

(*b*) *The joint stock company.* This is a device for financing an enterprise with a stock of capital contributed by many investors. They participate in profits in proportion to their subscription.

By the seventeenth century, this principle was widely applied in overseas trade, e.g. the Hudson's Bay Company and the East India Company.

(*c*) *Insurance.* The risks of overseas trading were reduced by marine insurance, which was first practised in England in the sixteenth century.

Assisted by these institutions, trade and industry prospered, with control increasingly concentrated in the hands of a class of entrepreneurs. Long before the Industrial Revolution of 1760, therefore, the organisation of industry and commerce was capitalistic and individualistic. This assertion may be supported by further evidence.

24. Further evidence of early industrial capitalism.

(*a*) *Antagonism between employer and employee.* Medieval harmony was replaced by open antagonism as the domestic system expanded the wage-earning class. The woollen industry was the first to succumb but was swiftly followed by linen and, in the seventeenth century, the nascent silk and cotton industries. In coal, iron, copper, brass, salt, paper, glass and soap, the need for large investments in raw materials and equipment brought forth an industrial proletariat.

Medieval custom, which had hitherto protected the worker's interest, fell into disuse. Discontent made itself manifest in numerous attempts to organise labour in opposition to the employer, e.g. fifteenth-century gilds of journeymen.

By the early eighteenth century, there was much trade union activity, evidenced by repeated measures to suppress it. Of these, the Combination Laws of 1799 and 1800, which outlawed it completely, were the climax.

(*b*) *Cartels.* Cartels or price rings are often considered an exclusive feature of modern capitalism, but they can be traced to the fourteenth century, when one was established in the coal industry. It restricted output, fixed prices, and allocated quotas to members. These techniques were employed with varying degrees of finesse by producers and distributors of iron, copper and some foodstuffs.

(*c*) *Social problems.* Many of the social problems of capitalism were present before 1760, for example, the following.

(*i*) Unemployment: although nominally independent, under the domestic system the worker was completely dependent upon the entrepreneur for employment. This in turn depended upon the fluctuations of the market.

(*ii*) Trade disputes: the workman was constantly involved in disputes over his depressed wages, which caused the working day to be long and arduous (*see* XIX, **4, 5**).

(*iii*) Child labour in the factories: children were employed from as early an age and for as long hours as they were at a later period. Their parents were their employers but it was claimed that they made the hardest taskmasters.

(*iv*) Monotonous work: many of the routines of the handicrafts were as dully repetitive as those of today's assembly line and frequently produced occupational complaints.

THE GROWTH OF INDIVIDUALISM IN AGRICULTURE

25. Decay of the manorial system. The communal character of agriculture restrained progress and improvement by the individual. The complete acceptance of customary practice implied stagnation.

By the fourteenth century, the competitive spirit which had invaded industry and commerce in the towns began to permeate agriculture. It was argued that land should be viewed in the same practical commercial fashion as every other branch of the economy. The more ambitious cultivators added to their strips in the open fields and exchanged strips with their neighbours in order to consolidate a holding. Small, compact farms, hedged around with hawthorn, began to appear. They justified themselves by the greater efficiency with which they could be cultivated.

26. The sixteenth-century enclosure movement. The incentive to enclose the open fields was powerfully reinforced in the sixteenth century by industry's growing demand for wool. Hitherto, sheepfarming had been chiefly confined to remote hill areas. Now sheep invaded the cornfields. The lord of the manor began to enclose the waste land and to devote it and the demesne to the more profitable activity of wool production.

Men made rich in trade found in the land a profitable area for investment, particularly following the dissolution of the monasteries, when large church estates were sold and passed from the plough to pasture.

27. The eighteenth-century enclosure movement. In the eighteenth century, the movement to enclose the land gathered momentum in response to the growth in population and the greater demand for food. The economies of large-scale production induced the consolidation of holdings into large farms. The freehold farmer was persuaded to sell his land. The tenant farmer was evicted when his lease expired. The lord then farmed the land himself or leased it to another large-scale operator, from whom rents would be more certain and more easily collected.

This movement was reinforced by an awakened interest in new techniques and a more scientific approach to farming.

28. The growth of an agricultural proletariat. The enclosure movements undoubtedly resulted in more efficient farming, but it was achieved at considerable social cost. The English peasantry was separated from the land on which it had always subsisted. In its place, there arose an agricultural proletariat: landless labourers who worked the large estates for a wage or who were driven from the land completely to seek work in the towns. Robbed of independence and exposed to insecurity of employment, the rural population experienced great hardship, and impetus was given to many of the social problems which came to a head in the nineteenth century.

THE RISE AND DECLINE OF MERCANTILISM

29. Growth of the nation state. In the stable and disciplined calm of the Middle Ages, the competitive spirit had been absent, as had—to a large extent—a sense of nationhood. The aim was *local* self-sufficiency and men throughout Europe tended to see themselves bound together by their common Christianity rather than separated by their nationality.

The slow decay of the manorial and craft systems gradually substituted national for local allegiance. Wider markets and greater travel made men aware of their dependence upon neighbouring regions, while in overseas trade the competition of the foreigner demonstrated that European interests might not always be in harmony, despite a common Christian heritage.

By the sixteenth century, the concept of the "nation state" was firmly established throughout much of Europe and, with it, a fear of the potential hostility of other nations.

In this spirit was evolved the doctrine of mercantilism which in some of its aspects was to survive into the nineteenth century.

30. The aim of mercantilism. The breakdown of the manorial system and the diminishing power of the gilds implied an equivalent relaxation of local controls over economic life.

Mercantilist policy advocated the assumption and extension of these controls by a strong central government which would apply them in the interests of the nation at large. Local self-sufficiency would be replaced by national self-sufficiency in the face of a hostile world. To this end, there would be no more freedom of individual action than there had been in medieval times. Society, represented by the State, would always take precedence.

31. The devices of mercantilism.

(a) *Encouragement of agriculture.* National self-sufficiency demanded an adequate food supply. Moreover, a large and healthy population could best be supported in close proximity to the land. Movements which separated the peasantry from the land (e.g. the sixteenth-century enclosure movement) were therefore to be discouraged.

(b) *Regulation of industry.* From 1563, industry was governed by the Statute of Artificers (*see* XIX, 2) and by supplementary directives which were administered by local Justices of the Peace.

(c) *Development of naval strength.* To an island, this was of great importance whenever invasion might threaten and also as an instrument of overseas trade.

Acts of Parliament from 1381 encouraged shipbuilding and, in Tudor times, legislation restricted the uses of timber in order to conserve it for naval purposes.

(d) *Overseas trade.* Mercantilism has been most criticised on this count. "Gold and silver," said Sir Thomas Mun, a prominent mercantilist, "are the sinews of war." A nation without gold and silver mines could only finance wars if it earned these metals from the foreigner. This could be achieved by ensuring a favourable balance of exports over imports. Hence it was necessary to restrict the one and subsidise the other as required.

Beyond domestic policy, control of trade overseas was exercised by vesting monopolies in a few chartered companies (*see* XI, 1), whose activities could be more easily supervised than those of a large number of independent traders.

(e) *Colonial policy.* Loss of population by emigration was only permissible if overseas settlement provided the home country with commodities which she could not produce herself. The natural corollary was a close supervision of the trade of the colonies to ensure that England derived the maximum benefit.

32. The revolt against authority. With mercantilist devices, the Crown attempted to preserve the legacy of the Middle Ages, namely, a society made stable by a strictly disciplined economic life. The following forces impelling change prevented its success.

(a) *Economic forces.* The rising tide of individualism, already observed in industry, trade and agriculture, was held back by mercantilist restrictions. The increasingly confident, successful and influential entrepreneur chafed at restraints, which, by the seventeenth century, began to weaken.

It was still maintained that the interests of society should take precedence over those of the individual, but what was now in question was whether there need be any conflict between the two. Would not society be best served by permitting the fullest possible development of the interests of the individual? Since every man knew his own interest best, he should not be impeded by State meddling.

(b) *Political and religious forces.* The growing strength of individualism also expressed itself in the desire of the middle class for political and religious liberty. The struggle continued for over a century and culminated in the Civil War, when the revolt against the authority of Crown and Church was brought to a climax.

33. The triumph of laissez-faire. The new political order which accompanied the Restoration in 1660 weakened the power of the Crown and provided an environment in which the new economic ideals could flourish. The relaxation of authority meant that never again could the nation's productive efforts be channelled into the narrow confines which had previously bound them.

The eighteenth century, therefore, opened upon a highly individualistic society with a firm belief in the merits of *laissez-faire* and whose economic affairs were widely organised on a capitalistic basis.

Further economic progress then depended upon technological advance.

34. The union of technical innovation and capitalist organisation. In the eighteenth century came a series of inventions: Watt's steam engine, textile machinery by Hargreaves, Arkwright and Crompton, iron processes by Darby and Cort, to name only the most striking advances. They came as the climax to two centuries of experiment and were born into an eagerly receptive capitalist environment. The union of technical innovation and capitalist

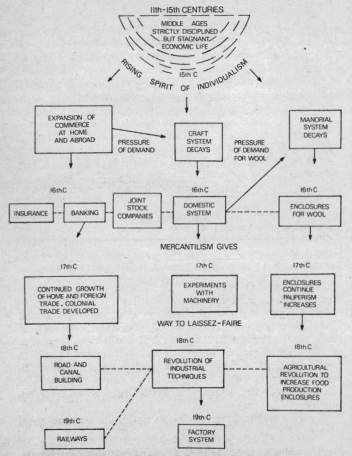

FIG. 1—Evolution of the capitalist system

organisation made certain Britain's economic supremacy in the nineteenth century and laid the foundations of the affluence of modern times.

Her industry outstripped that of her keenest competitors. Her mercantile marine grew to be the largest in the world and carried a substantial portion of the world's trade. The £ sterling was as good as gold, inspiring such confidence that the rest of the world preferred to use it in conducting its own foreign trade. London consequently became the world's financial and commercial capital. Supported by her economic power, Britain's political power grew to its greatest extent, while the standard of living of the British people was unequalled anywhere else in Europe.

The subsequent chapters of this book outline these developments in agriculture, industry, commerce and transport and go on to consider the social by-products which inspired, from an early date, the inevitable reaction to the spirit of *laissez-faire*.

PROGRESS TEST 1

1. Describe the functions of the entrepreneur. **(2)**

2. What was the economic implication of the doctrine of *laissez-faire*? **(4)**

3. What was the economic objective of the medieval manor? **(7)**

4. Account for the growth of medieval towns. **(13)**

5. How did the towns acquire powers of self-regulation? **(14)**

6. How did the craft gilds control medieval industry? **(18)**

7. Describe the principal features of economic life in the Middle Ages. **(12, 15, 17, 20)**

8. What caused the decline of the craft gilds? **(20)**

9. How did the increasing scale of production contribute to the decline of the craft system? **(21)**

10. What social evidence is there of an early capitalist system? **(24)**

11. Differentiate between the motives for enclosures in the sixteenth and the eighteenth centuries. **(26, 27)**

12. What was the driving force behind the doctrine of mercantilism? **(29, 30)**

13. Explain the methods of mercantilism. **(31)**

14. Account for the decline of mercantilist doctrine. **(32)**

15. "Technical improvements alone were not responsible for the Industrial Revolution." Explain. **(33, 34)**

PART TWO

AGRICULTURE

CHAPTER II

The Development of Agricultural Techniques and Organisation

THE AGRICULTURAL REVOLUTION, 1700–1860

1. Character of agriculture before 1700.

(*a*) *Fragmented landholding.* Since the Middle Ages, an enclosure movement had been breaking down the manorial system of land tenure. Out of the open fields, many large estates and farms had been created, in the interest of more intensive sheep farming. Especially during the sixteenth century, greater wool production was necessary to meet the growing needs of industry.

NOTE: Nevertheless, half the agricultural land of England was still cultivated communally in open fields and about 4 million hectares (a quarter of the country's area) were waste.

(*b*) *Uneconomic agricultural practice.* Cereals and animals provided the base of all farming but the yields were low.

(*i*) Seed wastage: seed was scattered and much consumed by birds. The yield was only about five times the seed sown.

(*ii*) Poor tools: sickles were used for harvesting and many other tools were of wood, not iron. There were few mechanical appliances.

(*iii*) Fallowing: fields normally lay fallow one year in three in order to recover their fertility.

(*iv*) Haphazard breeding: all animals grazed together and breeding was completely unselective.

(*v*) Lack of fodder: in winter the best animals were slaughtered for meat, since it was impossible to support large herds throughout the winter. Livestock therefore increased only slowly.

(*v*) Lack of experiment: since agriculture was communal and decisions were made collectively, there was little opportunity for individual experiment.

2. Incentives to change. From the beginning of the eighteenth century, agriculture assumed a new importance which provided strong incentives to change.

(*a*) *Early eighteenth century*. There was a general quickening of scientific interest, which in agriculture expressed itself in a desire to lower production costs and to utilise the vast areas of waste land.

(*b*) *After 1760*. Rapidly expanding population, growing towns and better communications increased the demand for foodstuffs.

(*c*) *Bad weather and rising prices, 1765–92*. In this period, there were only two good harvest and wheat prices rose as follows:

Before 1765	1770s	1780s	1790s
35s. a quarter	51s.	43s.	47s.

NOTE: 1 quarter = 12.7 kg; 1s. = 5p.

Higher prices were an incentive to greater efforts.

(*d*) *Wars with France, 1793–1815*. Increased home production had to replace restricted imports. The effort was handicapped by further bad weather which gave fourteen poor harvests between 1793 and 1814. Shortages and inflation of the currency raised prices from 47s. a quarter to an average of 97s.

3. Significant features of change.

(*a*) *Transition to a market economy*. The enclosure movement, which had continued without interruption for three centuries, slowly separated the peasantry from the land upon which they had always subsisted. The eighteenth- and nineteenth-century enclosures completed their transformation to a class of wage-earning agricultural and industrial labourers.

Simultaneously, the land was required to produce not for its tenants but for the market. The development of a market economy gave rise to the difficulty of adjusting supply to demand, a problem which was even more acute in agriculture than in industry.

(*b*) *Transition to capitalism*. The creation of an agricultural proletariat also marked the transition to a capitalist system of agricultural production (i.e. a system where labour and the instruments of production are provided by two separate classes of people).

(c) Division of agriculture and industry. As the revolution in industry and agriculture progressed, so a cleavage developed between the two. The increasing scale of operation in each sphere precluded simultaneous activity on the part of an individual as both farmer and manufacturer.

Similarly, the craftsman of the domestic system, who had also been a small farmer, was forced into the factory or on to the farm as a wage earner, since he had not the capital to be independent either as farmer or craftsman.

4. The chronology of change. In the light of recent research there is now a tendency to assign a date earlier than previously accepted to the start of the Agricultural Revolution.

In the first instance it must be recognised that different writers will make different interpretations in attempting to identify the precise moment at which revolutionary change began. The true criterion must be the point at which major influences upon the general conditions of economic life can be observed. Isolated precedents for the innovations of the Agricultural and Industrial Revolutions antedate those Revolutions by many centuries.

(a) Significant change unlikely to have occurred before the early eighteenth-century. Evidence suggests that Calorie consumption per person at the beginning of the eighteenth century was not much above the minimum necessary to sustain life. It is also known that during the nineteenth century agricultural production grew at an annual average rate of 1 per cent. If we assume that during the seventeenth century, the growth rate of agricultural production was, say, 0.5 per cent, then as late as 1650 the per capita production of Calories would have been insufficient for human survival. This is clearly impossible and we must therefore conclude that throughout the seventeenth century annual agricultural output remained virtually static at about subsistence level.

(b) Significant change must have been earlier than 1750. Quantitative data is available which demonstrates the rise in the productivity of agricultural labour between 1700 and 1750. During the seventeenth century the export of English cereals was insignificant. By 1750, it had risen to a total of 200,000 tons per annum or 30 kg per head. Related to per capita consumption of Calories at that time this represented the export of 13 per cent of food production surplus to domestic consumption.

Moreover, in the same period population had increased by

some 5–7 per cent. There had also been an increase in Calorie
consumption while the proportion of the population engaged in
agriculture had diminished. At the same time exports such as
wool and other livestock products increased showing that higher
sales of cereals were not achieved at their expense.

We are therefore led to conclude that widespread changes in
the English agricultural economy can be perceived about 1700 or
at the earliest a quarter of a century before. This conclusion does
not, of course, preclude the possibility of *some* technical progress
at an even earlier date.

THE REVOLUTION IN TECHNIQUES

5. The influence of the Low Countries. Put simply, the revolution
in agricultural techniques represented the accelerated application
in countries with low population density of methods gradually
developed in densely populated countries.

It is probable that the development of the overseas trade of the
Low Countries in the fifteenth and sixteenth centuries facilitated
the expansion of a population dependent upon imported cereals.
This expansion in turn intensified the demands made upon domestic agriculture with the result that from the sixteenth century the
densely populated plains of Brabant and Flanders were the focal
point of European agricultural experts.

It is undoubtedly the case that during the seventeenth and
eighteenth centuries the whole of England learned much from
Flemish methods and by applying them in a much less densely
populated environment achieved striking improvements in per
capita output. That England was led to utilise this expertise is
explained fundamentally by the changes in the structure and
motivation of society which were observed in I. As in industry, so
in agriculture a highly individualistic society, widely organised on
a capitalist basis, demanded accelerated technological progress.
Necessity became the mother of invention.

The opportunity to acquire Flemish expertise arose from
England's frequent contacts with the Low Countries, and in particular from the influx of Protestant refugees escaping from
Spanish domination. The diffusion of knowledge during the eighteenth century was assisted by many English writers and in-
novators (*see* **20–29**) so that from about 1730 down to the middle
of the nineteenth century it was England which became the
Mecca of agricultural experts.

The main elements of the new techniques are summarised in 6–10.

6. Crop rotation and the elimination of fallowing. In place of the traditional system of allowing a field to regenerate by lying fallow for one year in two or three, crop rotation was introduced. The crops used in the rotation system had a different chemical consumption at different depths and some themselves exercised a regenerative effect on the soil. The inclusion of fodder crops furthered livestock rearing and therefore permitted more intensive manuring.

Rotation fostered the cultivation of crops which were new to most of Europe. These included turnips, clover, hops, maize, buckwheat, cabbages, carrots and potatoes.

7. Land reclamation and improvement. New techniques were employed to drain marshy land.

8. Improvement of farm instruments. Of greatest importance were the improvement in the structure of the plough and its substitution for the hoe in more backward areas. The scythe replaced the sickle and the sower replaced broadcast sowing. A second wave of innovations after 1830 brought a greater use of farm machinery.

9. Use of horses. In ploughing, the speed of horses is about 50 per cent greater than that of oxen. Their wider use led to a rise in agricultural productivity.

10. Scientific breeding and seed selection. This process continues today. In its early stages the most striking results were in livestock breeding which resulted in higher meat and milk yields.

THE EIGHTEENTH-CENTURY ENCLOSURE MOVEMENT

11. Its purpose. Fear of food shortage had checked the sixteenth-century movement to enclose the land for wool production. However, in the eighteenth century, it was fear of food shortage that provided a stimulus for further enclosures designed to increase the area under cultivation.

Consolidated farms, it was thought, would be more productive than strips scattered throughout the open fields. Waste land would also be brought into use.

12. Enclosure of arable land. Much of the open fields had been enclosed by mutual agreement to exchange strips in order to consolidate a holding.

However, in the eighteenth century, as in the sixteenth century, pressure was frequently exerted by landlords to evict their tenants in order to secure the land for their own use or to let it to more substantial farmers. Since land titles were often vague and tenants ignorant, this might easily be accomplished.

13. Enclosure of waste land. Squatters could be evicted legally and with little difficulty. Moreover, the smallholder with a legal title often required use of the waste to supplement his few strips. Denied this, he was easily dispossessed of his arable land by an offer of cash.

14. Private Enclosure Acts. Big landlords were able to secure the passage of private enclosure Bills, often without the knowledge of their tenants. In any case, the legal costs of opposition would have proved prohibitive.

This rapidly became the accepted method, as can be seen from the following.

> *Enclosure Acts*
> 1700–1760: about 4 a year
> 1760–1792: ,,   40 ,,
> 1792–1815: ,,   80 ,,

The pace then slackened, but by 1845 some 4,000 Acts had accounted for about one-fifth of the area of England and the movement was virtually complete.

15. General Enclosure Acts. Parliament favoured the enclosure movement but appreciated the disadvantage of poor tenants who might want to enclose but lacked the funds to promote a private Bill. This was remedied by the following.

(*a*) *A General Enclosure Act 1836.* With the agreement of two-thirds of the holders of open fields rights, the land could be enclosed under the supervision of commissioners. They could dispense with the latter if seven-eighths were in agreement.

(*b*) *A General Enclosure Act 1845.* The system was extended to the waste land. The waste was enclosed so rapidly, and often illegitimately, by rich landlords that special parliamentary approval again became necessary in 1852.

16. Economic effects. Consolidation of holdings transferred the initiative to the individual farmer. He could then experiment and improve freely and efficiently, being no longer bounded by the conservative decisions of those with whom he had shared the open fields. The following had been the disadvantages of the old system.

(*a*) Traditionally, the stubble of the arable land had been used for grazing. This had precluded winter crops.

(*b*) Efficient drainage of an open field had been impossible unless everyone co-operated fully.

(*c*) The farmer found it more difficult and time consuming to work his land when having to move from strip to strip.

However, improvements called for considerable investment of capital in buildings, fencing, fertilising, tools, drainage and livestock.

While the economic effects of enclosures and the accompanying capitalistic methods of farming were entirely beneficial, the social consequences were serious.

17. Social effects. The eighteenth- and nineteenth-century enclosures completed a movement which had caused the decay of the yeomanry and created in its place an agricultural proletariat.

The small farmer lacked the resources to develop his land, and his competitive position in a market economy was therefore weakened. This was especially important in the war years, 1793–1815, when the emphasis was upon efficient large-scale production. When peace came, prices fell but costs remained high.

NOTE: the Speenhamland policy (*see* XVI, **8, 9**) kept local rates at an intolerable level.

18. Contributory causes of rural reorganisation.

(*a*) *Political.* The 1688 revolution had placed political power squarely in the hands of the landed class. Wealthy industrialists sought to buy their way into this privileged class and in so doing dispossessed the small farmer.

(*b*) *Loss of supplementary employment.* The small farmer had frequently supplemented his income in the carrying trade and by domestic industry. These occupations were now closed as a result of improved communications and the rising factory system.

19. The agricultural proletariat. From the upheaval of the

Agricultural Revolution emerged a system in which the land was owned by a few large landlords (in 1873, over half of England and Wales was in the hands of some 2,250 people), farmed by substantial tenants with the aid of a class of landless labourers.

The lot of this agricultural proletariat was never easy, as can be seen from the following:

(a) 1790–1850.

(i) They now bought food at retail market prices and the general tendency after 1770 was for prices to rise.

(ii) The demand for labour did not keep pace with the supply.

(iii) Gilbert's Act (1782) and the Speenhamland decision (1795) made a pauper of the labourer until 1834 (see XVI, 8–10).

(iv) They had to compete with "roundsmen" (gangs of paupers who were hired out by the Poor Law authorities at whatever rates they could obtain).

(b) 1850–70. Although this was a period of agricultural prosperity, the labourer had little share in it.

(i) Unlike the industrial worker, he was difficult to organise in unions.

(ii) He was usually overawed by the local gentry.

(iii) He occupied a cottage tied to the farm he worked on. He could not therefore easily change his job.

(c) 1875–96. The low prices of the Great Depression (see 39; XII, 16) restrained any possible advance in wages.

The result of these depressed conditions was a steady drift away from the land which persisted until 1914.

AGRICULTURAL WRITERS AND INNOVATORS

20. Eighteenth-century writers. Agricultural literature played an important part in diffusing ideas. All writers stressed that improvement should be made in the following two ways.

(a) *Technological*, e.g. drilling instead of broadcasting seed, fertilising and better crop rotation.

(b) *Land use*. Elimination of the waste and the open fields, together with grazing rights on arable land. Large farms and long leases were advocated.

Some of the more important of these writers are dealt with in 21–25 below.

21. Jethro Tull (1674–1741). A landowner, he observed farming methods throughout the country and then made his own experiments. The essence of his advice was to plough and hoe intensively. In 1701, he invented a seed drill and, in 1714, a horse hoe. He also did valuable experimental work with crop rotation.

22. Viscount Charles Townshend (1674–1738). On his Norfolk estate he applied methods he had observed in Holland. Sandy soil was improved with marl. Waste land was enclosed and the Norfolk rotation of crops invented, i.e. cereals, grasses and roots, which obviated the necessity for fallowing. The grass and root crops could be used as winter fodder.

23. Robert Bakewell (1725–95). Between 1760 and 1790, he accomplished major changes. The wider market which accompanied better communications, together with the expanding population, changed the emphasis in sheep-rearing from wool and manure to meat. By selective breeding, he increased the yield, his notable contribution being the Leicester sheep.

24. Arthur Young (1741–1820). One of the greatest of the agricultural writers, his 45-volume *Annals of agriculture* was the product of his observations of farming methods throughout Europe.

He strongly favoured enclosures, capitalistic farming and more scientific methods. He was widely read and exercised much influence, especially after his appointment as Secretary of the Board of Agriculture in 1793.

25. Thomas Coke (1752–1843). Like Townshend, he transformed his estate at Holkham, Norfolk, from sand dune and marsh to model farm land. He improved livestock, mainly through fodder grasses, and gave long leases, prizes and courses of instruction to his tenants. The "Holkham gatherings", when farmers assembled annually in their thousands to discuss agricultural techniques, became famed throughout Europe.

26. Agricultural machinery. Before 1830, there was little mechanisation save for Meikle's threshing machine, a hay tosser by Salmon and a plough by Small. A variety of other machines had been invented but were not in regular use.

(a) *In the 1830s* the most important advance was the substitution of iron for wooden tools.

(b) *In 1853* a mechanical reaper and sheaver was invented.

(c) *Between 1850 and 1870* steam power was applied to a variety of machines, although its use was never widespread.

(*d*) *In 1879* a string binder was invented which proved of great value.

(*e*) *In 1880* power presses were applied to the baling of hay and straw.

Mechanisation of British agriculture proceeded slowly. Only since 1945 has real progress been made.

27. Drainage. Great advances were made between 1760 and 1830.

(*a*) *Elkington* in Warwickshire initiated deep drainage with trenches to a depth of one and a half metres.

(*b*) *Smith* built shallow covered drains.

(*c*) *Drainpipes* were in common use by the 1850s following the development of cheap manufacturing methods.

28. Agricultural chemistry. The year 1840 was a landmark. In Germany, Justus von Liebig analysed soil and concluded that it could be improved or restored chemically in order better to support plant life.

Lawes and Gilbert introduced this thinking to Britain and in 1843 the Rothamsted Experimental Station was founded.

From then on, increasing use was made of Chilean nitrates, Peruvian guano, German potash and superphosphates.

Both pasture and arable land were improved and there was no longer any need for fallowing.

29. Diffusion of knowledge.

(*a*) *The Royal Agricultural Society*, founded in 1840, encouraged scientific farming.

(*b*) *Board of Agriculture*. A new Board was set up in 1889 to prevent the spread of disease and to supervise agricultural experiments.

POST-WAR DEPRESSION, 1816–40

30. Falling prices. For the first time, the effects of falling prices in a market economy were experienced. At its maximum, during the war, the price of wheat had risen to 126*s*. 6*d*. a quarter. The average for the first post-war decade was only 70*s*.

High prices had encouraged an excessive wheat-growing capacity which low prices could not support when there was no corresponding fall in costs.

NOTE: Distress was not uniform but affected cereal farmers most acutely.

31. High costs.

(*a*) *Rents*. It was impossible to make them respond immediately to falling prices.

(*b*) *Repayment of loans*. Money had been borrowed for wartime expansion in depreciated inconvertible currency. It now had to be repaid in *appreciated* convertible notes (*see* IX, **8**).

(*c*) *Taxation* was high, and hit agricultural produce.

(*d*) *Local rates* were high, and were contributed chiefly by the farmer.

(*e*) *Poor harvests*. A series of wet seasons led to poor harvests.

In consequence of high costs and falling prices much marginal wheat land went out of production.

32. The Corn Law 1815. Grain imports were prohibited until English prices had risen to the following per quarter.

Wheat	Barley	Oats	Rye
80*s*. a quarter	40*s*.	26*s*.	53*s*.

The law's primary purpose was to prevent cheap imports from accelerating the fall in price in years when home output was excessive. Conversely, by permitting imports in years of shortage, undue price increases would be avoided.

33. Ineffectiveness of the Corn Law. In fact it offered agriculture no protection which was not already afforded by distance and transport costs (i.e. the only source of grain not likely to be affected by weather similar to that of the British Isles was North America).

Wheat supplies, and therefore prices, still fluctuated with the weather. Farming was a gamble and when prices rose more land was cultivated. When they fell, land went out of use.

34. Repeal of the Corn Law, 1846. As part of the general movement towards free trade (*see* XI, **6, 7**) and in response to the demand of manufacturers for low food prices which would enable them to check wages, the Corn Law was repealed.

35. Recovery. After 1836 began a slow recovery.

(*a*) *The burden of taxation* was reduced as the country moved towards free trade.

(b) *Local rates* were reduced following the Poor Law Amendment Act 1834 (*see* XVI, **12**).

(c) *Rents* by then had fallen into line with lower prices.

THE GOLDEN AGE OF AGRICULTURE, 1850–70

36. The condition of agriculture in the 1850s. Although in many respects agricultural organisation and practice had been revolutionised, progress had not been uniform throughout the country.

The influential agricultural writer, James Caird, gave a gloomy account of what he observed on his travels. He argued that the solution to the farmer's problems lay in efficiency, not protection. Caird's voice was heard and the farmer, reconciled to the fact that salvation lay in his own hands, rapidly adopted the new techniques already described.

The results were seen in rapidly expanded corn production and more and better quality livestock.

37. Supplementary causes of prosperity.

(a) *Railways* widened the market.

(b) *Rising prices* resulted from gold discoveries in Australia and California with a consequent increase in the quantity of money (*see also* XII, **11**).

(c) *Industrial prosperity* increased the demand for food.

(d) *Lack of foreign competition*, since Europe was in political upheaval and transport costs still limited imports from farther afield.

(e) *Intensive capitalisation.* The land was owned by the wealthy classes who had many sources of income and frequently were content to improve the value of their estates without too great a regard for the rents received.

38. The weakness of "high farming". Success in meat and wheat production led to excessive specialisation. This proved disastrous in the following age, when improved communications flooded the market with cheap foreign imports of these commodities in particular.

THE GREAT DEPRESSION, 1873–96

39. Effects of free trade and poor harvests. The full effects of free trade, experienced after 1875, coincided with a series of poor harvests. In 1874–82 there were only two good crops.

(*a*) *Wheat*. Imports flooded in from the Baltic, south Russia and North America, where transcontinental railways and Great Lakes freighters had opened up the prairie.

Ocean freight rates fell simultaneously. The transatlantic freight for a bushel of wheat fell from 33 cents in 1870 to 14 cents in 1881 and 2 cents in 1904.

The poor harvests experienced by the British farmer were no longer compensated by a rise in price, since home shortages were met by more imports. Many farmers were ruined and much land went out of use.

(*b*) *Meat*. Reece's refrigerating machine of 1867 was followed by various improvements and by the next decade frozen meat was being imported in ever increasing quantities.

40. Ulterior causes of depression in agriculture.

(*a*) *Growth of a world market*. Improved communications replaced national markets by a world market. Instability in one country was therefore reflected everywhere, e.g. a decline in the rate of industrial growth in America forced more labour into agriculture. The consequent increase in agricultural output had to be unloaded on to world markets.

(*b*) *Inadequate purchasing power*. The tremendous increase in world productivity had far outstripped the supply of money and the general level of prices fell accordingly.

(*c*) *Rents*, which in Britain had risen in the previous period of prosperity, remained high.

(*d*) *Protection* was resorted to elsewhere but in Britain was no answer. Agricultural produce was imported as the only means of interest payment on overseas investment.

41. Results of depression.

(*a*) *The area under wheat* was halved.

(*b*) *The total area of arable land* was cut by a quarter.

(*c*) *The capital value of land* was cut from £2,000 million to £1,000 million.

(*d*) *The agricultural labour force* was reduced from 1 million to 600,000 in a period when the population rose by 11 million.

(*e*) *Rents* were ultimately reduced or remitted.

REMEDIES FOR THE PROBLEMS OF
AGRICULTURE, 1896–1939

42. Partial recovery, 1896–1914. The fortunes of farming improved for the following three main reasons.

(a) *Rising prices.* The increase in the world supply of money, following the exploitation of the Rand goldfields, caused the general price level to turn upwards (*see also* XII, **17**).

(b) *Diversification of farming.* From concentration on meat and wheat, the British farmer turned more to perishables which were not so exposed to foreign competition, e.g. dairy produce, fruit and vegetables. Such activities were assisted by (c).

(c) *Urbanisation.* The continued growth of towns and speedier transport brought the farmer closer to a concentrated market.

In a very small degree, recovery was assisted by legislation. The Smallholdings Act 1907 was intended to check the drift from the land by assisting with housing, capital and marketing.

43. The 1914–18 war. The dangers inherent in a weak agriculture became apparent. Home production had to be expanded and about 800,000 extra hectares were brought under the plough.

Imports were consequently cut—wheat by a fifth, beef and sugar by a third, mutton and butter by a half, eggs and apples by three-quarters.

The national importance of a healthy agriculture was acknowledged in a most important Act, the Corn Production Act 1917, by which prices were guaranteed (as was a minimum agricultural wage).

Although the Act was repealed in 1921, a precedent had been established.

44. Decline in the 1920s. The artificial prosperity induced by wartime conditions disappeared and much arable land was deserted.

(a) *Prices* fell throughout the world (*see* XII, **21**).

(b) *Wages*, however, remained relatively high.

(c) *Loans* raised for expansion during the wartime boom had to be serviced at high interest rates.

(d) *Capital investment*, which might have promoted greater efficiency and lower costs, was restricted. The traditional source of agricultural capital was the wealthy landowner, but his capacity to invest had been reduced by Harcourt's death duties (*see* XXI, **22**).

45. Government assistance.

(*a*) *Agricultural Credit Acts 1923 and 1928*. Loans were made for improvements.

(*b*) *Agricultural Rates Act 1929*. Farm lands and buildings were exempted from local rates.

These measures scarcely touched the basic problem of giving agriculture some stability, a problem which soon came to a head.

46. The 1929–32 slump.
Agriculture was adversely affected in two ways. Depression in the industrial sector of the economy curtailed the purchasing power of the industrial worker. Simultaneously there was an increase in the supply of foreign produce at cut prices.

Since depression was world-wide, countries like the U.S.A., with a highly mechanised agriculture, unloaded their surpluses on world markets.

(*a*) *Cereals* were especially affected by foreign imports and there was an outcry for protection. The Government, torn between the desire to assist agriculture and yet restrain prices in the interest of the industrial population, compromised with the Wheat Quota Act 1932. The price of a quota of British wheat was guaranteed at 45*s*. a quarter. This scheme was financed by a levy on flour.

(*b*) *Mixed farming* also suffered. This was largely the result of high costs caused by small-scale production and poor marketing. The Government assisted with the Agricultural Marketing Acts 1931 and 1933. Marketing boards were set up to regulate the price and distribution of a number of products, e.g. the Milk Marketing Board and the British Egg Marketing Board.

The Board of Trade was also given power to regulate agricultural imports, and the Ministry of Agriculture power to regulate the total quantity marketed when this was in the national interest.

47. Slow recovery, 1933–9.
In a situation in which the State largely regulated supply and price, agriculture began to recover. Even so, by 1939, Britain produced only a third of her own food. Cultivated land was down to about 5 million hectares, the lowest figure in modern history, and, while the number of livestock reached a record level, a third of its fodder had to be imported.

PLANNING AND PRICE STABILITY

48. The 1939–45 war. Agriculture was again faced with the necessity of increasing output in order to minimise imports.

(a) *Increased production.* There was a 60 per cent increase in ploughed land and the output of wheat and potatoes was doubled. There was also a great expansion in sugar beet and vegetables. However, owing to the difficulties of importing fodder, the number of livestock fell.

(b) *Supervision.* County War Agricultural Committees were set up, empowered to:

(i) direct farmers, control land use and, if necessary, replace inefficient farmers;

(ii) organise the supply of machinery and fertilisers.

(c) *Labour.* Previously there had been too few agricultural labourers and now more left for war service. The acute shortage was made good by the Women's Land Army, prisoners of war and volunteer harvest workers.

Wages gradually rose to a more attractive level.

49. The new importance of agriculture. The return of peace posed the following four fundamental problems.

(a) *Britain could not feed her population* from her own resources.

(b) *Her overseas earning capacity* had been impaired by the sale of overseas investments and the running down of export industries.

(c) *The increase in the world population* brought greater pressure on food supplies.

(d) *The world's primary producers* were better organised to control supply and therefore keep up prices. This contrasted with the 1930s, when the terms of trade were in Britain's favour and her population had been fed at cut prices.

Agriculture could not be permitted to relapse into depression but had to be improved to produce as much as possible of the nation's requirements.

The results were (i) intensive mechanisation, and (ii) a comprehensive Government agricultural plan.

50. The Agriculture Act 1947. The aims were to bring long-term stability and to produce as much as possible at home.

(a) *Price stability*. Prices were controlled and guaranteed. The Annual Price Review made any changes which the Minister of Agriculture thought were in the national interest (*see* **63**).

(b) *Supervision*. It was argued that the nation could no longer afford inefficient farming. A National Agricultural Advisory Service was established and representatives of landowners, farmers and labourers formed County Agricultural Committees to carry on the work of the County War Committees.

An inefficient farmer might be placed under supervision and, in the last resort, dispossessed.

These powers were relaxed by the Agriculture Act 1957, which replaced force with inducements.

(c) *Smallholdings*. Before the First World War, efforts had been made to re-establish a peasant class on small farms (Smallholdings Act 1907). After the war, it was hoped to settle ex-servicemen on the land, and in the 1930s the smallholding was seen as a means of alleviating unemployment.

With all these schemes, the primary considerations were social and not agricultural. The 1947 Act differed in trying to attract to the land men who were skilled in agriculture.

County councils were to provide smallholdings at fair rents to agricultural workers and other experienced people, but *not* to ex-servicemen as such.

51. The Hill Farming Act 1946.
A large part of the nation's pasture land lies on the hillsides of the north. In the twentieth century, its quality has declined. Therefore, in the interest of stimulating meat production, the 1946 Act:

(a) *provided for capital grants* of up to 50 per cent of the cost of approved schemes: farm buildings, cottages, drainage, roads, sheep shelters, bracken cutting;

(b) *stressed the necessity* of hill farmers themselves taking the initiative in improving pasture by ploughing, re-seeding and fertilising.

In 1956, the scheme was extended and the amount of capital available increased. It was estimated that ultimately the hill farms would support five to six times the number of sheep and cattle as they did formerly.

52. 1956 White Paper.
The Minister described the proposals as the most massive measures of support since the 1947 Act.

They were long-term assurances of Government intentions and were to operate from the 1957 price review:

(a) *Further long-term price stability* was guaranteed. Any reduction would be of a maximum 4 per cent in any one year.

(b) *The amount which the Government would contribute* to the cost of farm improvements was increased to one-third of the total.

The Government's long-term policy was "to support and assist the industry to achieve maximum economic output".

These proposals were incorporated in the Agriculture Act 1957.

53. Rationalisation. In August 1965, the Government published three White Papers: *Voluntary Amalgamation of Small Farms*, *The Development of Upland Areas* and *Aid to Agricultural and Horticultural Co-operatives*. The White Papers showed that about 340,000 holdings out of a total of 455,000 were small farms producing only 30 per cent of home grown food. In many of these cases farmers had no hope of making a reasonable living at prices which the public could afford to pay.

It was therefore proposed to promote the voluntary rationalisation of the industry in order to achieve greater efficiency.

(a) *Financial assistance.* Aid would be given in the enlargement of farms through the acquisition of more land when available and for resettlement or retirement in the case of those wishing to give up unremunerative holdings.

There would also be new forms of grant aid to encourage the formation of co-operative groups in production and marketing.

(b) *Rural Development Boards.* Boards would be set up to deal with the special problems of upland areas, drawing up plans which would cover farming, forestry, recreation and tourism.

54. National Plan, 1965. The National Plan saw that agriculture would continue to play a vital part in the development of the whole economy. British agriculture at that time provided for one half of the nation's food requirements and it was anticipated that it ought to be able to meet the major part of additional demand by 1970. If it were successful, then pressures on imports would be relieved. Moreover, increasing productivity ought to facilitate the release of more labour for other work.

There would therefore be a selective expansion programme for the production of cereals, beef and veal, mutton and lamb, pig meat, poultry, meat offals, eggs, milk, fruit and vegetables planned at a rate equivalent to the growth rate of the preceding few years.

For such a programme, resources had to be made available and this would be borne in mind in subsequent price reviews.

55. Agriculture Act 1967. The Act was based upon the White Papers of August 1965.

Its main provisions were as follows.

(a) *A Meat and Livestock Commission* was set up. This was a new body to improve the production and marketing of meat.

(b) *Amalgamation grants*. The Minister was empowered to make grants of up to 50 per cent and loans for the remainder for the purpose of making amalgamations.

(c) *Other grants*. There was an increase from £90 million to £170 million in the sum available for improving farms which were already economic. In common with industrial machinery, farm machinery was to benefit from investment grants, i.e. a Government contribution to total cost.

(d) *Rural Development Boards* were established.

(e) *A Central Council for Agricultural and Horticultural Co-operatives* was also set up.

56. Government agricultural policy in the 1970s. Summarised, the Government's agricultural policy has been founded upon the Agriculture Acts of 1947, 1957 and 1967 and increasingly since 1973 upon the provisions of the E.E.C.'s Common Agricultural Policy (*see* **58–64**). The principal objective, set out in the 1947 Act, continues to be "a stable and efficient agricultural industry capable of producing such part of the nation's food and other agricultural produce as in the national interest it is desirable to produce in the United Kingdom and of producing it at minimum prices consistent with proper remuneration and living conditions for farmers and workers in agriculture and an adequate return on capital invested in the industry".

57. Market stabilisation. An aspect of the Government's broader policy for agriculture has been its attempts to establish more orderly marketing arrangements. Agricultural products are marketed mainly through private trade channels such as corn merchants, livestock auctions and bacon factories. However, for certain commodities marketing is conducted by boards operating under the Agricultural Marketing Act 1958. These boards are

producers' organisations with a majority of members elected by
the producers themselves and a minority by the relevant minister.
They have statutory powers to regulate the marketing of particular products, and are divided into the following two categories.

(a) *Boards which are statutorily the sole buyers of the regulated
product.* These include the boards for hops, milk and wool, and
in Northern Ireland, the pig and seed potato boards.

(b) *Boards with only a general influence over marketing conditions.* One example is the Potato Marketing Board.

For other commodities there are broadly based organisations
representing producer, distributor and independent interests. One
example is the Home Grown Cereals Authority set up in 1965.
This board also acts as an agent for the Intervention Board for
Agricultural Produce which engages in support buying (*see* 60).

THE COMMON AGRICULTURAL POLICY

58. Reasons for a Common Agricultural Policy (C.A.P.). The
policy of the E.E.C. in respect of agriculture has been determined
by a technological revolution in European farming methods
which raised productivity and depressed prices. Without substantial intervention, free trade would have had severely disruptive effects upon the economies of the member nations. The problem has therefore been to achieve free trade and at the same
time assure the economic position of the Community's farmers.

In essence the policy has meant protection from overseas competition and the setting of "intervention prices" for all the main
agricultural products. The intervention price is the guaranteed
minimum selling price at which the Community will purchase all
surpluses.

59. Objectives. The objectives of the C.A.P. were similar to those
established for British agriculture in the 1947 Act, namely increased productivity, a fair return to farmers, market stability
and security of supplies at reasonable prices.

As in Britain, the other members of the Community had for
many years been operating their own agricultural support
policies. It was necessary to harmonise these. In principle, markets are managed in such a way as to secure the desired level of
prices. When world prices are low, variable import levies are
imposed to ensure that Community prices are not undermined.
At the same time subsidies may be paid to Community exporters

to enable them to compete in world markets. When world prices are high, export levies may be imposed in order to discourage exports and ensure home supplies.

Exceptions to these policies arise where the Community is largely dependent upon the import of particular commodities.

60. Intervention Board for Agricultural Produce. An Intervention Board was set up in 1972 with the function of carrying out the support arrangements of the C.A.P. These include the following.

(*a*) *Import and export licensing* in respect of trade with third countries together with the payment of export refunds and the fixing of rates of import levy and export refund.

(*b*) *Support buying, storage and resale* of cereals, pig meat, beef, milk products and sugar.

(*c*) *Administration of production subsidies* in respect of a number of commodities.

61. The European Agricultural Guidance and Guarantee Fund. This is known as F.E.O.G.A.—the French initials. The Fund is that part of the Community's budget which finances the C.A.P. and in 1976 accounted for 68 per cent of the total budget. Expenditure falls under the following two main headings.

(*a*) *Support expenditure.* The larger guarantee section is used to finance market support arrangements through the national intervention bodies.

(*b*) *Structural reform.* The guidance section finances expenditure on structural reform which includes the rationalisation of production and marketing structures and the provision of retraining and resettlement facilities for agricultural workers.

62. British accession arrangements. The adoption of the C.A.P. meant the introduction of new techniques of market management and a move to a substantially higher level of support prices. Too sudden a change from "cheap" food policies would have been politically unacceptable and therefore from February 1973 a transitional period of five years was allowed to achieve full harmonisation with Community prices.

63. Residual elements of the annual price review. Domestic price support policies remain in respect of those commodities for which the Community has no common market organisation and include price guarantees for milk, potatoes, fat sheep and wool.

Domestic guarantees for fat cattle, rye, eggs, sugar beet, fat pigs, wheat, barley and oats had by 1976 been replaced by intervention under the C.A.P.

In 1976, the cost of domestic support policies for agriculture was £201 million against receipts under the guidance section of F.E.O.G.A. of £4 million. Expenditure on market regulation under the C.A.P. was £311 million against receipts from F.E.O.G.A. of £260 million. The figure of £311 million includes aid for private storage, production subsidies, import and export refunds on trade with third countries and the net cost of commodities bought through intervention and subsequently sold.

64. Renegotiation and the C.A.P. Following the signing of the Treaty of Accession in 1972 there lingered the belief that the C.A.P., in cutting Britain off from the traditional sources of cheap food, left much to be desired.

The incoming Government of 1974 therefore sought a renegotiation. The improvements which it claimed to have achieved were outlined in a 1975 White Paper, *Membership of the European Community: Report on Renegotiation*. They included the following.

(*a*) *Holding down C.A.P. prices.* Agreement was achieved to hold prices at levels which took greater account of consumers as well as producers.

(*b*) *Greater price flexibility* to meet the varying needs of producers in different parts of the Community.

(*c*) *Greater flexibility in the use of subsidies* for high cost producers, thus reducing prices to the consumer.

(*d*) *Discouragement of the creation of surplus stocks* as a means of supporting prices, the consumer again deriving the benefit.

(*e*) *Access to the Community for Commonwealth sugar* on favourable terms for an indefinite period. There was also progress in improving access arrangements for New Zealand dairy products.

The White Paper concluded that the relationship between world prices and Community prices was likely to be much closer than in the past and that on balance British prices were unlikely to have been lower even had she remained outside the Community. Moreover, the Community as a major food producer offered greater stability of price levels and greater security of supply in times of shortage.

CONCLUSION

65. Review and commentary. To put what has been said in this chapter into perspective, the following observations may be made upon the development of British agriculture over two centuries.

(a) *The foundations for an industrialised state.* Whether the Agricultural Revolution preceded or was concurrent with the revolution in industry (*see* **4**), it is clear that the latter could not have occurred without a vastly increased capacity to support an expanding industrial proletariat and a growing population for which greater food supplies were both a cause and a subsequent necessity.

(b) *The roots of agricultural progress.* As with the Industrial Revolution, the source of change is to be found in the rising tide of individualism which is associated with the European Renaissance. By the dawn of the eighteenth century, social, political and economic structures had been so transformed that this individualism could be given full expression (*see* I).

(c) *Technical progress.* Throughout the eighteenth century and into the nineteenth, Britain led the way in agricultural innovation.

(d) *The shift to industry and its consequences.* Agricultural improvements having facilitated the Industrial Revolution, the drift from the land into industry gathered pace. Britain, "the workshop of the world", then began to place greater reliance upon agricultural imports in exchange for her manufactures. This tendency accelerated towards the end of the nineteenth century with the improvement in the quantity and the variety of the nation's diet. Foodstuffs were consumed which could only be produced in non-temperate zones of the world. Britain became ever less self-sufficient.

Three checks to this process occurred, all pointing to the importance of a balanced economy in which an efficient agriculture would have a major role. The first two of these checks were the two world wars which necessitated improvements in domestic agricultural output. On the third occasion, after 1945, it became apparent that Britain's relative importance as an industrial and trading nation was in decline. A strong agriculture which would reduce dependence upon imports was now vital. Government policy, at first independently and subsequently through negotiation with the E.E.C., has been designed to achieve this end.

PROGRESS TEST 2

1. Agricultural practice before 1700 was backward and un-economic. Give reasons for this statement.   (1)

2. What were the forces which inspired agricultural change in the late eighteenth century?   (2)

3. Why did the eighteenth-century enclosure movement signify the transition to a market economy?   (3)

4. What arguments can be advanced for dating the beginning of the Agricultural Revolution at 1700?   (4)

5. What were Parliamentary enclosures and why were they often inequitable?   (14, 15)

6. "The beneficial economic effects of the eighteenth-century enclosures were achieved at great social cost." Evaluate this statement.   (I, 28; 16, 17)

7. Account for the nineteenth-century "drift from the land".   (19)

8. What were the two bases of improvement in eighteenth-century agriculture?   (20)

9. By what means did (a) Arthur Young and (b) Thomas Coke influence agricultural techniques?   (24, 25)

10. What was the contribution to agricultural progress of Justus von Liebig?   (28)

11. Account for the depression in wheat farming after the Napoleonic wars.   (30, 31)

12. Why was the 1815 Corn Law irrelevant to the problems of wheat farming?   (32, 33)

13. What factors contributed to the recovery of agriculture in the 1840s and led to a "golden age" after 1850?   (35, 36, 37)

14. Agricultural success in the mid-nineteenth century contained the seeds of its own undoing. Explain this assertion.   (38, 39)

15. "Circumstances beyond the control of British agriculture contributed to its depression between 1873 and 1896." Explain.   (40)

16. Outline the causes of recovery during the period 1896–1918.   (42, 43)

17. How did the Government respond to the problems of agriculture during the depression of the 1920s and 1930s?   (45, 46)

18. In the nineteenth century, agricultural interests had been

sacrificed to manufacturing interests. Why and with what results did the Government view agriculture in a different light after 1945? (49)

19. What was the broad intention of the Agriculture Act 1947, and how was it to be achieved? (50)

20. To what extent has hill farming been actively encouraged since 1945? (51)

21. What are the main features of the U.K. agricultural policy in the 1970s? (56, 57)

22. Outline the main features of the C.A.P. (58, 59)

23. Explain the functions of F.E.O.G.A. (61)

PART THREE

INDUSTRY

CHAPTER III

Location of Industry

REGIONAL SPECIALISATION, 1760–1939

1. Controlling factors. The possibility of certain economic activities is limited by geographical and geological environment.

(a) *Agriculture* depends primarily upon climate and soil.

(b) *Mining* depends upon geological suitability.

(c) *Manufacturing industry*, on the other hand, would seem to offer a much wider choice of site. At least in theory, any industry may be carried on in any locality. In practice, location was determined in the period 1760–1939 by comparative costs.

2. Comparative costs and the revolution in transport. Until the eighteenth century, British industry was widely dispersed. Little regard was paid to the costs of production of one region compared with another, since poor communications insulated the less efficient from the competition of the more efficient.

The construction of better roads, canals (in the eighteenth century) and railways (in the nineteenth century) brought regions throughout the country into close competition. It then became difficult for an industry to survive locally unless conditions favoured low costs.

EXAMPLE: Wool was spun and woven wherever there were sheep. The major centres of production were, however, the more densely populated areas of the south and south-west of England.

When improved communications widened the market, so woollen manufacture died out in the older areas and concentrated in the West Riding of Yorkshire.

The determinants of cost in the nineteenth century were fundamentally different from those in the period 1920–39. Until 1914, there were three governing factors:

(a) proximity to source of power;
(b) proximity to raw materials;
(c) miscellaneous historical and geographical factors.

3. Proximity to power. Mechanisation began with water power and for a time during the eighteenth century industry, e.g. cotton and wool, was drawn to the swift-flowing streams of the Pennines.

Nineteenth-century steampower demanded a site close to coal, a bulky and costly commodity to transport.

The country's coalfields lay in the midlands of Scotland, South Wales and in a great arc around the Pennines.

In this period, heavy industry was localised upon these coalfields, as follows.

(a) *Cotton* in south and north-east Lancashire.
(b) *Wools* in west Yorkshire.
(c) *Iron and steel* in the North-East, Scotland, South Wales, south Yorkshire, the Midlands (*see* V, **13**).
(d) *Pottery* in north Staffordshire.
(e) *Shipbuilding and heavy engineering* on Clydeside and Tyneside.
(f) *Chemicals* in south Lancashire.

4. Proximity to raw materials. This explained the distribution of the above industries between the coalfields. When the raw material was bulky and costly to transport, then if it was found in association with coal, this was the determining factor.

EXAMPLES: (1) Iron ore and limestone in conjunction with coal gave rise to the iron industry of the Black Country and Scotland. (2) Liverpool, a deep-water port facing west across the Atlantic, gave access to raw cotton and therefore fostered the growth of that industry. (3) The chemical industry of south Lancashire was based not only upon coal but also upon the raw salt of the adjacent Cheshire saltfield.

5. Miscellaneous geographical and historical influences. These also played a part in providing some areas with lower production costs in particular industries.

EXAMPLES: (1) Lancashire's humid climate favoured the spinning of cotton thread which did not easily break. (2) Clydeside was similarly favoured but had greater attractions for shipbuilding and engineering (i.e. a good waterway with adjacent coal, iron and steel). (3) The genius of Josiah Wedgwood played no small part in attracting other pottery manufacturers to the same area of Staffordshire. (4) The lace and hosiery industries of Nottingham were favoured by the presence of political and religious refugees from Europe who were skilled in these crafts.

6. External economies of scale. An industry, having selected a site favourable to low costs, gradually expanded the scale of its operations. As it did so, other cost-reducing advantages (the "economies of scale") began to accrue, as follows.

(*a*) *A local pool of skilled labour.* All the areas previously mentioned developed labour skills associated with their particular industries.

(*b*) *Disintegration of an industry.* When there was a sufficient concentration of any one industry, specialisation was taken to a very great length. Towns, and even firms, narrowed the range of their production to a single type of article or component, e.g. fine cotton spinning in Bolton (*see* VII, **19**) and shoddies in Dewsbury (*see* VIII, **9**).

(*c*) *Growth of contributory industry.* This was especially important with the rise of the machine tool industry from the 1790s (*see* VI, **12, 13**), e.g. boot and shoe manufacturing machinery in Leicester; cotton textile machinery in Manchester.

(*d*) *Local financial services.* British banking developed locally in the hands of men with a special knowledge of local industries.

(*e*) *Specialised marketing facilities.* Industrial concentration encouraged the growth of specialised commodity markets, e.g. Liverpool Cotton Exchange, Leeds Wool Exchange.

All these forces led to a very high degree of regional specialisation before 1914.

7. Danger of regional specialisation. Economic progress demands that at all times some industries should be decaying while new industries take their place, e.g. a decline in the production of gas mantles was followed by an increase in the production of electric light bulbs.

If, in the course of change, a region finds that its staple industry is in decline, this will affect all the dependent trades and all who rely for a living upon the workers' expenditure.

The remedy lies in diversification of local industry.

Unemployment in contracting industries will then be absorbed by those which are expanding.

8. Determinants of comparative costs, 1920–39. During this period, additions to heavy industry were still made on the traditional coalfield sites. However, this period was significant for the growth of new industries of quite different character.

They catered in the main for the consumer, e.g. food trades, furniture, clothing, electrical and radio, domestic apparatus.

Different factors now governed costs, factors which tended to move industry to completely new locations.

(a) *Improved communications*, which had been vital to industry's nineteenth-century localisation, now tended to disperse it. The development of road transport brought such flexibility that materials and workers could be carried to the industry with relative ease.

(b) *Alternative sources of power*. Gas, oil, and especially electricity, made a coalfield site no longer important.

(c) *Proximity to markets*. Since the new industries were aimed at the consumer, this was the important consideration. London consequently exercised the greatest attraction throughout this period since it had both the largest market and the biggest port to handle any export traffic.

(d) *Old labour skills* in the traditional areas were not considered suitable for the new industries.

(e) *The growth of business combines*, which frequently had their head offices in London, was conducive to setting up factories close at hand.

A PLANNED LOCATION FOR INDUSTRY

9. The uneven burden of depression. The period 1920–39 was one of world trade depression. In such circumstances, the first industries affected are those producing capital goods. There is no longer an incentive to renew machinery if it is still functioning, and certainly no incentive to expand.

Consequently, the areas in which unemployment was most severe were the coalfield sites of the north of England, Scotland and South Wales which had specialised almost exclusively in heavy industry. In the south and Midlands where the new light industry was growing the problem was not nearly so acute.

There was therefore a strong tendency for labour to drift to the south. From a social point of view such a tendency may not be desirable, since it can result in the creation of derelict areas with a great waste of social capital (i.e. houses, schools, roads, etc.).

The only remedy is to take new industry to areas of unemployment and, as a first step, the Government intervened with several measures outlined in 10–13 below.

10. Special Areas (Development and Improvement) Act 1936. The parts of the country with unemployment figures above the national average were designated Special Areas.

In some, trading estates were built (e.g. Aycliffe, County Durham) and to firms willing to occupy the new factories the Government offered the inducement of low rents, relief on rates and taxes, and loans on favourable terms.

In addition, it set up retraining centres for men who had been employed in the declining industries.

11. Evaluation of the scheme. These measures had only a limited success in attracting new industry to the Special Areas. The implication was that, despite the many concessions, industry still preferred, for sound economic reasons, to go elsewhere.

Moreover, the Government was in no position to insist upon co-operation, since, in a time of unemployment, business expansion anywhere was preferable to none at all.

In the brief period of rearmament before 1939, some impetus was given to the estates when the Government itself operated some of the factories.

12. "Employment Policy", 1944. A most important White Paper outlined the Government's proposals for preventing the reappearance of heavy concentrations of local unemployment after the war.

(a) Nineteenth-century tendencies to over-specialisation should be reversed and every region should have its industry diversified.

(b) Specifically, industrial expansion in the London area should be checked for social, economic and strategic reasons.

These proposals were embodied in an important Act of Parliament (1945) which to a great extent has determined the location of new industry in the post-war period.

13. Distribution of Industry Act 1945. The Special Areas were renamed Development Areas and ultimately included: (i) the North-east, (ii) west Cumberland, (iii) South Wales and Monmouth, (iv) Scottish coalfield and Dundee, (v) south Lancashire excluding Manchester, (vi) Merseyside, (vii)

Wrexham, (viii) Scottish Highlands, (ix) north-east Lancashire.

All these areas had in common the fact that, despite the post-war boom conditions, pockets of unemployment persisted.

The problem of the Highlands differed in that lack of local employment opportunity caused a drift south to the Scottish coalfield and aggravated unemployment there.

The Act empowered the Government to:

(a) build factories;
(b) make loans to private industrial estate companies;
(c) improve local services, e.g. transport, power, housing;
(d) give financial assistance to firms already established.

Firms seeking to construct buildings beyond a certain size had to obtain an Industrial Development Certificate from the Board of Trade. The Town and Country Planning Acts then limited industrial building to firms with such certificates.

14. Successful results. In the period 1945–8, 52 per cent of the country's industrial expansion was in the Development Areas. That the Government had more success than was achieved under the 1936 Act was due to the following.

(a) Its greater legal powers (*see also* X, 35).
(b) Far more important, post-war labour shortages induced industry to expand quite willingly into areas where labour was more readily obtainable.

Between 1949 and 1955, 28 per cent of industrial growth was in the Development Areas. This slackening in the rate of expansion was due to the now relatively small residual unemployment in these areas and therefore the less rigorous application of controls.

15. Local Employment Acts 1960 and 1963. With the object of giving greater flexibility to Government assistance, the 1960 Act substituted Development Districts for Development Areas. Aid could now be concentrated as required upon relatively small districts whose need was greatest. These were defined as districts with unemployment in excess of 4.5 per cent. The 1963 Act standardised grants.

16. The National Plan. The publication of the National Plan in September 1965 introduced the new concept that the problem of regional imbalance could only be solved within the framework of planning at national level designed to develop the economy as a whole. The emphasis was upon a positive approach to achieving economic growth, the regions playing their part, rather than fragmented attempts to alleviate the problem of unemployment.

17. Regional planning. Eight regions were defined: Scotland, Northern, North-west, East Midlands, West Midlands, Yorkshire and Humberside, Wales and South-west. For each region the following two planning authorities were created.

(*a*) *Regional planning board.* This body was made up of senior Civil Servants from the region and had the function of drawing up a regional economic growth plan.

(*b*) *Regional economic planning council.* The Council had twenty-five part-time members drawn from local businesses, trades and professions. Their function was to advise and assist in the preparation of the regional plan and to study the effect of national policies upon the regions.

The early failure of the National Plan explains the rapid loss of influence of these planning bodies, and as early as 1966 governmental policies had begun to revert to the traditional approach.

18. Industrial Development Act 1966. Development Areas were now established to cover the following regions.

(*a*) *Scotland.* The whole of Scotland with the exception of an area around Edinburgh.

(*b*) *The Northern region* with the addition of the Furness peninsula.

(*c*) *Merseyside.*

(*d*) *The greater part of Wales.*

(*e*) *The South-west* including most of Cornwall and parts of north Devon.

A scheme of investment incentives in the form of direct cash grants gave preferential treatment to these areas. In 1970, grants were replaced by improved capital allowances which were offset against tax liability.

19. Special Development Areas. In 1967, certain labour exchange districts within the Development Areas and which were experiencing particularly acute unemployment problems were designated Special Development Areas and qualified for special assistance.

20. Local Employment Act 1970. For a number of years various local authorities had complained that while their areas were economically depressed they could not qualify for financial aid since their unemployment rates were not quite high enough. In 1969, the Hunt commission published the results of its inquiry into these "intermediate areas" (or grey areas) and certain of its recommendations were adopted in the Local Employment Act 1970.

(*a*) Firms expanding in certain districts of the intermediate areas would receive a 25 per cent grant towards new buildings.

(*b*) A grant of 75 per cent would be paid to local authorities in the intermediate areas towards the cost of clearing derelict land.

The list of intermediate areas was extended in 1971.

21. Industrial and regional development. In the early 1970s, the Government made a thorough review of persisting regional problems and in 1972 issued a White Paper, *Industrial and Regional Development*, setting out what was described as the most comprehensive programme ever undertaken to regenerate the regions.

22. Industry Act 1972. This Act was designed to stimulate industrial investment in general but in the depressed regions in particular. In addition to national and regional incentives, the Act provided a new framework for extending special Government assistance to firms and industries which were failing to compete. It also rationalised the administrative framework with the formation of a new Industrial Development Executive (I.D.E.). The assisted areas were extended and greater provision made for retraining.

23. Extension of assisted areas. The Act granted intermediate area status to almost the whole of the North-west and the Yorkshire and Humberside planning areas outside of the existing development areas. Merseyside and parts of north-west Wales were uprated to Special Development Areas, while Cardiff and Edinburgh were uprated to Development Areas.

24. Financial assistance. The 1972 Act introduced a new system of regional development grants, cash payments towards the cost of plant, and buildings for specified qualifying activities in manufacturing, construction and mining.

Additionally, selective assistance was made available for employment-creating projects in the form of loans at concessionary interest rates and removal grants.

25. Industry Act 1975. The incoming Government of 1974 outlined its "industrial strategy" in a White Paper, *The Regeneration of British Industry*. The proposals were given effect in the Industry Act 1975.

The basic proposition of the strategy was that private investment had failed to sustain the economy at an adequate level. The Government would therefore intervene more directly using the following two new instruments.

(*a*) *The National Enterprise Board* (*N.E.B.*). The Board not only would provide selective financial assistance to ailing industries, but more positively would buy into healthy industry with the intention of promoting greater dynamism. It would also help to stimulate investment and employment in the assisted areas.

(*b*) *Planning agreements*. Closer co-operation between labour, capital and Government would be promoted through voluntary agreements. Regional development grants and selective financial assistance would, however, depend upon such agreements being concluded.

It may be noted that by this time the whole of the United Kingdom with the exception of the East and West Midlands, East Anglia and South-east England qualified for assistance as either an intermediate area, a development area or a special development area.

26. Appraisal of the effectiveness of legislation. Although it may be shown that since 1945 a large number of jobs have been created in development areas, the available evidence suggests that when account is taken of the rate of fresh redundancies and comparison is made with the national unemployment rate, the regions have barely held their own despite massive injections of Government expenditure. A number of explanations may be considered.

(*a*) *Higher costs of production*. If the assumption is made that without Government intervention a firm will choose a location which offers the lowest costs of production, then financial inducements which artificially influence those costs may lead it to an area which in the long run proves unsuitable. For example, a number of firms which were persuaded to expand into Merseyside subsequently transferred these operations to the south-east and the Midlands which offered better natural advantages.

Moreover, many large firms which were drawn to the development areas opened only branch factories, their main centres of production remaining elsewhere. During recessions, it has been in these branches that production has been cut back first.

(b) *A single solution for all areas.* While superficially displaying the same symptoms, the problems of the various areas are distinct, e.g. while Wales suffers from the collapse of hill farming Merseyside has a problem of unskilled labour.

(c) *Policy vacillations.* Conservative Governments have argued that aid could be applied most effectively by concentrating it upon growth points from which the beneficial effects would work outwards to the surrounding regions. Conversely, Labour Governments have preferred to give support to wider growth areas. Faced with the uncertainty of the effects that a change of Government might have, industrial confidence has been weakened.

(d) *National demand management policy.* "Stop-go" demand management policies arose from the attempt to steer a middle course between inflation and balance of payments crises on the one hand and excessive unemployment and stagnation on the other. The simultaneous attainment of growth with full employment at stable prices has eluded all governments. Hence when it became necessary to check the level of demand at a time when national unemployment was running at about 1.2 per cent while that in the regions stood at 5 per cent or more the inevitable result was a sharp upturn in regional unemployment. A conflict may therefore be observed between national and regional economic policies.

REGIONAL POLICY AND THE EUROPEAN ECONOMIC COMMUNITY

27. Background. Like Britain, the member states of the Community have pursued regional economic policies for many years. They have had the same broad objectives of attempting to secure a more balanced development between regions and a more effective use of resources. All members provide a range of incentives to industrial development.

28. Co-ordination of regional policies. At a Paris meeting in October 1972 it was agreed that the enlarged Community of Nine should adopt a regional policy to correct structural and regional imbalances which might obstruct progress towards full monetary and economic union. The national regional policies of the members would now be co-ordinated.

29. Regional Development Fund. In March 1975 the Council of Ministers adopted the Fund Regulation which fixed the size of a Regional Development Fund at 1,300 million units of account, about £540 million. (Unit of account—u.a.—is the monetary unit used by the E.E.C., in this case equal to 0.888671 grams of fine gold.) The Regulation also established the share each member state could claim.

30. Use of the Fund. Members may call upon the Regional Development Fund to contribute to the cost of industrial, handicraft and service industry and infrastructure projects which are receiving regional aids from the member state Government. The contribution may be used either to supplement national aid or as a partial repayment of it.

All applications must be made by the Government. In Britain, government departments select suitable projects for the Fund's consideration in consultation with the projects' promoters and, in the case of infrastructure works, the appropriate public authority.

Britain's share of 28 per cent of the Fund is the second largest after Italy.

31. Other E.E.C. assistance. Regional problems within the E.E.C. have benefited from several other funds, including the following.

(*a*) *European Coal and Steel Community* (*E.C.S.C.*). Through its responsibility for modernising the coal and steel industries, E.C.S.C. was the first institution to concern itself with regional problems. It has given substantial retraining and rehousing aid to southern Belgium and northern France where the coal industry has declined rapidly.

(*b*) *European Investment Bank*. The Bank has provided loans for the industrialisation of agricultural regions and the modernisation of obsolete industry. It has financed most of the south Italian *autostrada* (motorways).

(*c*) *European Social Fund*. This fund is designed to help unemployed workers and to improve labour mobility. It is financed from the Community budget and can assist with retraining and resettlement expenditure.

(*d*) *European Agricultural Guidance and Guarantee Fund.* (*See also* II, **61.**) The guidance section of this fund has had significance for regional development through its expenditure on agricultural modernisation and improved marketing structures.

PROGRESS TEST 3

1. Explain the phrase "comparative costs". (**2**)

2. Comparative costs were of little consequence until the revolution in transport. Why did they then become important? (**2**)

3. The period in which Britain's heavy industry was constructed was one of intensive regional specialisation. Why was this so? (**3–5**)

4. Define the phrase "economies of scale" and explain why they accelerated the pace of nineteenth-century regional specialisation. (**6**)

5. Why may the benefits of economic progress conflict with those of regional specialisation? (**7**)

6. What factor chiefly explained the location of new industry between 1920 and 1939? (**8**)

7. In the 1920s and 1930s, unemployment was much less acute in the south of England than in the north. Why? (**9**)

8. In a period of depression, the Government cannot hope to influence industry's choice of site. Explain this statement with reference to the Special Areas Act 1936. (**10, 11**)

9. What was the intention of the Distribution of Industry Act 1945, and how was it to be accomplished? (**13**)

10. What principal reason explains the success of the 1945 Act? (**14**)

11. Outline the provisions of the Industry Act 1972. (**22, 23, 24**)

12. What was the basic purpose of the Industry Act 1975? (**25**)

13. What assistance is available to Britain from the E.E.C. for regional development? (**27–31**)

CHAPTER IV

Coal

EXPANSION AND CONTRACTION OF PRODUCTION, 1760–1960

1. Domestic use. Coal was a household fuel from early times, but its use was limited by transportation difficulties.

By the eighteenth century, the exhaustion of much of England's timber, together with the growth of population, increased the demand for coal. Marketing was now made possible by canals, improved roads and, in the nineteenth century, by railways and improved coastal shipping.

Its use for domestic purposes was increased by the nineteenth-century development of the following two dependent industries.

(*a*) *Gas.* Invented by William Murdock in 1800, gas lighting was in common use after 1850. The invention by Welsbach in 1885 of the incandescent mantle and, at the end of the nineteenth century, the introduction of the gas stove further increased demand.

(*b*) *Electricity.* Davy had produced an arc light as early as 1810, but only in 1870 was there discovered an economic means of generating current. The Edison and Swan lamp of 1883 then gave impetus to electric lighting.

2. Industrial use. Eighteenth-century industrialisation provided the great impetus to increased production. Indeed, the Industrial Revolution was founded on Britain's coal and iron resources. Demand developed from a number of directions.

(*a*) *The iron industry.* In the early eighteenth century, Darby's new process made it possible for coal to be used for smelting (*see* V, **9**). The growing demand for iron machinery was thus reflected in a parallel demand for coal.

(*b*) *Steam power.* The steam engine simultaneously made possible increased output, by facilitating the drainage of mineshafts, and itself created a demand for coal. The first engines were applied to pumping out mines and then, later, to manufacturing industry, railways and shipping.

(c) *By-products.* Between 1856 and 1870, coal was chemically analysed. In 1856, Perkins discovered a method of preparing an-aline dyes, which were invaluable in the textile industries. From that time, the list of uses has been extended to include, amongst other items, fertilisers, drugs, tar, fibres and oils.

The use of gas and electricity in industry also increased the nineteenth-century demand for coal.

3. Nineteenth-century expansion.

	Output (million tons per annum)	Labour force
Early 19th century	10	
1850		200,000
1860	80	
1880	147	
1900	225	
1913	287	1,127,000

NOTE: 1 ton = 1.016 tonnes.

4. Exports.

Mid-19th century	1900	1913
10 million tons p.a.	50	98

After 1860, industrialisation in Europe and a demand for coal from countries with underdeveloped mining industries provide the principal explanation of the great upsurge in production.

By 1913, a third of Britain's coal output was exported, to pro-vide about 10 per cent of the total value of exports.

The coal export trade proved vital to further industrialisation. Britain imported bulk cargoes but her general export trade was in relatively lightweight manufactures. Coal exports obviated the necessity of ships sailing outward in ballast and so freight rates were kept low. Britain's competitive strength was therefore maintained and further industrial specialisation encouraged. This was in turn reflected in a greater demand for coal.

5. Falling productivity.
The continuing high level of demand obs-cured the fact that after 1880 British mining began to suffer from diminishing returns (i.e. surface seams had been exhausted and deeper mines meant higher costs). Output per manshift reached a maximum in the early 1880s but thereafter declined.

In such circumstances, production may only expand if either the customer or the industry bears the extra cost.

(*a*) *Before 1900*. This was a deflationary period in which the general price level fell (*see* XII, **16**) but the fall in coal prices was less than the average. In other words, the customer bore the extra real cost of mining.

(*b*) *1900–13*. Coal production continued to increase (by about one quarter) and although its money value grew by almost a half, this was less than the rise in the general price level. In other words, the industry was beginning to bear the extra real cost of mining in lower wages and profits per ton.

Lacking flexibility in its organisation and methods, British coalmining was not, at this crucial stage, amenable to cost-reducing change.

6. War production, 1914–18. The mines suffered from a lack of capital investment and manpower was concentrated on the easiest seams, regardless of future consequences. Nevertheless, output declined and restrictions were imposed to conserve supplies for vital needs.

7. Delayed adjustment to new market conditions. After the war, Government controls were at first continued. Home prices were set at low levels and exports were restricted by quotas.

The 1920s brought world trade depression, and the Government dropped its export restrictions. This was the opportunity to face up to the task of reorganisation in order to meet the pressures of a more competitive world market, but these pressures were artificially and temporarily removed by the following.

(*a*) *1922*. A strike in the U.S. mines lent impetus to British production.

(*b*) *1923*. Curtailment of German production after the French occupation of the Ruhr bolstered demand.

(*c*) *1925*. Production was subsidised by the Government until 1926.

(*d*) *1926*. A protracted strike reduced supplies.

Only after 1927 did the industry tackle the problem of readjustment to inter-war market conditions.

8. Inter-war market conditions. Despite the growth in population and industry, consumption of British coal was about 16 per cent less in 1938 than it had been in 1913. This was explained by the following factors.

(a) *Fuel economies.* Better equipment made economies possible in iron and steel, gas, electricity, shipping and railways.

(b) *Alternative sources of power.* The internal combustion engine and cheap oil revolutionised transport. Traffic moved from rail to road. In any case, the railways themselves, like the shipping companies, were beginning to replace steam with diesel engines.

In manufacturing industry, electricity widely replaced steam power, and electricity could be produced with greater economies in coal, or with turbines driven by oil or water.

(c) *Loss of export markets.* This was the principal cause of contraction.

	1913	1929	1937
Export index	100	84	57

The explanation for this lay in the following causes.

(i) As in the home market, the growing use of alternative fuels.

(ii) Other countries (e.g. the U.S.A., Germany, Poland) had growing mining industries in which production costs were falling. Not only did they provide all their own domestic needs, they also encroached on long-established British markets.

In a period of falling prices, Britain's competitive position was weak and her exports declined not only absolutely but also relatively.

	1913	1937
Share of world market	55%	40%

9. 1939–45: wartime shortages. With the export trade closed, many pits in the exporting areas went out of production. Loss of manpower and a decline in productivity from 22 cwt (about 1,100 kg) per manshift in 1938 to 20 cwt (about 1,000 kg) accelerated the decline in output with the result that, by 1942, there was a coal shortage. It was remedied by:

(a) direction of labour;
(b) opencast mining;
(c) fuel economy.

10. 1945–58: peacetime shortages.

(a) *Production and productivity.* After the grave shortages of the severe winter of 1947, there was a slow recovery and productivity increased steadily until 1950. Output per manshift then remained almost static until 1957. Since there was a shortage of labour, coal output never recovered its pre-war level.

(b) *Home and foreign demand.* While foreign demand remained static, vast industrial expansion stimulated home demand. By 1951, it was estimated that production fell short of demand by about one-fifth. Supply and demand were only adjusted by:

(i) *restricting exports;* by 1957, they had shrunk to 7 million tons.

(ii) *imports;* quantities varied, but in one year, 1955, the tonnage imported exceeded that exported and was of greater value.

11. Stabilising production since 1958. With the end of the industrial boom in 1958, the demand for coal fell. Since then, the emphasis has lain upon:

(a) *streamlining production* in order to make coal a more competitively-priced fuel;

(b) *stabilising output* at a level consistent with the nation's requirements. In the absence of a coherent national energy policy it remains difficult to establish what the most economic level of output would be. The issue is confused by political considerations with a powerful coalmining lobby pressing for a greater share of the energy market.

LABOUR CONDITIONS AND STATE INTERVENTION

12. Systems of employment, hours and wages. In the early nineteenth century, the miner worked directly for the coal-owner, as in Northumberland and Durham, or under the "butty" system (*see* below), as in the Midlands. In neither case, despite the thirteen or fourteen hour day worked underground by men, women and children, was there any public concern. Relatively, the miner was considered well paid and well fed, and his job, though dangerous, was not thought unhealthy.

(a) *The butty system* gave rise to the worst conditions. A contractor, or "butty", agreed to work the mine, giving the owner a fixed return on each ton. Thus committed, he drove a hard wage bargain and exacted every ounce of work from his employees.

"Truck payments" (i.e. payments in kind) developed and there was a complete lack of precautions against accident.

(b) *Direct employment* under the coal-owner was usually better, although the miner was often tied to his job by an annual bond and by the fact that his cottage belonged to the mine.

13. Protective legislation. Throughout the nineteenth century, conditions of work were slowly improved by a series of protective measures.

(a) *1842.* An Act prohibited underground work for women and girls and boys under ten.

(b) *1850.* An Act gave powers of inspection to the Board of Trade.

(c) *1860 and 1872.* Coal-mines Regulation Acts controlled various aspects of mine management with a view to reducing the grave accident rate.

(d) *1881.* An Act empowered the Home Secretary to inquire into the causes of mine accidents.

(e) *1908.* The Eight Hours Act limited the working day.

(f) *1911 and 1914.* Coal-mines Regulation Acts codified existing legislation, detailing the safety regulations and methods of working which were to be adopted.

14. The Sankey Report, 1920. In view of continuing unrest, underlined by more militant trade union activity, a Royal Commission under Judge John Sankey inquired into conditions in the mines.

Interim reports by three different groups of the Commission were issued in 1919, and the final report was published in 1920.

(a) *First interim report.* Proposed a seven hour day, ultimately reducing to six, and an immediate wage increase. It also hinted at nationalisation.

(b) *Second interim report.* Proposed an immediate six hour day, substantial wage increases and nationalisation.

(c) *Third interim report.* Opposed nationalisation and shorter hours and made no wage proposals.

(d) *Final report, 1920.* Explicitly recommended nationalisation, shorter hours and wage increases.

The Government did not act on these recommendations, and relations between miners and employers grew more bitter as conditions deteriorated in consequence of the effects of the economic depression.

15. Effects of depression. In an intensively competitive market at a time when world prices were falling, the only cost-reducing solution offered by mine owners was wage-cutting. The miners resisted and partial stoppages of work were frequent (*see* XIX, 35).

In an effort to alleviate the situation, the Government initiated a subsidy in 1925 but on the recommendation of the Samuel Commission this was discontinued in April 1926.

The mine owners then announced a reduction in wages, whereupon the miners struck work.

16. The General Strike, 1926. Workers in the country's major industries supported the miners, but within a week the General Strike had been broken (*see* XIX, 36). The miners stayed out for many weeks longer but were finally starved into submission.

17. Coal Mines Act 1926. The miners' resistance broken, the Government sought to assist the employers by permitting an increase in the underground working day of one hour.

Despite low wages and extra hours, by the end of 1929 the industry was in danger of collapse. The Government intervened with further legislation.

18. Coal Mines Act 1930. The aims were twofold.

(*a*) *Technical reorganisation* in order to make the industry more competitive.

(*b*) *Price stability*. The country was divided into regions in each of which an Executive Board allocated production quotas to individual collieries and set minimum prices. Output of the separate regions was co-ordinated by a Central Council.

The Act also set up a Coal Mines Reorganisation Committee to advise on the production and marketing of coal and to promote colliery mergers when this seemed desirable.

The 1930 Act provided a stepping stone to nationalisation. The framework of the existing administrative machinery was retained.

THE NATIONALISED INDUSTRY AND ITS PROBLEMS

19. Coal Mines Nationalisation Act 1946. A National Coal Board was established, whose duty was to develop the industry and make available supplies of coal "in such quantities and at such prices as might seem best calculated to further the public interest".

The Act was deliberately vague in defining the responsibilities of the Board as distinct from those of the Minister of Fuel and Power. The intention was that experience should provide guidelines.

In practice, the Minister (who appoints all the members of the Board) retained the power of decision on matters of capital reorganisation, output targets and prices.

20. Three post-war problems. The N.C.B. has been faced with three main problems.

(a) *Labour:* the improvement of labour relations and the stabilisation of the labour force at a level which accords with production requirements.

(b) *Modernisation:* the reorganisation and streamlining of the industry in order to lower production costs.

(c) *Marketing:* assuring a place for coal in the face of competition from other fuels.

21. Marketing. The problem of the industry's marketing has lain in predicting with any accuracy the extent of the market for coal. Future sales have been governed in part by the strength of competition from other fuels and in part by the price at which coal could be supplied.

The figures illustrate how the market has contracted and hence production declined, particularly during the second half of the 1960s and into the 1970s.

Coal production 1938–77
(million tons)

1938	227	1970	140
1946	190	1972	109
1950	216	1974	97
1955	208	1976	112
1960	184	1977	106
1965	184		

Certain factors are noteworthy.

(a) *Short-term importance.* Coal has remained the principal source of energy and until 1958, demand outstripped supply.

(b) *Long-term view.* The intensity of competition from natural gas, electricity and particularly oil has increased while the very long term holds out the prospect of much wider application of nuclear energy.

(c) *Strategic considerations.* In favour of coal it may be argued that an excessive dependence upon foreign-produced oil is strategically undesirable.

On this evidence it seemed that, while coal would remain of vital importance in the short run, in the longer term the industry would continue to contract. However, from the mid-1970s the Government took a different view. The 1974 rise in world oil prices, the assessment that North Sea oil and gas were strictly finite and the political influence exercised by the coalmining industry all contributed to the decision to develop the country's coal reserves as the best energy prospect for the twenty-first century (*see* 33).

22. Modernisation and adjustment to a contracting market. If coal was to defend its position against its competitors then production costs had to be minimised. The root of this problem lay in the fact that mining is an industry very much subject to diminishing returns because of the greater depth of shafts as surface seams are exhausted and the lack of continuity of seams due to faulting.

Planning therefore required a decision on whether to aim at extracting as much as possible or whether to abandon poor seams and concentrate production in the richer ones. On the basis of this decision capital would be invested.

23. A plan for coal, 1950. The N.C.B. introduced a scheme for reconstruction and development which involved the investment of £365 million by 1960–5.

The existing 950 collieries would be reduced by 350–400 and ultimately 70 per cent of production would be derived from 250 pits.

A labour foorce reduced by 80,000 to 618,000 would by 1961–5 produce an estimated output of 240 million tons per annum at a cost of 35p a ton lower than in 1949.

In the first five years, new pits were sunk and 140 old ones reconstructed. Large sums were spent on mechanisation and improved welfare facilities. Nevertheless it became increasingly clear that the production target would not be attained. The mines were under-manned and there was too great a preoccupation with current production.

24. "Investing in Coal", 1955. An N.C.B. booklet outlined the revised estimates.

(*a*) *Forecast output* for 1965 was now 230 million tons.

(*b*) *Investment expenditure* was expected to be more than double the previous estimate. The new figure of £1,350 million was explained by inflation and by new schemes which were becoming necessary to offset loss of productive capacity.

(*c*) *Labour*. The new estimate was much higher at 682,000.

25. Revised plan for coal, 1960. After 1958, there were coal surpluses for the first time since the war and this necessitated yet another review of the industry's plans.

(*a*) *Projected investment* was cut back by £200 million.

(*b*) *The production target* was reduced to between 200 and 215 million tons by 1965—the maximum which it was felt the market would then absorb.

The plan emphasised that "no severe contraction of the industry is envisaged" but that there would be between thirty-five and seventy collieries fewer than originally intended and with a labour force reduced from the existing 652,000 to between 587,000 and 626,000.

Stress was laid upon efficiency and it was hoped to achieve the target figure at a productivity rate of 30 to 31 cwt (about 1,550 kg) per manshift.

26. National Plan, 1965. The National Plan predicted that over the following five years total energy requirements would increase at an annual average rate of $13\frac{1}{2}$ per cent from 286 million tons of coal equivalent to 324 million tons. On the other hand the decline in the consumption of coal was expected to continue and unlikely to be in excess of 170–80 million tons by 1970.

27. Fuel Policy White Paper, 1965. Following publication of the National Plan, two White Papers set out the Government's fuel policy in general and plans for the reorganisation of the coal industry's finances. Of the N.C.B.'s £927 million capital debt, £406 million was to be written off. This measure would improve the prospect of profitable operation. Moreover the Government was prepared to make funds available to speed up the closure of uneconomic collieries. These were to be used to minimise the social cost of the run-down.

On general fuel policy there was a recognition of the inevitability of the industry's further decline and projections of future consumption were in line with those of the National Plan.

28. Fuel Policy White Paper, 1967. Two years later forecasts of the demand for coal had again been modified. It was now estimated that demand in 1975 would not exceed 120 million tons.

Despite the measures taken in 1965 to support the industry through reorganisation and the closure of uneconomic pits demand had already fallen below the 1965 projection.

Although the industry was more than 75 per cent mechanised, coal alone of the fuel industries remained labour intensive. Moreover there existed the problem that even though closures had improved productivity, overheads were now spread over a smaller total output with a consequent adverse effect on unit costs. Additionally, there was a labour shortage in some of the most productive collieries.

The solution did not lie in subsidisation and protection but rather in further contraction and concentration in the best collieries. In this way costs could be held down and coal made more competitive.

Within this context the White Paper outlined the Government's policy for the transition period to 1970.

(a) *Manpower.* A reduction in the labour force at the rate of 35,000 per year would be tolerable subject to Government assistance in those areas particularly affected.

(b) *Coal utilisation by gas and electricity industries.* The gas and electricity industries would be encouraged to make greater use of coal. Up to £45 million would be made available to them to offset any resulting increase in their costs.

(c) *Adjustment of production to demand.* The excessive stock-piling of coal was to be avoided since this was bad for morale in the industry.

(d) *Increased borrowing powers.* The limit of the N.C.B.'s borrowing powers was raised from £750 million to £900 million.

The Coal Industry Act 1968 introduced those measures in the Fuel Policy White Paper which related to coal.

29. National Coal Board Reports, 1965–6 and 1966–7. These two reports emphasised that the industry's future depended upon the following.

(a) *Increasing productivity.* Further mechanisation and automation as in the remote-controlled Bevercotes Colliery, which would continue to increase productivity.

(b) *The ability-to man the most productive collieries.*

(c) *The development of markets.*

30. Increasing productivity. The following figures illustrate how massive investment by the N.C.B. has raised labour productivity.

Output per manshift
1947–76

	cwt		cwt
1947	21.5	1968	42.5
1955	24.5	1969	43.4
1959	26.9	1970	44.1
1960	28.6	1971	41.9
1962	31.2	1972	45.8
1963	33.4	1973	42.3
1964	34.8	1974	45.0
1965	36.1	1976	43.6
1967	39.6		

Source: Annual Abstract of Statistics.

NOTE: 1 cwt = 50.8 kg.

Fluctuations in the 1970s principally reflect the disturbed state of labour relations.

31. Stabilisation of the labour force.

Average number of wage earners on
colliery books
(thousands)

1938	782	1971	287
1946	697	1972	281
1948	724	1973	268
1950	697	1974	252
1955	699	1975	246
1960	602	1976	247
1965	491	1977	242
1970	305		

The figures reflect both the contraction in the industry and the substantial increase in productivity achieved during the 1960s. They also point dramatically to the uncertainty of mining as a career and explain the failure of the N.C.B. to maintain an adequate recruitment programme.

From 1939–45 the problem was to maintain the labour force at a level sufficient to satisfy the demand for coal. A temporary solution was found in the direction of labour. The problem persisted in the post-war years and was magnified by the ageing of the labour force and the difficulty of recruitment to compensate for retirements. In a situation of over-full employment the competitive pull of more attractive jobs with a more certain future was too great.

During the 1960s the streamlining of the industry exacerbated the problem of manpower planning. Concurrent with the over-all reduction of the labour force existed the need to assure a sufficient labour supply to the colleries in which production was to be concentrated.

32. Labour relations. Nationalisation did not eliminate friction, and production has been frequently handicapped by strikes. Public ownership did not satisfy what may have been the syndicalist feeling of many miners that the industry should be operated in their interest rather than that of the nation.

Although wages rose steeply and miners established themselves amongst the highest paid workers this favourable differential was gradually eroded by the inflationary pressures of the 1960s and culminated in the most serious stoppage since the war when over 100,000 miners struck in 1971 and more than 1 million working days were lost.

The table below shows comparative average wages since 1938 and may help to explain the growing dissatisfaction of miners during the 1960s.

Average weekly earnings 1938–76
(£)

	Mining	Adult males in all other industries
1938	2.90	3.45
1946	6.15	6.45
1950	9.10	7.50
1955	13.05	11.15
1960	15.55	14.50
1965	19.13	20.16
1970	25.45	28.91
1976	78.30	60.23

Source: Annual Abstract of Statistics.

Inflation accelerated during the 1970s, Government attempts to suppress it being confined to prices and incomes policies. Such measures implied the further compression of differentials, something which the highly organised manual unions were not prepared to accept, particularly from a Conservative Government.

Of these unions the National Union of Mineworkers (N.U.M.) proved the most militant and in 1973, rejecting pay restraints, struck again. The effect upon electricity supplies put the whole of British industry in some difficulty. Production was reorganised on the basis of a three-day week. Strangely, output was little affected, i.e. overnight, productivity was almost doubled.

The ensuing general election returned a Labour Government which acceded to N.U.M. pressures. Differentials were once again widened and in general miners now gave support to national pay policies.

33. A national energy policy. Post-1945 attempts at a national energy policy have not proved entirely successful, largely because of the changes of direction of different governments in the development of publicly owned industries. On one view, Government intervention has been all too frequently politically motivated and has impeded a rational economic strategy.

In the mid-1970s policy was based upon the following considerations.

(a) *Oil.* Offshore discoveries are finite and need to be conserved.

(b) *Electricity.* The Government is unwilling to permit the Central Electricity Generating Board to develop its capacity using the primary fuels of its choice. While world price rises in 1973–4 made oil uncompetitive, subsequent stabilisation and the increased wage costs of coal production restored its position. The Government is, however, concerned to exploit coal resources.

(c) *Gas.* Proven reserves of natural gas are calculated to be sufficient to satisfy present levels of consumption well into the twenty-first century. Nevertheless the same arguments have been applied, if less convincingly, as those used against oil. Prices were therefore raised artificially in 1977 to make it less competitive with electricity and hence coal.

(d) *Coal.* Vast reserves around Selby in Yorkshire are scheduled for development. It is upon coal that the Government bases its long-term strategy.

(e) *Nuclear energy.* Similar pressures have inhibited the more rapid development of nuclear energy which despite its much lower cost per kilowatt has been opposed by a powerful anti-pollution pro-mining lobby.

PROGRESS TEST 4

1. To what extent was coal of economic value before 1760? (1)

2. Without coal there would have been no Industrial Revolution. Support this statement. (2)

3. How did the coal export trade contribute to Britain's industrialisation? (4)

4. Diminishing returns in the coal industry after 1880 were at first concealed by the customer's preparedness to bear the extra cost of mining. What evidence is there for this assertion? (5)

5. What factors postponed the coal industry's exposure to the full effects of depression in the early 1920s? (7)

6. What was the principal cause of the contraction in demand in the period 1913–37? (8)

7. Between 1945 and 1958, supply and demand on the British coal market did not equate. What was the explanation? (10)

8. What was the "butty" system of mining? (12)

9. Conditions of employment in the mines were improved slowly but only in consequence of State intervention. Explain. (13)

10. The Sankey Report, 1920, held out hopes of improvement which were soon dispelled. Give reasons. (14, 15)

11. What was the Government's response to the plight of the coal industry in 1929? (18)

12. Describe the two principal aspects of the labour problem which has confronted the National Coal Board. (20)

13. Modernisation plans for the coal mines encountered difficulties which called for their frequent revision. What were the plans and why have they been revised? (22–25)

14. What lay at the roots of labour problems in the 1970s? (32)

15. Explain the nature of energy policy in 1978. (33)

CHAPTER V

Iron and Steel

THE NATURE OF THE INDUSTRY

1. Composition of iron ore. Iron is found in ores which contain varying percentages of the metal in conjunction with oxygen, silicon, sulphur and other materials. A rich ore may contain as much as 75 per cent metal. Ores with as little as 30 per cent require favourable local conditions to make smelting worth while. Ores with a smaller iron content are seldom worth working.

2. Definition of the industry. This industry has always tended to practise vertical integration, i.e. to link closely in one direction with coal and coke production and iron ore mining and, in the other direction, with shipbuilding and engineering, hardware and allied trades. In the interest of analysis, it is best defined as follows (*see also* Fig. 2).

(*a*) *Smelting of ore* to produce iron, cast in "pigs" (moulds), with some consideration of the provision of coke and ore.

(*b*) *Wrought iron and crude steel production* (the latter in "ingots", or slabs).

(*c*) *Finishing processes*, e.g. castings, forgings, plate, tube, wire.

3. A key industry. Industrialisation has been conditioned by the growth of the iron and steel industry. It is a basic industry upon which many others depend and consequently its development has often been viewed as an index of a country's economic growth. Its vital national role provides the basis of the argument in favour of public ownership.

4. Importance of changing techniques. The most important aspect of the history of the industry is that successive discoveries have intimately affected its structure, its size and its location. In other industries (e.g. cotton) improvements have been made to basic inventions without consequence to organisation and location.

The industry therefore has an inherent instability which is dangerous to established producers in times of technical change. The natural advantages enjoyed by certain regions or nations may be quickly lost upon the introduction of new production processes.

PRODUCTION BEFORE THE EIGHTEENTH CENTURY

5. Growing demand. Iron was produced in England from an early date. There was smelting in Roman times and it continued through the Anglo-Saxon period into the Middle Ages, when it flourished, owing to the growing demand for armaments. The home industry at this time found it increasingly difficult to meet demand and additional supplies had to be imported.

6. Production methods. Smelting was carried out in small charcoal-fired furnaces purely by trial-and-error methods. Blooms (thick bars) were produced, usually consisting of an iron core surrounded by a thin steel shell. This was cast or worked under a hammer to make it malleable.

7. Location.

(*a*) *The earliest centres of production* were naturally those where iron ore was found in conjunction with abundant timber, e.g. the Weald, the Forest of Dean, south Staffordshire.

(*b*) *The exhaustion of timber supplies* led to the gradual movement of the furnaces to areas which were still well forested, and production in Wales then began to expand. (NOTE: It was found cheaper to carry ore to the forests than timber to the iron workings.)

(*c*) This trend was reinforced in the late sixteenth century by legislation. The Crown, worried by the destruction of forests whose timber was urgently required for shipbuilding, restricted the number and the location of the furnaces.

Legislation served not only to disperse the industry, but also to curb production. By the eighteenth century, the industry was producing only 18,000 tons annually and the country was relying in large measure upon supplies from Spain, Russia and Sweden.

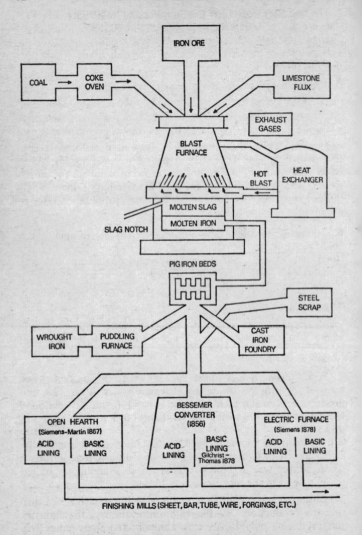

Fig. 2.—Iron and crude steel production

EIGHTEENTH-CENTURY CHANGES IN TECHNIQUE AND LOCATION

8. Need for change. Industrialisation increased the pressure of demand and underlined the iron industry's lack of productive capacity as well as the high cost of wide dispersion. There existed, therefore, a strong stimulus to technical change.

9. Abraham Darby. It had been impossible to use coal in the smelting process, since its sulphur content combined with the iron to make it too brittle. Early in the eighteenth century, Abraham Darby and his successors, ironmasters of Coalbrookdale, devised a method of converting coal to coke, which could be used for smelting.

For a considerable time, they managed to keep their discovery secret, but by the end of the century it was widely known and a great expansion of production was initiated.

This was assisted by the superiority for many purposes (e.g. hollow-ware) of the new iron over charcoal-smelted iron.

10. Henry Cort. Until 1783, malleable (i.e. wrought) iron could only be produced most uneconomically by working the pig under the hammer. In that year, Henry Cort devised the process of rolling and puddling. Pig iron was heated in a furnace and stirred, or "puddled", until the impurities were removed. The pure metal was then passed between rollers and became malleable.

This process led to a great expansion of output and to a much lower cost of production.

11. Homfray of Tredegar. In 1790, the benefits of Cort's process were augmented by Homfray's design of a refinery. This removed unwanted silicon from the pig prior to puddling and produced a considerable saving in the amount of pig used.

These inventions of Cort and Homfray gave rise to Britain's supremacy in the production of wrought iron until it was finally superseded by steel in the last quarter of the nineteenth century.

12. Fuel conservation and the "blast". One of the greatest problems of the eighteenth-century ironmasters was to raise temperature to the degree required and with a minimum of fuel. To this end, experiments were made by the Darbys with a blast of air. Initially, the blowing apparatus was operated by water power but by 1800 Watt's steam engine, already in use in other industries, was performing this task.

13. New locations for the industry. The new processes fundamentally affected the distribution of the iron industry. No longer was it dependent upon water power and supplies of timber. The determining consideration was now coal, both for smelting and for motive power, in proximity to deposits of iron ore.

From the end of the eighteenth century, the rapidly expanding industry began to concentrate more and more closely in areas which satisfied these requirements, e.g. South Wales, the Midlands and Yorkshire.

The concentration of smelting was accompanied by a similar concentration of the secondary processes, for which the coalfields offered the same advantages.

14. Steel. The difference between cast and wrought iron lies in their carbon content. Cast iron has between 2 per cent and 5 per cent carbon content; wrought iron has none. Steel is pure iron with an added carbon content of $1-1\frac{1}{2}$ per cent. Although steel has been known for centuries, its production was often defective, because the carbon content could not be accurately controlled.

An advance was made with the introduction of a crucible process in the 1740s by Benjamin Huntsman. This made possible the production of a high grade steel of known quality. The method was necessarily expensive and applicable only to small outputs, and until the end of the eighteenth century England was principally dependent upon foreign supplies, which were themselves produced in very restricted quantities.

NINETEENTH-CENTURY CHANGES IN TECHNIQUE AND LOCATION

15. Progress with fuel conservation.

(*a*) *J. B. Neilson.* Many detailed improvements were made in the design of blast operating equipment but it was in Scotland that the most revolutionary change occurred. Here, the industry had been handicapped by the difficulties experienced in smelting local iron ore with Lanark coal, a kind which would not coke.

In 1828, J. B. Neilson discovered that by using a hot furnace blast, coal could be used in place of coke. This most important discovery gave rise to the great Scottish industry, which quickly grew to rival and even outstrip those of the older established areas.

The hot blast was gradually introduced throughout Britain, although in England, because of the use of different varieties of ore and coal, the economies were not as great. (Today, the hot blast is used almost everywhere.)

(*b*) *Budd of Ystalyfera*. In 1845, further advance was made at Ystalyfera, near Swansea. Budd designed a furnace in which hot exhaust gases were utilised to heat the blast, instead of being dissipated in the atmosphere.

The new type of furnace with a closed top was accepted in step with the acceptance of the hot blast.

16. Wrought iron improvements.

(*a*) *Joseph Hall*. In south Staffordshire, Joseph Hall devised in 1825 an improved puddling process known as pigboiling. Previously, the floor of the puddling furnace had been lined with sand, a wasteful practice, since much metal was absorbed. For sand, he substituted a substance known as "bulldog" which absorbed the impurities in the pig but not the metal.

The immediate result of this discovery was to give the south Staffordshire wrought iron producers an immense advantage over their rivals in other parts of the country.

(*b*) *James Nasmyth*. In 1839, Nasmyth invented a steam hammer which was used to rid the puddled iron of slag before it passed to the rolling mill (the process was known as shingling).

17. Growth of the market. The nineteenth century witnessed an enormous increase in the demand for iron.

(*a*) *Armaments*. The period 1790–1815 was one of strained relations or open war with the French, in which there was a great demand for armaments.

(*b*) *Machinery*. As industrialisation gathered momentum, so the demand for machinery increased.

(*c*) *Railways*. From 1830, with the rapid development of the railways, grew a demand for railway material.

(*d*) *New uses*. Wilkinson (*see* VI, **8**), introduced to the country many uses for iron which at first were considered quite unpractical but later were enthusiastically accepted, e.g. bridges, barges, ships, building.

(*e*) *Exports*. Britain's inventions, coal, iron ore and political stability established her lead in the iron industry. Well into the second half of the century, her production outstripped that of France, the U.S.A. and Germany, her nearest rivals. Until 1870, she was able largely to monopolise the world export market in iron products.

18. The 1850s and new areas of production. The growth of demand gave the following new areas an opportunity to compete.

(*a*) *Northumberland and Durham.* This area had distinct advantages:

(*i*) Durham coal;

(*ii*) ore from the Cleveland Hills;

(*iii*) proximity to ports which provided an export outlet and which had a growing shipbuilding industry.

(*b*) *The West Riding of Yorkshire*, which had the advantage of an extensive coalfield.

(*c*) *Lancashire and Cumberland.* Here there were coalfields and, in Cumberland, deposits of non-phosphoric iron ore. This was an important consideration in the light of subsequent technical developments in steel production (*see* below).

19. New processes for steel production.

(*a*) *Bessemer converter.* In 1856, Sir Henry Bessemer devised a new process for producing malleable iron and steel without puddling. In a converter, a very powerful blast was used to burn out the impurities from the molten pig iron. To produce steel, he added a quantity of spiegeleisen, an alloy of iron, manganese and carbon. Since the carbon content of the alloy was known, its addition to the pure iron could be regulated.

Bessemer steel proved to be immensely superior to malleable iron in strength and reliability. In the 1860s it began slowly to replace iron for rails, girders, plates and other products whose strength was important.

Disadvantage of the Bessemer process. The converter was lined with an acid material which was ineffective in removing the phosphorus left in pig iron after smelting. The phosphorus affected the quality of the steel. Since much of Britain's ore was phosphoric, resort had to be made to imports from Spain and Sweden.

(*b*) *Siemens-Martin open hearth.* In 1867, Sir William Siemens in Britain and Pierre Martin in France both made similar experiments. Pig iron was melted with ore in a shallow hearth lined with silica bricks (an acid material) to give acid steel.

Comparison with Bessemer process. It had the same disadvantage in that the acid lining would not remove phosphorus but the advantage that the open hearth permitted control during the conversion process.

(c) Gilchrist and Thomas basic steel. In 1878, Sidney Thomas and Percy Gilchrist lined a converter with a basic substance (dolomite) and clay. This method successfully eliminated phosphorus and the way was then open to the large-scale production of steel.

20. Transition from wrought iron to steel. In the 1860s there was a resistance to the introduction of steel from producers who had vast sums invested in the wrought iron processes. At first, steel production remained small while wrought iron production continued to expand, reaching its peak in the Franco-Prussian War 1870–1.

The general depression in trade which marked the last quarter of the nineteenth century brought a steady decline in the fortunes of wrought iron, hastened by the introduction of basic steel.

There were early prejudices against basic steel, and acid steel continued to enjoy preference when strength was important. However, mild steel made by the basic process had many applications previously reserved to wrought iron. By the end of the century, wrought iron had been very largely displaced.

21. Changes in location 1870–1913. The dependence of the steel producers in the 1860s upon imported non-phosphoric ores led to yet another change in the relative importance of producing regions. Now it became important to have a site close to a port.

The introduction of the basic steel process did not reverse this trend, since, with the exhaustion of many domestic sources of ore, imports grew steadily.

During this period, the Midlands industry declined in importance. In the North-east, however, port facilities led to a steady expansion of both pig iron and steel production, until in 1913 it was the chief British centre.

New areas of pig iron production were also being developed. Fuel economies made it possible to carry the smaller amount of coal required to the little-worked ore fields of Northamptonshire and Lincolnshire.

22. The electric furnace. In 1878, Siemens developed an electric furnace which produced very high temperatures. By the 1890s it was in restricted use. Its disadvantage lay in the very high cost of electric current, but it has proved of great value in the production of high grade steels when only moderate quantities are required.

23. Decline of the Bessemer process in Britain. During the 1880s

the open hearth overtook the Bessemer converter in importance.
There were the following three main reasons.

(a) Technical superiority, since it gave the opportunity to test
for quality during production.

(b) The British market lay chiefly in high grade steels which
could best be produced by the open hearth method.

(c) The growth of foreign competition induced specialisation.
In the 1870s and 1880s, the German and U.S. iron and steel
industries made rapid progress, but the nature of their ore reserves disposed them towards basic open hearth and acid and
basic Bessemer steels. Britain was led to concentrate upon steels
of a very different character which could best be produced in an
acid open hearth.

24. Decline in Britain's superiority. In 1870, Britain was the
world's leading producer of iron and steel, but by 1913 stood
third in output to the U.S.A. and Germany. These three countries then supplied the greater part of the rapidly growing world
market. Although Britain responded to the increase in demand,
she did not do so as effectively as her competitors. This is explained by the following.

(a) *Small-scale production.* The industry had developed in the
hands of a large number of small family firms and, by 1880, the
pattern of organisation was fairly rigid. Amalgamation was not
easy because of the heavy investment in immovable capital
equipment.

In contrast, the developing U.S. and German industries were
organised on a large scale from the beginning, e.g. the U.S. Steel
Corporation and Stahlwerksverband, which sited coking ovens,
blast furnaces and steelworks in close proximity.

(b) *Exhaustion of raw materials.* From the 1880s the effect
upon costs of shrinking reserves of raw materials was becoming
more marked. Many iron ore deposits were exhausted and deeper
coalmining raised fuel costs. Again, there was a contrast with the
vast accessible natural resources of the U.S.A. and Germany.

MARKET FLUCTUATIONS, 1900–39

25. Expansion, 1900–14. Despite its relative loss of advantage,
the British industry remained sound. Exports were growing and
blast furnace capacity was expanded to meet rising demand. By
1913, pig iron production had grown to $10\frac{1}{4}$ million tons.

26. War production, 1914–18. During the war years were sown the seeds of subsequent problems.

(a) *The difficulty of importing ore* brought a greater reliance upon domestic sources. Since these were largely phosphoric, there was therefore, a swing from the established acid open hearth to the basic open hearth, which had never been Britain's speciality. Furthermore, the existing steelworks were not sited close to suitable iron ore fields and there was a consequent adverse effect upon costs.

(b) *The demands of war* led to a great expansion of world steel capacity amongst both belligerents and neutrals.

27. Wartime co-operation. One beneficial result of war was closer co-operation and the integration of technical research throughout the industry. This led in 1918 to the foundation of the National Federation of Iron and Steel Manufacturers.

28. Post-war depression. Immediate post-war requirements having been satisfied, the market collapsed. World capacity was too great for a period in which credit facilities were lacking.

All European production was checked, but Britain was particularly hard hit, as can be seen from the following table.

	1913	1919	1921
Pig iron output (million tons):	10¼	9	2½
Crude steel output (million tons):	7½	9½	3½

NOTE: 1 ton = 1.016 tonnes.

29. Reasons for Britain's plight.

(a) *Failure of demand* for Britain's specialities, wrought iron and acid steels.

(b) *Britain's relatively high costs* in the production of basic steels for which there *was* some demand.

(c) *Invasion of the home market* by cheap German basic Bessemer steel.

30. Attempted remedies.

(a) *Rationalisation.* A reduction in costs was sought through amalgamations to create large-scale units of production. The attempt was only partially successful, since there was a lack of capital for thorough reorganisation.

(b) *Price stabilising.* In order to attract capital by a guaranteed return, the main heavy goods producers agreed a scale of prices.

As a result of these measures, by 1929 there was some revival in the industry, but it was short-lived.

31. World slump, 1929–32. Loss of confidence on the New York Stock Exchange brought a crash which led to a world-wide slump. The effects on the British iron and steel industry were disastrous.

(*a*) *There was an immediate collapse of demand* for heavy capital equipment.

(*b*) *Competition from cheap imports* increased as European producers unloaded stocks on world markets at any price. British steel output plummeted:

> 1929: 9¼ million tons
> 1930: 7¼ million tons
> 1931: 5¼ million tons

In these circumstances, there was an outcry for protection from unfair competition.

32. Protection. In 1932, the Import Duties Advisory Committee was asked to grant protection to the industry. It agreed, provided that lower costs were secured through a fundamental reorganisation. The British Iron and Steel Federation was created in 1934 and in consultation with I.D.A.C. became responsible for:

(*a*) supervising the redevelopment of the industry;
(*b*) regulating output;
(*c*) fixing prices;
(*d*) subsidising high-cost producers.

In 1935, the tariff was reinforced by import quotas.

33. Revival after 1933. The basis of revival was the elimination of European competition at home and the gradual recovery of domestic markets in shipbuilding, heavy engineering, motor vehicles and—in 1938—rearmament.

There was not, however, any comparable expansion of exports, since British prices remained uncompetitive.

34. Export failure. The industry's lack of competitive strength in international markets may be explained by the following.

(*a*) *Loss of cheap crude steel.* In the 1920s, exports had chiefly comprised finished steel products based upon cheap, imported crude steel. Protection denied these supplies (the Continentals then diverted their excess output to their finishing processes).

(b) *Uneconomic production.* Some attempts were made at reorganisation of the industry in large-scale units of production (e.g. the Stewarts & Lloyds steel and tube works at Corby), but in general too little attention was paid to plant specialisation and the relocation of the industry on more favourably placed sites.

Guaranteed prices and protection from foreign competition reduced the pressure on the industry to make economies.

POST-WAR RECONSTRUCTION AND EXPANSION

35. The 1939–45 war. The Government assumed control through the Ministry of Supply, which supervised prices. As in other industries, war retarded growth. There was little expansion of capacity and maintenance difficulties were encountered.

36. A period of achievement, 1945–58. Despite the insecure foundations of the pre-war period, there was a remarkable expansion of output to a level four-fifths greater than in 1938. Growth was induced by a continuous extension of home demand until 1958. To achieve this success, the industry had to face three problems:

(a) structure and control;
(b) technical innovation;
(c) location.

37. Structure and control. The Labour Government of 1945 sought to nationalise the industry at the earliest opportunity. As an interim measure, an Iron and Steel Board was appointed to supervise reorganisation while the industry remained in private hands. It set production targets and required the British Iron and Steel Federation to submit plans for their realisation by 1950–2.

(a) *First development plan.* Six million tons of steel capacity (4 million tons of which to replace obsolete plant) was to be created, thus raising the industry's potential from 14 million tons to 16 million tons annually. Considerable plant specialisation was envisaged, with the concentration of production in fewer but larger mills. The development plan was accomplished ahead of schedule and target figures exceeded.

NOTE: For a short time, the industry was under public ownership. In 1949, the Iron and Steel Corporation was formed to buy out the firms making heavy primary products. With the election in 1951 of a Conservative Government, the majority of these firms were returned to private ownership.

(b) *Second development plan.* In 1952, fresh targets were set for 1957 of 20½ million tons of steel and 15 million tons of pig iron.

(c) *The continuing increase in demand* until 1958 led to plans for a capacity in 1962–3 of 29 million tons of steel and 19 million tons of pig iron.

38. Price control. In 1953, the Iron and Steel Board was formed to regulate capital investment and to control home prices, since it was argued that there was insufficient competition to safeguard the consumer. A maximum price for each class of product was geared to the average cost of its producers. High-cost producers were subsidised from an industry fund whose revenue was derived from producers of ingots. These methods displayed:

(a) *the advantage of stable prices,* an important consideration to manufacturing industries which made use of steel;

(b) *the disadvantage* that insufficient pressure is placed on the high-cost producer.

39. Technical innovation. Into the 1960s substantial capital investment in new techniques accounted for the high productivity of labour and the relatively low costs of the British industry. Technical innovations included the following.

(a) *The oxygen blast.* Higher temperatures can be raised more economically than with air.

(b) *Preparation of pig iron.* Sinter, a mixture of ore and burning coke, is fed to the furnaces, yielding economies in both fuel and ore.

(c) *Power.* In the finishing processes, oil proved more economical than steam.

(d) *Continuous rolling mills.* These mills cover vast areas and permit the steel ingot to be reduced stage by stage on a straight "conveyor belt" principle.

(e) *Scale of equipment.* There has been a great increase in the size of blast furnaces, open hearths and Bessemer converters.

(f) *Automation.* In many processes, automation of production has reached an advanced stage.

40. The problem of location. Much discussion has centred on the comparative costs of the various producing regions. Since the history of the industry demonstrates clearly that today's regional advantage may tomorrow be obsolete, the choice of site for expansion is crucial. The following are some of the pertinent and often conflicting considerations.

(a) *Fuel efficiency.* The more efficient the use of fuel, the less important is a coalfield site.

(b) *Grade of ore.* Low-grade ore demands an ore field site in order to reduce transport costs.

(c) *Imported ores and freight rates.* The advantage of a coastal site may be cancelled when freight rates are high.

(d) *Scrap prices and choice of process.* Price permitting, scrap may be substituted for pig iron, but scrap is suited to the open hearth rather than the Bessemer converter.

41. Changes in location 1938–58. Reference to the tables of figures illustrates both the growth in total output of iron and steel and the contribution to this output of various producing areas.

Pig iron production (*thousand tons*)
1938–58

	1938	1945	1950	1955	1958
East Midlands	1,598	1,697	2,209	2,342	2,080
Lincolnshire	868	1,039	1,239	1,880	2,048
N.E. Coast	1,833	1,664	2,402	2,824	2,848
Yorkshire }	349	349	437	148	169
Lancs., Cheshire, N. Wales. }				843	1,104
N.W. Coast	722	613	824	964	801
Staffs, Worcs., Warwicks.	317	339	551	567	438
S. Wales & Monmouth	665	864	1,232	1,975	2,511
Scotland	409	542	739	927	976
Total	6,761	7,107	9,633	12,470	12,975

Source: Annual Abstract of Statistics.

It will be observed that while the expansion of pig iron capacity was unevenly distributed the most significant growth was in Lincolnshire and S. Wales while the N.W. Coast and Staffs., Worcs., and Warwicks, showed a relative decline.

Crude steel production (thousand tons)
1938–58

	1938	1945	1950	1955	1958
East Midlands	444	558	756	1,000	938
Lincolnshire	1,083	1,099	1,561	2,003	2,252
N.E. Coast	2,279	2,353	3,354	3,992	3,875
Sheffield	1,523	1,714	2,218	2,636	2,505
Yorkshire Lancs., Cheshire, N. Wales.	806	1,000	1,292	1,801	2,108
N.W. Coast	279	317	423	365	327
Staffs., Worcs., Warwicks.	625	656	856	1,043	966
S. Wales & Monmouth	1,759	2,380	3,407	4,607	4,479
Scotland	1,601	1,747	2,426	2,344	2,116
Total	10,399	11,824	16,293	19,791	19,566

Source: Annual Abstract of Statistics.

The figures reveal that by 1958 the seller's market of the post-war years had begun to harden and crude steel production in fact declined from its 1957 record level of 21,699,000 tons. However, it will also be seen that in the twenty year period production almost doubled, the greater part of this expansion occurring after 1945 and that the most spectacular growth was in Lincolnshire and S. Wales. Nevertheless, with the exception of the N.W. Coast, all areas benefited.

42. Slower growth in the 1960s. During the 1960s the iron and steel industry experienced a substantially lower growth rate as is evidenced by the figures.

Pig iron and crude steel production (thousand tons)
1961–71

	1961	1962	1963	1964	1965	1966
Pig iron	14,747	13,692	14,591	17,274	17,460	15,710
Crude steel	22,086	20,491	22,520	26,230	27,006	24,315

	1967	1968	1969	1970	1971
Pig iron	15,153	16,432	16,390	17,393	15,173
Crude steel	23,895	25,862	26,422	27,869	23,793

Source: Annual Abstract of Statistics.

Certain major factors should be considered.

(a) *Slow U.K. economic growth rate.* The domestic market for steel is highly sensitive to shifts in economic policy. It has suffered in consequence during periods of recession when the level of demand has been restrained and investment in capital goods therefore discouraged. Had the economy achieved a more rapid and stable growth rate there would have been a corresponding expansion of the demand for steel and the industry would have had a better chance of increasing its productive capacity more evenly.

(b) *Keener international competition.* By the close of the 1950s the European and Japanese economies were beginning to forge ahead and world markets in steel and steel products were becoming increasingly competitive.

(c) *Structural problems.* The scale of production of many older units was small and uncompetitive. Although productivity increased by 20 per cent between 1957 and 1965, in that year output per man hour was still only half that of the U.S.A. and substantially less than that of E.C.S.C. and Japan. Rationalisation of the industry to achieve greater output at lower unit cost called for vast investment and the concentration of production. It was felt by some that this would not be achieved while the industry remained in private hands.

43. Steel Nationalisation White Paper, April 1965. The Labour Government set out its proposals to renationalise the thirteen major companies which (with the firm of Richard Thomas and Baldwin which had not been denationalised), accounted for over 90 per cent of iron and steel production.

The White Paper analysis made the following points.

(a) *Structure of the industry.* There were 300 works carrying out iron ore mining, pig iron and crude steel production and steel finishing. Of these only 22 were integrated plants carrying out three processes. 38 made steel and finished it while there were 92 rolling plants and about 150 specialist units which overlapped with the engineering industry. They were owned by 260 limited liability companies which were members of the British Iron and Steel Federation.

(b) *Role in the economy.* The industry was one of the largest in the economy with 1964 sales in excess of £1,000 million and with 315,000 employees. Its average capital investment in 1960–4 was £130 million per annum or 11 per cent of all manufacturing invest-

ment. Key industries, particularly in the engineering sector, were
dependent upon steel and they accounted for two-fifths of all
manufactures. The steel industry was therefore of critical importance to exports.

(c) *Public supervision.* The history of the industry showed that
for more than thirty years it had been "generally accepted" that
by its nature it required a special degree of public supervision.
This had led to nationalisation in 1949. However, the Iron and
Steel Act 1953 had transferred the industry's assets to the Iron
and Steel Realisation Agency whose function was to return them
to private industry. With the exception of Richard Thomas and
Baldwin, this process had been largely completed by 1961.

The 1953 Act had also provided for the supervision of the
industry by an Iron and Steel Board appointed by the Minister of
Fuel and Power. Its functions were to hold a watching brief on
production, capacity and arrangements for procuring and dis-
tributing raw materials and fuel. Of greatest importance, it also
set maximum prices.

(d) *Defects of the existing system.* It was argued that the
system had the following three major defects.

(i) The powers of the Iron and Steel Board were purely
negative. It could not insist on development which might be in
the interest of the economy as a whole when it proved commercially unattractive to individual steel companies.

(ii) The scale of production was now so great (e.g. in 1965 a new
integrated plant would cost £150 million) that it was increasingly
difficult to secure adequate private funds to finance investment.

(iii) The firms in the industry showed little tendency to compete. The maximum prices set by the Iron and Steel Board had in
fact been treated as the actual prices at which all companies sold.
If monopoly was inherent in the industry then it was better that
this power should be publicly exercised.

44. Objectives of the Government's proposals. The 1965 White
Paper concluded by outlining the Government's objectives.

(a) *Investment.* The rate of development and the location of
new capacity would be planned centrally in harmony with the
needs of the whole economy.

(b) *Production and marketing.* Central planning would eliminate wasteful practices such as cross hauling and would enable
computers and new management techniques to be used to best
advantage.

(c) *Exports.* The competitive strength of the industry in increasingly competitive world markets would be improved by the scale of operation which nationalisation would permit.

The Iron and Steel Bill which gave effect to the White Paper proposals was published in July 1966 and enacted in March 1967. On the vesting date, 28th July 1967, the new British Steel Corporation (B.S.C.) assumed control of the thirteen major companies together with Richard Thomas and Baldwin.

45. Formation and dissolution of iron and steel bodies subsequent to nationalisation. As a result of nationalisation some existing organisations were dissolved while new ones were set up.

(a) *British Iron and Steel Federation.* This body was dissolved on the 31st October 1967 and the majority of its functions transferred to the British Steel Corporation.

(b) *British Independent Steel Producers Association.* Covering about 150 producers with 100,000 employees, this association was formed in July 1967.

(c) *Iron and Steel Advisory Committee.* Formed in October 1967 and comprising representatives of the public and private sectors of the industry, of trade unions and government departments, its terms of reference were to consider the situation, outlook, plans and policies of the industry in relation to the national economic planning as a whole.

(d) *Iron and Steel Consumer Council.* The Council was set up in October 1967 to consider any matter affecting the consumer's interests including prices.

46. Reorganisation and rationalisation. In August 1967 B.S.C. published its initial proposals for reorganisation in the form of a White Paper.

(a) *Grouping of companies.* The fourteen companies would be concentrated in two stages into four geographical groups to be known as Midland Group; Northern and Tubes Group; Scottish and North West Group; South Wales Group.

(b) *Management.* The organisation of the management structure was also set out in detail.

Two years later in a second report on organisation (March 1969) it was argued that an industrial structure based on the old companies grouped in multi-product geographical areas was uneconomic. It was therefore proposed to replace the existing system with four product divisions, special steels, strip mills, general steels, tubes.

These recommendations were incorporated in the Iron and Steel Act 1969.

47. First Annual Report of B.S.C., March 1969. The report envisaged improved profitability as the domestic economy expanded and as the benefits of rationalisation were experienced. Assuming an annual 3 per cent increase in gross domestic product the anticipated output of crude steel in 1975 would be in the region of 30–4 million tonnes. This would call for major new developments and the concentration of production in fewer and larger modern complexes.

Proposals were also made for the capital reorganisation of the industry. These were subsequently embodied in the Iron and Steel Act 1969.

48. Iron and Steel Act 1969. Enacted in July, provision was made for the structural and financial reorganisation of the industry.

(*a*) *Borrowing powers.* The Act authorised an increase in B.S.C.'s borrowing powers from £400 million to £500 million, while there was provision for a further increase, if necessary, subject to parliamentary approval.

(*b*) *Overseas borrowing.* Authority was given to raise capital overseas.

(*c*) *Debt conversion.* Authority was also given for the conversion of £750 milion of B.S.C.'s capital debt of £834 million to "public dividend capital", a form of equity analogous to ordinary share capital.

(*d*) *Dissolution of old companies.* The Minister was empowered to transfer the assets of the companies taken over by B.S.C. and subsequently to dissolve the companies themselves.

The intention was to promote the pace of rationalisation in order to secure as quickly as possible the benefits of bulk purchase, of co-ordinating the development of new capacity and of economising in the use of existing capital.

There was, however, no blueprint for the future location of the industry and no list of proposed closures.

49. Investment plans, 1969–75. The 1969 Act provided, it was hoped, the means for the realisation of the industry's investment plans which had been published in the previous month.

The annual rate of investment over the six years to 1975 was expected to be between £150 million and £175 million. It was not expected that new works would be built on "green field" sites or that there would be major closures. There was, however, the prospect of substantial expansion of sites adjacent to the deep water ore terminals at Port Talbot and Lackenby and of a major new plant at Scunthorpe and a new ore terminal on the Clyde.

The results of this investment were the expected elimination of 40,000 jobs and the raising of productivity from 90 tonnes per man year to 150 tonnes by the mid-1970s.

50. Ten-year investment strategy, 1972. Previous plans were updated and extended. It was proposed to invest £3,000 million in ion in the decade to 1982 with the intention of increasing capacity to some 36–8 million tonnes. Obsolete open hearth furnaces were to be closed by 1980 and replaced by oxygen and electric arc processes.

51. Financial performance of B.S.C. The Corporation's turnover rose from £1,071 million in 1967–8 to £1,478 million in 1972–3, at which point it made a pre-tax profit of £9 million after charging depreciation of £90 million and interest of £44 million. Despite the poor net return on capital invested, this was an improvement on the loss of £10 million in 1970–1 and £68 million in 1971–2.

Subsequently B.S.C.'s financial results steadily deteriorated until in 1977–8, after politically embarrassing attempts at concealment, a loss of some £500 million was disclosed with a comparable if smaller loss predicted for 1978–9.

52. Interpretation of financial results. The Corporation's catastrophic performance in the mid-1970s can be explained by the following.

(*a*) *Intervention for socio-political reasons*. In common with other publicly owned industries, B.S.C. has suffered from Government interference with its commercial and investment strategies for social and political reasons. The Corporation's investment strategy called for large-scale closures of obsolete and inefficient plant and the concentration of production on a limited number of sites. Where closure would have resulted in unemployment in politically sensitive constituencies, works were kept open and continued to operate at a loss.

(*b*) *World recession*. Following the fourfold increase in oil prices in 1973–4 the pace of economic expansion slackened throughout the Western world. Demand for steel did not grow at the rate previously anticipated.

(c) *Excess world capacity.* During the 1970s world steelmaking capacity continued to grow not only amongst established producers but also in developing countries such as South Korea. B.S.C. found it more difficult to compete with more modern, lower-cost producers, even in the home market which continued to import large steel tonnages.

(d) *Diseconomies of scale.* B.S.C. is by far the largest single producer in the E.E.C. with a capacity twice that of its nearest rival. During the 1970s economists have come to question the extent to which, at least in Britain, unit costs are lowered by increasing the scale of enterprise.

53. The private sector. The The Iron and Steel Act 1967 left in private ownership over 100 companies with some 160 works. They range in scale from the very small to those whose output fell just short of the criterion for nationalisation. In character, they cover large integrated concerns which incorporate steelmaking with engineering and small firms engaged in specialist steelmaking.

While accounting for only about 10 per cent of total tonnage, private firms produce about one-quarter of Britain's deliveries of finished steel and about one-third of the value of total turnover. The private sector is particularly strong in the manufacture of finished products for the engineering industry and in the production of alloy and stainless steels.

THE EUROPEAN COAL AND STEEL COMMUNITY (E.C.S.C.)

54. Treaty of Paris 1951. The European Coal and Steel Community (E.C.S.C.), of which Britain became a full member on 1st January 1973, was created by the Treaty of Paris 1951 (*see* XI, **31**). It provided for the abolition of duties and quantitative restrictions on trade in coal and steel between members. Also prohibited was discrimination by producers in prices, delivery terms and transport rates.

In 1967, the European Commission was made E.C.S.C.'s executive body with the European Parliament exercising supervisory powers.

55. Funding. To finance the operation of E.C.S.C., coal and steel producers pay to the Commission a percentage levy on output, the funds being used to finance administration, the provision of

cheap loans to finance the retraining and resettlement of redundant labour and the building of factories in declining coal and
steel areas.

Britain has benefited from these payments in respect of closures which occurred after the beginning of 1973.

56. Administrative powers. The Treaty of Paris affords wide-
ranging powers to the Community.

(a) *Structural change.* Prior authorisation of the Commission
must be secured for mergers which would result in a single undertaking gaining control of more than 13 per cent of the Community capacity in a single product.

(b) *Quotas.* Only in times of "manifest crisis" may the Commission establish a system of production quotas, a procedure
which as yet has never been adopted.

(c) *Pricing.* The primary intention is to protect consumers
against price discrimination and producers against unfair competition. In principle, producers set their own prices but the
Commission may in circumstances of shortage or over-supply
intervene to set maximum or minimum price levels.

The Treaty's objective of ensuring free movement of steel products throughout the Community was incompatible with the
U.K. Government's powers under the 1967 nationalisation statute to issue directives to B.S.C. on pricing. These powers were
therefore revoked in the European Communities Act 1972. At
the same time, this Act wound up the statutory Iron and Steel
Consumer Council on whose price recommendations the
Government acted (*see* 45(*d*)). It was replaced by an independent
advisory body, the British Iron and Steel Consumer Council.

CONCLUSION

57. The continuing historical problems of iron and steelmaking.
From the preceding account it will be observed that the iron and
steelmaking industry has suffered throughout its history from
certain inherent problems, such as the following.

(a) *The problem of technological change.* Repeatedly the discovery of new processes has rapidly transformed low-cost areas
into high-cost areas. When these innovations have been first applied overseas the whole U.K. industry has become uncompetitive.

(b) *Resistance to innovation and reorganisation.* There has been a tendency from the following three directions to resist the pace of change.

(i) Capital: the industry is capital intensive. There has been a natural reluctance to agree to the writing-off of vast investment in obsolescent plant.

(ii) Labour: equally, skilled labour has been reluctant to see itself replaced by more advanced equipment.

(iii) Government: while displaying interest in the long-term response of the industry to changing conditions, in the short term the Government has been aware of the social and political consequences of permitting change to occur too rapidly.

(c) *Market fluctuations.* With a high proportion of fixed capital costs the industry has a strong interest in a stable market which will facilitate a stable output. In practice the demand for iron and steel fluctuates with the prevailing economic climate.

(d) *The optimal scale of production.* The volume of capital investment implies a larger rather than smaller scale of production. The growth in the late nineteenth century of foreign competition organised from the outset on a large scale placed the characteristic U.K. family company at a disadvantage.

Only after 1945 was real progress made in rationalising the structure of the industry, culminating in the formation of the present British Steel Corporation. The opposite question now arises. Is the industry organised on too large and unwieldy a scale to permit sufficient flexibility and responsiveness to changing circumstances?

PROGRESS TEST 5

1. Describe vertical integration as it may apply to the iron and steel industry. (2)

2. What are the three principal stages in iron and steel production? (2)

3. Why may the prosperity of a country's iron and steel industry be an indication of its general prosperity? (3)

4. What is the significance to the iron and steel industry of a change in its production processes? (4)

5. What factors governed the location of the industry before the eighteenth century? (7)

6. Evaluate the importance of Abraham Darby and Henry Cort to Britain's industrialisation. (3, 9, 10, 17)

7. How did Darby's discovery affect the location of the iron industry? **(13)**

8. How did the invention of the "hot blast" affect the location of the iron industry? **(15)**

9. What was the problem of early steel production? **(14)**

10. How did Bessemer solve the problem and what was the drawback to his process? **(19)**

11. In what way was the open hearth superior to the converter? **(19)**

12. What was the significance of the Gilchrist-Thomas process? **(19, 20)**

13. How did the Bessemer process affect the location of the iron and steel industry? **(21)**

14. What was the nature of Britain's steel specialisation from the 1880s and why was specialisation made necessary? **(23)**

15. By 1913, Britain's iron and steel industry had been surpassed by the industries of Germany and America. What two factors chiefly explain this? **(24)**

16. Why did the steel industry suffer so acutely from the depression of the 1920s? **(26, 29)**

17. What was the effect of the 1929 slump upon the steel industry? **(31)**

18. How did the Government respond to the steel industry's predicament? **(32)**

19. Account for the failure of export markets to recover in step with home markets during the 1930s. **(33, 34)**

20. Give a reason for the steel industry's successful expansion of output after 1945. **(37, 39)**

21. How and why were steel prices regulated after 1953? **(38)**

22. Why may the choice of site for steel expansion today be a crucial and complex question? **(40)**

23. Account for the poor financial performance of B.S.C. **(52)**

24. Outline the operation of the E.C.S.C. **(54–56)**

25. From what basic problems does the steel industry suffer? **(57)**

CHAPTER VI

Engineering

NATURE, SCOPE AND SIGNIFICANCE TO INDUSTRIALISM

1. Definition. Unlike other industries such as coal or textiles, the limits of the engineering industry cannot easily be defined. The nature of its growth was such that its various branches were frequently born in other industries (e.g. textile machines made by mill owners) before being detached to become part of the engineering trades.

Broadly, engineering may be said to comprise the production of transport equipment and of machinery which itself contributes to further production.

In modern times, there may possibly be added the growing range of "consumer durables", e.g. refrigerators, television sets.

2. Engineering and the Industrial Revolution. Before 1760, scientific engineering was virtually non-existent. The economic pressures which then brought forth progress in coal mining, spinning and weaving, and iron production, simultaneously demanded greater precision in engineering.

Engineering was especially associated with the new processes in the iron industry (*see* V, **8–14**), for the machine age depended upon iron. This dependence has remained to the present day, when engineering progress frequently waits upon advance in metallurgy, e.g. heat resistant metals in high-speed aircraft.

3. Expanding range of engineering.

(*a*) *Steam engineering* after 1760 marks the beginning of the industry. Its development encouraged the invention of machines in other industries and this was in turn reflected in a greater demand for steam engines. It also necessitated greater engineering precision.

(*b*) *The machine tool industry* dates from the 1790s. Machine tools are precision tools used in the construction of other machines.

(*c*) *Textile machinery*. From the 1800s, the construction of the new textile machines began to be detached from the textile firms.

(*d*) *Locomotive construction* became important in the 1830s.

(*e*) *Shipbuilding and marine engineering* from the 1850s.

(*f*) *Gas engines* from the 1870s.

(*g*) *Automobile engineering* from the 1890s.

(*h*) *Aircraft and radio* from the 1900s.

(*i*) *Electronic and nuclear engineering* from the 1940s.

4. Interchangeability of parts and mass production. The components of the early machines were made by hand and each machine was assembled individually. In the event of breakdown, a new part had to be fashioned to fit the particular machine.

The precision developed by the machine tool industry made possible the standardisation of parts, which in turn gave rise to mass production techniques.

In the application of such techniques, the U.S.A. (with its vast markets) led the way from the 1850s but increasingly in the twentieth century Britain has followed suit, e.g. in the automobile industry.

FOUNDATIONS AND EARLY DEVELOPMENT

5. Importance of steam. Unlike other forms of power which had previously been employed (e.g. watermills, windmills), steam was independent of unpredictable natural forces.

Its development provided the key to the Industrial Revolution, since it was the harnessing of steam power to machines and not the machines themselves which brought the transition to the factory system.

6. Early inventors. Forms of steam pump were devised as early as 1663 by the Marquis of Worcester and 1698 by Thomas Savery.

The first to be used for its intended purpose of pumping dry mine shafts was patented by Thomas Newcomen in 1705. It was, however, like its predecessors, a steam *pump* and not an engine in the proper sense. In any case, it proved to be dangerous, inefficient and uneconomical.

7. Boulton and Watt. A mathematical instrument maker by trade, James Watt studied the Newcomen pump and in 1769 considerably improved upon it. In 1775, he formed a partnership with Matthew Boulton, a Birmingham hardware manufacturer, in order to exploit his patent.

The major difficulty of this early period was the lack of skilled engineers and mechanics, and reliance had to be placed upon blacksmiths. To Boulton belongs the credit of training workmen to some degree of precision. He also had the commercial acumen to make a success of marketing Watt's engines.

Boulton's Soho Works was blessed with a foreman of great mechanical skill, William Murdock. He it was who inspired Watt to his revolutionary invention in 1781 of an improved steam engine with a "sun and planet" rotary motion, later replaced by a crankshaft. The means were then at hand to drive machinery other than pumps and to do so efficiently, since Watt was always concerned with the economical use of fuel.

8. John Wilkinson of Broseley. An ironmaster, he had made use of one of Watt's early engines for operating the bellows of his furnace.

After experiment, he devised a method of boring a cylinder accurately, and thereafter the steam engine became a commercial proposition.

9. Marketing. Until the 1780s steam power was restricted to pumping mines, waterworks and the bellows of iron works.

The rotary engine extended its use and by 1800 the Soho Works had supplied 325, mostly to textile mills (114) but also to corn mills, breweries and potteries.

In the nineteenth century, its acceptance depended upon the relative costs of labour and the ease with which an industry's tools could be adapted to power.

10. The new engineering workers. They were drawn from the following three categories.

(a) *Millwrights,* who had hitherto constructed and maintained the water mills, became the mechanics.

(b) *Clockmakers and mathematical instrument makers* became the precision toolmakers.

(c) *Military* engineers became the road, bridge, canal and railway engineers.

11. London, centre for machine tools. If the new machines which were being devised were to work efficiently, they had to be made accurately. This depended upon the successful development of precision tools.

London became, at this stage, the centre of the machine tool industry, upon which the machinery for all other industries wholly depended. This was for the following three reasons.

(*a*) In the 1880s, London had the biggest pool of skilled labour: silversmiths and goldsmiths, clockmakers and instrument makers.

(*b*) The pool was swelled by workmen from the north of England with practical experience of the operation of new machines. They were drawn to London by the capital's higher wage levels.

(*c*) In London were the workshops of a small number of master craftsmen of outstanding ability (e.g. Henry Maudslay, Joseph Bramah, John Martineau). From these workshops came the machines and tools which made manufacture of other machines a task for unskilled labour.

12. Machine tool inventions, 1790–1800.

(*a*) *Joseph Bramah* (1748–1814) invented a wheel-cutting machine, a machine for making locks and the hydraulic press.

(*b*) *Henry Maudslay* (1771–1831), trained by Bramah, was perhaps the most important of these early engineers. He devised a screw cutting lathe which gave rise ultimately to the universal thread and a slide-rest for use with a lathe. A simple instrument for holding the cutting tool in place, when used in conjunction with a measuring device, it permitted precision to within 0.025 mm. It was described as comparable in importance to the steam engine itself and is the parent of all precision tools.

The other significant development in this period was the general substitution of metal for wood in the construction of machinery.

13. Nineteenth-century machine tool inventions.

(*a*) *Maudslay and Brunel* in 1808 invented a mortising machine.

(*b*) *Roberts* invented a planing machine and templets for standardising machine parts (he also built a self-acting mule: *see* VII, 13).

(*c*) *Whitworth*, in Manchester, dominated the second half of the century. He devised numerous instruments for metalworking, exact measurement and standardisation (e.g. the Whitworth thread).

(*d*) *Armstrong*, in Newcastle, developed the science of hydraulics in lifts, cranes and pumps.

By 1900, the engineering shop itself was employing hydrauli-

cally operated tools, although in general it resisted its own mechanisation.

PRODUCTION AND EXPORTS

14. Expansion to 1920. A distinct engineering industry had evolved by the mid-nineteenth century, as is evidenced by the merging of many small trade unions into the Amalgamated Society of
Engineers in 1851.

There was rapid expansion from that time. To the ever-increasing demands of home industry were added those of countries
overseas, and after 1880 exports grew briskly, especially in respect of steam engines, locomotives, ships and textile machinery.

By 1914, the engineering trades employed 1¼ million people.
The First World War engendered a great expansion, and by 1918
the labour force had swelled to 2 million.

15. Inter-war output. Trade depression after 1920 affected the
heavy engineering section (steam engines, locomotives and textile
machinery) most severely. There was some compensatory expansion in the newer branches, e.g. cars and electrical apparatus.

After 1924, a general expansion lasted until the world slump of
1929. In the 1930s, there followed a great advance, and by 1937
output was about 60 per cent above 1924 levels. This was due to
expansion in aircraft, cars and electrical and some branches of
mechanical engineering (e.g. textile machinery), since steam engineering continued to decline.

16. Weakened export position. The growth of production was due
to increased home consumption. In certain branches, exports
expanded, but not sufficiently to compensate for losses in other
branches.

(*a*) The development of alternative sources of power caused a
big decline in the export of Britain's speciality, steam engineering
equipment.

(*b*) Shipbuilding declined owing to the stagnation of world
trade.

(*c*) British exports of agricultural machinery were to some
extent replaced by U.S., French and German products.

(*d*) In the 1930s, Germany overtook Britain as the leading
exporter of textile machinery.

(*e*) International demand for machine tools grew, but this market was already dominated by Germany and the U.S.A.

(*f*) The world automobile market expanded but was entirely dominated by the U.S.A.

(*g*) Britain participated in the growing trade in electrical equipment, but behind Germany and the U.S.A.

The decline in the importance of the British industry relative to that of Germany and the U.S.A. is explained by the decline in international demand for those products in the production of which Britain had a comparative advantage.

17. Wartime expansion, 1939–45. The needs of war once again gave great impetus to the industry and brought into being new branches, e.g. electronics and jet propulsion. Production capacity was increased by about 50 per cent.

18. Post-war expansion. After a brief lull, buoyant demand gave rise to further expansion which continued into the 1960s. The reasons were as follows.

(*a*) Industrial equipment was urgently needed for reconstruction.

(*b*) Need for the replacement of consumer durables, e.g. cars, household apparatus.

(*c*) Labour shortage throughout the economy encouraged the mechanisation and automation of industry.

(*d*) New industries, e.g. television, synthetic textile fibres, oil refining, nuclear power stations.

(*e*) German production capacity did not recover until the 1950s. World demand had therefore to be met by the U.S.A. and Britain.

(*f*) The Korean war added impetus to demand.

By the 1970s a stagnant national economy was reflected in low levels of investment and hence a tapering off of demand for engineering products. While progress continued in some specialist areas such as electronics, the traditional machine tool industry encountered severe problems.

19. Post-war exports. Industrialisation in underdeveloped countries created a growing demand for machinery. This was met principally by the U.S.A., Britain and West Germany, although in the 1960s competition increased, particularly from Japan but also from France, Italy, Czechoslovakia and Sweden. By the

1970s Britain was experiencing difficulty in retaining her share of world markets.

PROGRESS TEST 6

1. What activities fall within the scope of the engineering industry? **(1)**

2. Give examples of the fields in which engineering contributed to industrialisation and say how it played a vital part in promoting production for mass markets. **(3, 4)**

3. Why was the role of the steam engine so vital to industrialisation? **(5)**

4. In which fundamental respect did Watt's 1781 invention differ from all its predecessors? **(6, 7)**

5. What factors governed the rate at which industry was mechanised? **(9)**

6. Define a machine tool. What were the early attractions of London to the machine tool industry? **(11)**

7. What was the nature of Henry Maudslay's contribution to industrialisation? **(12)**

8. How was the structure of the engineering industry affected by the years of depression, 1920–39? **(15, 16)**

9. What factors account for the prosperity of the engineering trades after 1945? **(18, 19)**

Cotton

COTTON AND THE INDUSTRIAL REVOLUTION

1. Significance of cotton to industrialisation. Textiles were Britain's oldest industry and second in economic importance only to agriculture.

Eighteenth-century industrialism made its most spectacular impact upon cotton manufacturing, since it was here that machinery first replaced hand methods of production. When power was harnessed to machines, the factory became a necessary adjunct and, again, cotton reaped the benefit.

So dramatic was the progress made that cotton has frequently been seen as the industry upon which the Revolution hinged. This is to overstate the case, since without concurrent progress in transport, the metal trades and engineering, advances in cotton manufacture would have been delayed. They are all best viewed as interlocking industries, progress in one having stimulated further development in the others.

2. Obstacles to early development. At the beginning of the eighteenth century, cotton manufacture was relatively unimportant, for the following four reasons.

(*a*) *Raw cotton was imported chiefly from the East Indies* and distance made supplies uncertain.

(*b*) *The East India Company was hostile* to home manufactures, since it had long imported Indian cotton piece goods.

(*c*) *The hostility of the wool trade.* In response to pressure from wool interests, printed cotton imports were prohibited in 1700. However, white cotton imports continued and were printed in this country. An Act of 1721 then outlawed the wearing of printed cloth.

(*d*) *Technical inability* to spin a strong cotton thread. After 1721, there was an increasingly prosperous trade in a mixed linen and cotton cloth, the manufacture of which was perfectly legal. It was favoured by changing public taste—from wool to cotton—and the weakening of Indian competition by heavy import duties.

3. Changed market conditions. By the second half of the eighteenth century, the following factors radically changed the prospects for the development of home manufacturing.

(a) *Competition from Indian piece goods was gradually elimin-ated* after the death of the Emperor Aurangzeb in 1707. The power struggle between France and Britain which followed strangled Indian trade and led merchants to turn to home industry.

(b) *In 1774, the repeal of the Act* which prohibited printed cottons.

(c) *Technical advances: see* 4.

4. Technical advances. Cotton manufacture involved many processes, which may, however, be divided into four basic groups.

(a) *Preparation.* The separation of the seed from the fibre and the combing out of the fibre ready for spinning.

(b) *Spinning.* The fibres are twisted to give a yarn which can be woven. Difficulty arises in producing a thread of sufficient strength and fineness.

(c) *Weaving.* Horizontal strands (the weft) are woven between vertical strands (the warp) by means of a shuttle (a tool around which the thread is wound).

(d) *Finishing.* Bleaching, dyeing and printing.

Technical progress was not achieved by any sudden transfor-mation. Original machines were slowly modified and when per-formance in either spinning or weaving was improved it had to be complemented by equivalent progress in the other field.

5. John Kay of Bury. The first real progress was made in the wool trade. Kay's flying shuttle (1733) simplified weaving and economised in the use of labour.

After 1760, this loom was employed in the cotton trade, bring-ing pressure to bear upon the inadequate production capacity of spinners.

This deficiency was slowly remedied by a number of inventions (*see* 6–9).

6. John Wyatt and Louis Paul. These partners applied a revolu-tionary principle. Two pairs of rollers were substituted for spind-les. The first pair turned slowly and delivered the thread to the second pair which revolved more quickly, thus drawing it out. Paul also developed a process for carding or combing out raw cotton.

Though commercially unsuccessful, these experiments paved the way for later advance.

7. James Hargreaves of Blackburn. In 1767, Hargreaves produced the first commercially successful spinning machine, a "jenny" operated by hand and which could therefore be used in the cottage by domestic workers. The wheel turned 11 spindles, subsequently increased to 100. Its limitation lay in its unsuitability for producing warp.

8. Richard Arkwright of Preston. By the 1760s there was an acute shortage of yarn, especially for warp, which had to be spun by hand.

Utilising earlier ideas, in 1769 Arkwright devised a water frame which linked water power and the roller principle. He obtained commercial support and in 1771, with Strutt of Derby, opened a spinning mill which produced a pure cotton yarn for hosiery. He went on to open a mill at Bakewell, the New Lanark Mills in Scotland and became the first to employ steam power in spinning.

The fundamental significance of these developments was twofold.

(*a*) *A strong cotton yarn* without linen additive could be produced in quantities sufficient to meet the demands of the weavers.

(*b*) *Factory system.* In utilising first water power, then steam power, he introduced the modern factory system, since it was impracticable to make power available to domestic workers in their cottages.

9. Samuel Crompton of Bolton. The manufacture of muslin required a fine yarn which Hargreaves' jenny could not yield in sufficient quantity and for which Arkwright's water frame was unsuited.

The trade therefore depended upon Indian imports until, in 1776, Crompton cross-bred the jenny and the water frame to give the "mule" (hence the name).

The mule produced a strong, fine yarn and was subsequently improved by constructing it of metal and adding many more spindles. By 1800 it had displaced the jenny.

This invention relieved Britain of any dependence upon foreign imports, since she could now manufacture yarn and cloth of any quality.

10. Power looms. As the spinners' output increased, weavers were in demand and their wages consequently rose. Mechanisation of weaving was thereby hastened.

(*a*) *In 1785, Edmund Cartwright* developed a power loom and two years later opened a factory in Doncaster. However, this business failed.

(*b*) *In 1793, Robertson* successfully introduced power looms to mills in Glasgow and Dumbarton.

(*c*) *In the 1800s, Horrocks of Preston* constructed a power loom in metal which in the 1820s was further developed by Roberts and Sharp.

Not until the 1840s was a modern loom finally evolved and it was a decade later before the transformation to power was complete.

The chief reason for the delay was the drastic fall in handloom weavers' wages which accompanied partial mechanisation. There was little incentive to complete mechanisation when labour was so cheap.

11. Whitney's cotton gin. After 1793, the use of this device in the U.S.A. simplified and accelerated the separation of seeds and fibre and made available to British industry a virtually unlimited supply of raw cotton.

12. Finishing processes.

(*a*) *Bleaching.* Originally this took place by exposure to sun and air over a period of months. Vast areas of land would have been necessary to do this on a large scale. The problem was solved in 1799 by Tennant of Glasgow, who used chlorine.

(*b*) *Printing.* Originally, this was carried out by the laborious process of hand stamping. In 1783, Thomas Bell evolved a rotary press.

These developments, by accelerating output, were conducive to further advance in the preceding processes.

13. Nineteenth-century developments. Domestic production and hand methods took a long time to eliminate, but further mechanical improvements brought their eclipse in mid-century.

(*a*) *In 1825, Roberts devised a fully automatic mule*, thereby making spinning a steam-operated, factory process.

Raw cotton shortage and rising prices engendered by the American Civil War (1861–5) forced further cost-reducing improvements (*see* (*b*) and (*c*)).

(*b*) *Ring spinning*, which was invented in 1830 and which speeded up the operation, was now widely adopted.

(*c*) *Automatic cotton combing machines* which separated the long fibres for fine yarns were invented by Heilmann and Holden in 1848, and were now adopted.

CONTINUOUS EXPANSION UNTIL 1913

14. Reasons for Britain's early lead.

(*a*) Mercantile and colonial development in the seventeenth and eighteenth centuries had provided sources of raw cotton and markets for the finished product (*see* XI, **1, 2**).

(*b*) The countries which grew cotton were not themselves prepared for industrial development. The exception, India, was handicapped in adopting modern industrial methods and organisation by her social structure.

(*c*) Potential competition from Europe was restrained by political instability, e.g. the French Revolutionary and Napoleonic wars, which had a much more disturbing effect upon Europe than on Britain.

(*d*) Current advances in the iron industry (*see* V, **9, 11**) and engineering (textile machinery and the steam engine).

15. Britain's natural advantages.
Both Lancashire and southwest Scotland were ideally situated for cotton manufacture but, since Scotland had still greater attractions for iron, steel, shipbuilding and engineering, some 85 per cent of the industry was ultimately concentrated in Lancashire and adjacent parts of Cheshire and Derbyshire. The advantages were as follows.

(*a*) *A humid climate* suited to spinning, since it reduced the possibility of the thread breaking.

(*b*) *When water power was employed,* a sufficient rise and fall of land in the Pennines to produce it.

(*c*) *Local coal,* with the advent of steam.

(*d*) *Adequate supplies of soft water* from the Pennines for bleaching and dyeing.

(*e*) *Liverpool was a good deep-water port* for imported raw materials and exports.

(*f*) *Skilled local labour* with a tradition of spinning and weaving woollens.

(*g*) *A topography* which made the development of communications relatively easy.

16. Rate of growth.
Favoured by so many circumstances, the

cotton industry expanded uninterrupted except in the following periods.

(a) 1861–5. The American Civil War dislocated supplies of raw cotton. Mills were closed and there was considerable unemployment. Partly as a result, alternative sources were developed in India, Natal and Egypt, and ultimately, in 1902, the British Cotton Growing Association was set up to invest large sums in Uganda, Nigeria, Sudan and the West Indies.

(b) 1875–9; 1885–9. These were periods of steeply falling prices (see XII, 16) in which the effects of foreign competition were felt for the first time.

The 1900s, however, brought a massive recovery, with production increasing by more than a quarter by 1914 (see the figures below). This was a period in which the agricultural nations, favourably placed by the terms of trade, increased their demand for cheap cotton piece goods.

	1880s	1913
Number of spindles:	42¼ million	59 million
Number of looms:	546,000	805,000

17. The export trade. Success in export markets was the primary cause of the great expansion of production.

By 1815, cotton was the principal export and earned more than wool. By the 1830s, it represented half the total value of British exports, while the advent of free trade in mid-century brought even greater expansion (although cotton's share of the total declined as general trade increased).

In 1913, three-quarters of Britain's cotton production was exported, to yield about a quarter of her total export earnings.

18. Changing structure of foreign markets.

(a) Yarns. Until 1850 yarns represented about half the export value of piece goods, while in 1913 they represented about one-fifth the value. The decline in the relative importance of yarn exports is explained by changing markets.

(i) In the early nineteenth century, yarn was exported to European weavers, but they quickly developed home supplies.

(ii) During the period 1840–80, yarns were exported to India and the Near and Far East, but after 1880 they too developed home supplies.

(iii) During the period 1880–1913, there was some recovery of European demand, but only for fine yarns.

(b) *Piece goods.*

(*i*) In the early nineteenth century, Europe was the principal market, followed by the Americas.

(*ii*) In the mid-nineteenth century, the U.S.A. and Europe had developed their own protected industries and attention was turned chiefly to other countries in the Americas.

(*iii*) Since mid-century, trade with the East had steadily grown and by 1900 the Orient, the East Indies, Africa and the Near East absorbed three-quarters of British exports of piece goods.

(c) *Conclusions.*

(*i*) Before 1914, yarn exports accounted for the smaller share of the export market and went chiefly to Europe. Piece goods were of much greater value and were shipped to distant agricultural countries.

(*ii*) Although foreign industry was expanding, in no way did it impair British growth. It always proved possible to discover new markets or to adjust to meet changing needs.

19. Structure of the industry. The vast increase in output and the intensive use of capital in production led ultimately to an industry of immense structural complexity (i.e. the great number of processes in cotton manufacture would have made it impossible for one firm alone to invest in all the necessary machinery unless it had had a huge turnover).

In fact, the industry grew in the hands of a large number of relatively small-scale family businesses which by the 1880s were specialising in narrow fields.

(a) *Spinning* was established in the circle of towns around Manchester. There was further specialisation within the group, e.g. Bolton, fine yarns; Oldham and Rochdale, medium and coarse yarns; Haslingden, waste spinning.

(b) *Weaving.* North-east Lancashire: Preston, shirtings and sheetings; Blackburn and Burnley, plain cloths; Nelson and Colne, patterned cloths.

(c) *Finishing processes:* specialist firms located chiefly in the towns closest to the Pennines.

(d) *Marketing:* the piece goods merchants, to whose orders the manufacturer usually worked, concentrated in Manchester.

(e) *Cotton merchants.* In Liverpool grew firms which specialised in buying raw cotton for sale to the spinners.

CONTRACTION AND REORGANISATION
SINCE 1914

20. 1914–18 war. Capacity remained static but production and exports shrank, owing to the shortage of shipping space. In these circumstances, in 1917–19 the Cotton Control Board allocated supplies of raw cotton and concentrated production on the higher qualities.

Asia then looked for alternative sources.

21. Collapse of Britain's markets, 1920–39.

1920–4: Production of yarn was 30 per cent less and piece goods 33 per cent less than in 1913.

1937: Production of yarn was 31 per cent less and piece goods 61 per cent less than in 1913.

1920–4: Exports of yarn were 25 per cent less and piece goods 41 per cent less than in 1913.

1937: Exports of yarn were 27 per cent less and piece goods 71 per cent less than in 1913.

After a short post-war boom, in 1920 prices fell and the industry contracted continuously (save for brief recoveries in 1925 and 1932) until 1939.

During this time, the home market remained buoyant and in fact enjoyed some expansion. Lost exports therefore explained the decline.

Moreover, it was in piece goods that the chief losses were suffered. Britain retained her share of a world market in yarns which had been halved. However, her share of the piece goods trade fell from 65 per cent in 1913 to 26 per cent in 1938. This was her most important market and the one in which she proved to be most vulnerable.

22. Causes of lost markets. The chief markets to suffer were the Far and Near East, India and the Balkans. This was due to the following factors.

(a) *The rise of home industries.* For example, in 1913, Britain supplied 60 per cent of India's cotton requirements. In 1939, India met 80 per cent of her own needs.

(b) *Foreign tariffs.* In some markets, e.g. India and the U.S.A., British trade suffered (but in others, benefited) from tariff preferences.

(c) *Japanese competition.* During the war years, Japan had a free run of Britain's Asian markets and was determined not to be ousted. Thus in 1939 Japan provided more than half of such cotton as India did import.

(d) *Spread of European techniques* amongst Asian countries fostered the cotton industry.

(e) *Cheap labour* in competing countries meant low prices.

(f) *Local raw cotton*, e.g. in China and India.

(g) *Large local markets* reduced transport costs for Asian producers.

(h) *Increasing efficiency of competitors*, e.g. worker productivity doubled in Japan in the 1930s.

23. The burden of depression. The burden was not evenly spread.

(a) *Yarn.* Spinners of the coarse yarns which went into cheap piece goods were much more affected than fine yarn spinners.

(b) *Piece goods.* Weavers of coarse fabrics were hardest hit, but to some extent were able to turn to better qualities, rayons and cotton mixtures.

However, in the 1930s even the quality trade suffered from Japanese competition. Having lost markets in cheap cloths and yarns to local Indian and Chinese manufacturers, Japan turned to better-quality cottons.

24. Difficulties of reorganisation. After 1924, it was increasingly clear that reorganisation would be necessary if costs were to be reduced, but there were the following difficulties.

(a) *Over-specialisation.* The cotton towns offered no alternative employment if the industry were to be pruned.

(b) *Renewal of obsolete plant* would similarly increase unemployment.

(c) *Low Japanese wages* seemed to preclude any possibility of British recovery.

(d) *Excessive number of firms.* The industry was in the hands of a large number of firms whose scale of production was too small.

On this last point, the first remedial steps were taken in the 1930s.

25. Attempts at reorganisation in the 1930s.

(a) *Lancashire Cotton Corporation 1929.* The objective was a horizontal combination of spinning mills, followed by elimination of inefficient mills. The scheme was only partially successful in reducing the excessive number of spindles.

(b) *Cotton Industry Reorganisation Act 1936.* A Spindles Board was appointed by the Board of Trade to reduce spinning capacity. The less efficient firms were to be bought out and scrapped, the operation being financed by a levy on the whole spinning industry.

The activities of the Board resulted in the closure of seventy-eight mills by 1939.

(c) *Cotton Industry Reorganisation Act 1939*. The Act set up machinery establishing minimum compulsory prices, an admission that the industry could no longer survive in normal competitive circumstances.

26. 1939–45 war. In 1940, a Cotton Board was set up to regulate production and distribution on a system of priorities.

In accordance with a concentration of production policy in 1941, 40 per cent of the industry's capacity was closed.

By 1945, the output of yarn had been cut to 54 per cent and of cloth to 42 per cent of 1939 levels.

27. Post-war pressure of demand. There was a great demand both at home and abroad but the industry lacked capacity, particularly in view of the general labour shortage. The result was as follows.

(a) Yarn output in 1951 was 22 per cent short of pre-war levels.

(b) Piece goods output in 1951 was 32 per cent short of pre-war levels.

In the interests of the balance of payments and the export drive, clothes rationing continued but, even so, by 1951 exports were only half those of 1938.

28. Cotton depression after 1952. In 1952, there was a world textile recession from which the British cotton industry did not fully recover. The underlying cause was the radical change in the organisation of the world cotton trade effected by the war.

(a) The war destroyed the industries of Europe and Japan.

(b) Importing countries were compelled to develop home production.

(c) In particular, the U.S.A. effected a big expansion and was exporting more than in pre-war days.

The significant feature was that new capacity adequately compensated for that which had been destroyed. The world was much more independent of the exporting nations, and international trade in cotton shrank by one-fifth.

When Japan and Europe restored their industries in the 1950s, the competition for what remained of world trade was much keener and British exports were halved from their 1949 level.

Competition did not stop at export markets. After 1954, U.K. home markets were increasingly invaded by imports, particularly from India and Hong Kong. By 1960, the production of yarn and cloth was less than half and exports less than a third their pre-war levels.

Additionally and of major significance was the continuing post-1945 development of man-made fibres (*see* VIII, **21–28**). Until the Second World War, cotton was the fibre on which the textile industry mainly depended and even in the 1950s accounted for about 50 per cent of total fibre consumption. By 1977, the figure had fallen to about 15 per cent. Wool never rivalled cotton in the first half of the century and its decline was less marked from about 30 per cent of fibre consumption in the 1940s to about 17 per cent in 1977.

The wider availability of synthetics in the 1950s established them with about 25 per cent of the market, a figure which by 1977 had grown to 68 per cent.

29. Rationalisation after 1952. In response to falling prices, shrinking markets and increasing competition the industry began to eliminate surplus capacity. From a peak in the 1880s and 1890s when it is estimated that Britain controlled 50 per cent of the world's cotton spindles, by 1974 rationalisation and expansion by competitors had reduced this proportion to 3 per cent.

This contraction was accomplished through liquidations and mergers, the latter explaining the increased proportion of production now concentrated in large, vertically integrated, multi-fibre firms.

The future for the remaining small firms would seem to lie in short runs of specialised cotton products. Their survival was assisted by Government-sponsored modernisation and re-equipment programmes. In 1959, the Cotton Industry Act provided grants amounting to £30 million for this purpose.

PROGRESS TEST 7

1. To what extent may it be said that the cotton industry lay at the centre of the Industrial Revolution?   **(1)**
2. What reasons may be advanced for the late development of a cotton industry in Britain?   **(2)**

3. What new circumstances gave impetus to technical progress? **(3)**

4. Describe the principal stages in the manufacture of cotton cloth. **(4)**

5. Outline the technical progress made in spinning during the eighteenth century. **(6–9)**

6. What effect did progress in spinning have upon weaving? **(10)**

7. Describe the nature of the nineteenth-century innovations which finally eclipsed the domestic system of production. **(13)**

8. Account for Britain's lead in the cotton industry during the nineteenth century. **(14, 15)**

9. "The cotton industry expanded rapidly and without interruption until 1914." Evaluate this statement. **(16, 17)**

10. Explain the changes in the relative importance of yarn and piece goods exports during the nineteenth century. How did this react on the industry's prosperity in 1920–37? **(18, 21, 23)**

11. "The cotton industry was the supreme vindication of *laissez-faire*. A natural and voluntary co-ordination of activity was achieved without central control." Comment on this claim. **(19)**

12. Account for the difficulties of the cotton industry in the period between the wars. **(22)**

13. What attempts were made to rationalise the industry in the 1930s and what obstacles retarded progress? **(24, 25)**

14. What was the immediate problem of the industry after 1945? **(26, 27)**

15. Account for the continuing contraction of the industry after 1952. **(28)**

16. How did the industry respond to adverse conditions after 1952? **(29)**

CHAPTER VIII

Wool and Synthetics

WOOL AND INDUSTRIAL REVOLUTION

1. Early importance. Until the nineteenth century, the manufacture of woollen cloth was England's most important industry. As early as the Middle Ages, she was one of the principal centres of raw wool production, and by the sixteenth century had developed a considerable foreign trade in cloth. It remained the principal item of export until displaced by cotton in the nineteenth century.

2. Delayed mechanisation. The woollen industry adopted the eighteenth-century textile inventions much more slowly than did cotton. This may be explained by the following facts.

(*a*) *Dispersion*. The industry was widely scattered and knowledge of improvements spread very slowly.

(*b*) *Labour*. In the woollen areas, the supply of labour was far greater than in the cotton areas. This was especially true after the return of the soldiery in 1815. There was not therefore the same incentive to use capital.

(*c*) *Organisation*. The industry, unlike cotton, was rooted in the domestic system of production (*see* I, **21**). The gilds had a firm hold and resisted change.

(*d*) *Machinery*. Until 1830, reliable machinery was in short supply.

(*e*) *Part-time farming*. In Yorkshire, the weaver was also a part-time farmer. This activity did not accord with the factory system.

(*f*) *Climate*. The demand for woollens was largely limited by climatic considerations, while that for cotton was world-wide.

(*g*) *Raw materials*. Supplies of raw wool were severely restricted until new sources were tapped in the 1830s. Only then did mechanisation become practicable.

3. Worsted, woollens and shoddies. The distinction between these three types of cloth lies in the nature of the raw material, with consequent variations in the manufacturing processes.

(*a*) *Worsteds*. Originally, only long fibres were suitable, but later any length could be used provided it was possible to comb the fibres straight and parallel. They were then spun and woven.

113

(*b*) *Woollens*. The fibres were curled and easily felted. A fuller beat the cloth in water mixed with soap or fuller's earth, causing it to shrink and give a cloth in which the weave might be invisible.

(*c*) *Shoddies*. Yarn and cloth were made from reclaimed woollens.

4. Mechanisation of spinning (*see* VII, **4, 6, 9**). The spinning jenny was not in common use in Yorkshire until the 1780s and in the South-west until the 1790s. It was in any case a hand tool and continued to be used by domestic workers in their cottages.

By 1786, some use was being made of Arkwright's water frame and about 1800 Benjamin Gott applied power to spinning for the first time when he founded the industry in Leeds. Others who worked there, notably Brooks and Hirst, made use of the mule.

In woollens, the use of power was generally resisted, except for carding, and most yarn was still mule-spun by hand as late as 1850.

5. Mechanisation of combing. The most difficult part of worsted manufacture was combing (i.e. separation of straight parallel fibres—the *tops*—from the curly fibres, the *noils*).

In 1790, Edmund Cartwright devised a wool combing machine which in the 1840s was improved simultaneously by Heilmann in Germany and Donisthorpe and Samuel Lister in England.

One of Lister's mechanics, Noble, finally perfected a rotary comb (two circles, one carrying the wool, the other the comb) which could be employed on any kind and length of wool. It therefore eliminated the old distinction between woollen and worsted.

6. Mechanisation of weaving. Kay's flying shuttle (*see* VII, **5**) was devised for the woollen industry but, although widely used, this was not a power instrument.

In the 1820s some power looms were in use, but as late as 1841 the Royal Commission on Handloom Weavers reported that they were the exception rather than the rule.

By 1865, the transition in the worsted industry was almost accomplished but it still had to be followed by the changeover in woollens.

Delayed mechanisation in the woollen industry is evidenced by the labour force, which, from 1850 to 1914, remained almost stationary at about 250,000, even though production was increasing.

7. Localisation. From early times, woollen cloth was woven wherever there were sheep, but by 1700 the following three regions were pre-eminent.

(*a*) *South-west England.* Devon, Gloucester, Somerset and Wiltshire, the most renowned area.

(*b*) *East Anglia.* Trade was centred on Norwich.

(*c*) *West Riding of Yorkshire.* By 1800, even before the impact of machinery, this region was the equal of the others. By 1914, it possessed 50 per cent of the spindles and 60 per cent of the looms.

The West Riding enjoyed the following natural advantages.

(*i*) Raw wool from the local moorland.

(*ii*) When the local supplies proved insufficient, a central position facilitated the collection of wool from adjacent sheep-rearing areas.

(*iii*) Soft Pennine water for scouring the raw wool.

(*iv*) Water power.

(*v*) When steam power was accepted, local coal.

(*vi*) Hull, a convenient port for imported raw materials, and exported manufactures.

(*vii*) It was a region without competing agricultural potential.

(*viii*) The gilds were less firmly established here than in the south and therefore the industry was more amenable to change.

(*ix*) The dynamism of the adjacent cotton industry was infectious.

Since 1945 labour shortage has induced some migratory tendency to Belfast and south Yorkshire.

8. Eclipse of East Anglia and the South-west. The transition to steam power sealed the fate of these areas.

(*a*) *East Anglia* became too dependent upon supplies of yarn from Yorkshire, where power spinning was first adopted. Moreover, Norfolk was basically an agricultural county and progress in that direction was being made by men such as Coke and Townshend (*see* II, **22, 25**). Finally, nineteenth-century demand was for cheap mass-produced cloths, whereas East Anglia had always catered for the luxury trade. By the 1860s, the industry had been completely eliminated.

(b) *South-west England.* The conservatism of this old-established area strangled growth and, like East Anglia, it lacked local coal for steam. However, there continued a small output of high quality "West of England cloth".

9. Specialisation. To a limited extent, specialisation developed in a similar way to the cotton industry in that firms tended to restrict themselves to combing, spinning, weaving, finishing or merchanting. However, far more than in cotton, many firms engaged in two or more processes (after the Second World War, 418 out of a total of 1,067 manufacturing firms operated more than one process).

Like cotton, there was also considerable specialisation by certain towns, but in product rather than process.

(a) *Worsteds* were concentrated in the north and west, in the region of Keighley, Bradford and Halifax.

(b) *Woollens* developed in the south and east in the region of Leeds and Batley.

(c) *Shoddies:* the growth of the trade from the 1850s centred on Dewsbury.

(d) *Leeds* became the merchanting centre.

10. Raw wool supplies. Until the eighteenth century the industry depended upon the home clip. In an attempt to assure adequate supplies to an expanding industry, from 1662 to 1824 wool exports were prohibited.

Eighteenth-century concentration upon sheep for mutton (*see* II, **11**) caused a deterioration in quality, and the best wools were imported (Spanish merino wool was allowed in duty free).

The strain upon supplies remained until 1815, when new sources were developed in Australia, New Zealand, South Africa and the Argentine. By 1850, these imports equalled home production, at about 250 million lbs per annum, and by 1900 had quadrupled, while home output had declined.

In the twentieth century, supplies have increasingly included other fibres such as mohair, cotton, rayon and nylon, which are mixed with wool according to demand or the relative prices of the different fibres.

11. Production and exports to 1914. Production continued to expand steadily throughout the nineteenth century. In the later part of the century, expansion was induced by home demand since from the 1870s exports declined. This industry was the first to feel the effects of the world's growing independence of British manufactures.

The explanation lies in the fact that the wool-consuming nations were chiefly those with high standards of technical knowledge (e.g. Europe and the U.S.A.) and they were developing their own industries. Woollens, being more complicated to manufacture, fared better than worsteds.

Considerable international specialisation also developed within this period, with the result that Britain imported certain types of yarn and cloth. By 1914, Britain supplied 80 per cent of her own needs and exported 40 per cent of her output.

CONTRACTION AND RECOVERY, 1920–39

12. Effects of trade depression. When world prices fell and international trade declined after 1920, for a number of reasons the British woollen industry was not very seriously affected.

(a) Production capacity had not been expanded during the war.

(b) Wisely, in 1918, the industry was not tempted into overexpansion by the spurious and short-lived boom.

(c) Owing to difficulties in obtaining the right kind of machinery, there had been no great expansion in other parts of the world.

(d) The chief customers for woollens were those nations which had been involved in the war and whose production capacity, equally, had not expanded.

Although Britain retained her share of world markets, the reduction in the volume of international trade had some effect upon production. However, loss of exports alone was insufficient to explain the total decline in sales (*see* **13–15**).

13. Effects of a changing market structure.

(a) *Tops*. Output and sales were maintained.

(b) *Yarn*. Output grew slightly in response to the demands of the hosiery trade.

(c) *Cloth* sales, particularly of worsted, fell markedly. The decline could not be explained by current losses of established foreign markets since these were made good by expansion in Canada and the Far East, where European fashions were growing. The explanation lay in the home market, where a preference for knitted goods and other fabrics was developing.

14. Decline, 1924–9. There was a sharp decline in production, for the following reasons.

(*a*) *Growing European competition*, particularly from Germany and Czechoslovakia, caused a decline in exports.

(*b*) *Failure to hold the recently developed markets* of the Far East when local production increased.

(*c*) *Fashion trends* continued to move against wool.

15. Slump, 1929–32. Like other industries, wool suffered severely.

(*a*) *Uncertainty in the home trade* led to minimal buying at all stages of production.

(*b*) *Lack of purchasing* power in the depressed economies of Britain's overseas customers.

(*c*) *Protective tariffs* were raised in many countries.

(*d*) *Japanese competition* grew in the Far East.

(*e*) *Fashions* continued to be unfavourable to wool.

16. Recovery, 1932–9. The industry had made a substantial recovery by 1939, aided by the following factors.

(*a*) *The depreciation of sterling* after departure from the gold standard in 1931 increased foreign purchasing power (*see* IX, **20, 22**).

(*b*) *A steady improvement in domestic purchasing power.*

(*c*) *A 50 per cent ad valorem import duty* in 1931 (reduced the following year to 20 per cent without reviving competition) gave British producers a virtual monopoly of home markets.

(*d*) *Fashions* moved in favour of wool.

The result was that by 1937 the production of cloth was restored to a level only 16 per cent less than in 1913 while the output of tops was about the same and of yarn rather higher.

This was accomplished despite a substantial fall in exports and is explained by the displacement of foreign imports in the case of cloth, and by the growth of the hosiery trade in the case of yarn.

POST-WAR EXPANSION AND CONTRACTION

17. Labour shortage. As in other industries, the major reconstruction problem after the Second World War was labour shortage in an economy enjoying full employment.

Wartime contraction had reduced the labour force from 227,000 to 126,000. Those who remained were ageing and a high rate of recruitment was necessary simply to balance retirements.

Not until 1950 was the labour force restored to something like its 1939 level.

18. State of demand. Labour shortage accounted for the industry's inability to satisfy a rising home and foreign demand.

Rationing restricted the home market in order to restore the export trade and assist with current balance of payments difficulties.

Wool was affected by the textile depression of 1951–2 but unlike cotton made a good recovery in 1953 to maintain a fairly stable market until 1964. Since that year there has been a quite substantial contraction of production and exports.

19. Export trade. The successful expansion of the export trade was a major factor in the prosperity of the industry during the immediate post-war years and the 1950s. During these years exports reached a higher level than that of the 1930s, despite the growth of new production capacity abroad. The competitive strength of the industry until the 1960s may be explained by the following.

(a) Wage levels and hence costs were not appreciably different from those of her chief European rivals (cf. the disadvantage of the U.K. cotton industry in facing competition from relatively low-paid cotton workers in Japan and Hong Kong.)

(b) The productivity of British labour was high.

(c) The home market was insulated by tariffs.

(d) While the development of local industry in countries such as India and Japan lessened the demand for yarns and cloths, it increased the demand for tops, whose production requires a high rate of capital investment. At the time this investment was not being made.

From the mid-1960s, the industry was adversely affected by increased competition both from overseas producers and from man-made fibres, and by the rising world demand for raw wool reflected in a corresponding increase in prices.

20. Government assistance. In the 1970s the Government gave substantial financial assistance. On the recommendation of the Wool Textile Economic Development Committee (a committee of the National Economic Development Office) the Government in 1973 provided £15 million, increased in 1976 to £18 million, to encourage rationalisation and modernisation. It is estimated that this assistance generated new investment in plant and buildings of the order of £73 million.

SYNTHETICS

21. Types of synthetic fibre. Synthetic fibres fall into two basic categories.

(a) *Cellulosics*. These are made from cellulose fibres which occur naturally in cotton linters or wood pulp.

(b) *True synthetics*. They are made wholly by a chemical process involving the polymerisation of non-fibrous materials obtained mainly from oil but also from coal.

22. Cellulosics. The late nineteenth century brought the first development of man-made fibres stimulated by an unsatisfied demand for silk. The latter was the only fibre composed of a single continuous filament, a property which gave it a particular lustre which scientists attempted to reproduce.

The viscose process, whereby cellulose was treated with caustic soda, was discovered in Britain by Charles Cross and Edward Bevan in 1892. It was used to make rayon and was first put into large-scale production by Courtaulds at Coventry in 1905.

It found buyers particularly among hosiery manufacturers. Modern developments of this fibre include Vincel, Evlan and Durafil. In 1977, Courtaulds announced the development of a new fibre, Viloft, which is a modified viscose staple with absorption characteristics similar to cotton.

23. Acetates. The British acetate process was patented by Charles Cross in 1894 and developed commercially by Henry and Camille Dreyfus. This process gave rise to another range of cellulosics. It was first used as a coating for aeroplane fabrics in 1914–18 but in 1923 acetate yarns were manufactured commercially by British Celanese for use in fashion textiles.

By the late 1930s the traditional wool and cotton industries began to realise the potential of cellulosics as new fibres rather than being simply imitations of old ones. Research continued in Britain into ways of strengthening and modifying rayon. In 1955, cellulose triacetate was developed. It is stronger, more heat resistant and can be permanently pleated.

While retaining an important place in the textile industry, cellulosics have been overtaken by true synthetics.

24. Nylon. The first true synthetics were produced experimentally in the U.S.A. in the 1920s. Nylon was chosen for development in 1935 and was first manufactured under licence in the U.K. by I.C.I. in 1940. It was used militarily, particularly for parachutes, and after the war for the manufacture of hosiery and lingerie. Little by little it displaced viscose rayon as a tyre fabric and as production costs fell replaced cotton in the manufacture of cheap shirts and dresses.

25. Polyesters. Another wholly synthetic fibre, terylene, was discovered in Britain by John Whinfield and James Dickson in 1941. The war delayed its development and production did not reach a fully commercial scale until 1955.

26. Other synthetic fibres. Other important synthetic fibres include the following.

(a) *Acrylics.* Dupont's Orlon was first produced commercially in the U.S.A. in 1950.

(b) *Polyethylenes and polypropylenes.* These fibres have many industrial uses.

(c) *Modacrylics.* Teklan, a British modacrylic, was first marketed in 1962.

(d) *Polyurethanes.* These fibres can produce a lighter and stronger stretch fabric than rubber.

27. Melded fabrics. Research has continued in many areas, amongst them the production of non-woven fabrics by bonding fibres. In 1975, I.C.I. launched its new melded fabric Cambrelle.

Non-woven textiles have many outlets, but particularly for disposable articles such as cleaning cloths, tablecloths and napkins, disposable sheets and underwear.

28. Synthetics in relation to cotton and wool. The developments outlined in **27** represent the most important trends in the textile industry as a whole since the 1960s. The growth in the consumption of man-made fibres has been primarily at the expense of cotton but also to some extent of wool and silk. This can be seen in the following table.

Estimated consumption in the U.K. of cotton, wool and man-made fibres
(million kg)

	1970	1972	1974	1976
Cotton	165.8	130.0	112.2	114.1
Wool	166.3	164.6	120.6	130.1
Man-made fibres	448.0	486.3	491.5	516.0
Man-made fibres as percentage of total	57	62	68	68

Source: Department of Industry, Bulletin of Textile Statistics.

RESEARCH AND DEVELOPMENT IN THE TEXTILE INDUSTRY

29. Capital investment. Since the 1960s the textile industry has been transformed. There has been substantial investment in modernisation, e.g. £222 million in 1975, devoted largely to weaving cotton, linen and man-made fibres and to woollens and worsteds.

Since the textile industry has traditionally been labour intensive with the result that in the twentieth century high wage costs have undermined Western competitiveness, most investment is aimed at developing and introducing improved machinery.

30. Research associations. There are five main research associations: the Shirley Institute, the largest textile research centre in Europe, concerned mainly with cotton and synthetics; H.A.T.R.A., the Hosiery and Allied Trades Research Association; the Lambeg Industrial Research Association; W.I.R.A., the Woollen Industry Research Association; and the Textile Research Conference which is the umbrella organisation.

31. New machines. Since the 1950s there have been a number of revolutionary developments in textile machinery. In increasing output, speed is of primary importance. In this respect there has been considerable progress in the conversion of fibre to fabric and in texturing yarn, e.g. "throwsters" have improved from speeds of 100 metres per minute to 400–700 metres per minute. In yarn manufacture, carding speeds have increased from 4 kg an hour to 40 kg an hour.

Britain has been responsible for some of the most important developments in fibre-processing machinery, weft-knitting machines and carpet machinery. Computerised pattern preparation and other forms of automation have also been pioneered in Britain.

In spinning, the most important advance has been the introduction of open-end spinning which was developed in Czechoslovakia in the 1950s. This method differs from ring spinning in employing a rotor which revolves at speeds in excess of 40,000 revolutions per minute compared with the 15,000 revolutions of the conventional revolving spindle.

Similarly, in weaving a large number of machines have been designed to increase production speeds and improve the uniformity of the fabric.

INTERNATIONAL TRADING ARRANGEMENTS FOR TEXTILES

32. General Agreement on Tariffs and Trade (GATT). (*See also* XI, **29.**) The GATT Long-Term Arrangement for Trade in Cotton Textiles (L.T.A.) was introduced in the early 1960s with the intention of regularising the increasing use of quantitative restrictions. These had resulted from the sharp growth of low-cost imports into the developed countries of the world.

The L.T.A. which referred only to cotton textiles, was replaced in 1974 by the Multi-fibre Arrangement (M.F.A.). This was designed to lead to a long-term liberalisation of trade while avoiding disruption of the textile industries of the developed countries.

The M.F.A. provides that import restraints may be introduced as part of a bilateral agreement or they may be imposed unilaterally if they can be justified under very strict criteria laid down under the arrangement.

33. The European Community and the M.F.A. The European Commission signed the M.F.A. on behalf of all members including the U.K. Subsequently, more than twenty bilateral agreements were concluded with developing countries. Most of these agreements involve voluntary restraint but where they establish quotas the share allocated to each E.E.C. member was established by a 1974 formula which is regularly reviewed.

Textiles are included in the E.E.C.'s Generalised Scheme of Preference (G.S.P.). A proportion of a developing country's exports are admitted duty free.

PROGRESS TEST 8

1. New production methods were applied much more slowly to the woollen than to the cotton industry. How may this be explained? (2)

2. Distinguish between the principal branches of the industry. (3)

3. Compare the rate of technical progress in the various manufacturing processes. (4, 5, 6)

4. Account for the rise of the industry in the West Riding of Yorkshire and its destruction elsewhere. (7, 8)

5. Compare specialisation in the woollen industry with that in the cotton industry. (9)

6. What was the major problem of the eighteenth-century woollen industry and how was it solved? (10)

7. Assess the relative importance of wool and cotton exports in the nineteenth century. Why do they differ? (11)

8. How was the woollen industry affected by the trade depression in the 1920s? (12–15)

9. What circumstances favoured greater prosperity in the 1930s? (16)

10. Compare the relative positions of the woollen and cotton industries after 1945. Why did one expand and the other contract? (18, 19)

11. Outline the development of cellulosics. (22, 23)

12. Indicate the range of true synthetics. (24, 25)

13. What has been the impact of man-made fibres on cotton and wool? (28)

14. What evidence is there of technical progress in modern times? (31)

15. What arrangements cover the U.K.'s international trade in textiles? (32, 33)

PART FOUR
COMMERCE

CHAPTER IX

Money and Banking

ORIGINS

1. Nature of banking business. The essential function of the banks is to accept money on deposit, for which a rate of interest is paid, and to advance money on loan, for which a higher rate of interest is charged. The margin constitutes the bank's profit.

Throughout the Middle Ages, such practices were condemned, both in civil and canon law, as a Christian sin; it was not until Elizabethan times that this viewpoint began to change. The financial needs of an expanding commerce than brought statutes (in 1571 and again in 1624) which legalised interest charges and opened the way to the development of the modern banking system.

2. The Lombards. Forms of banking were practised in the Mediterranean in Classical times but the first bank in the modern sense was established in Venice in 1157. Thereafter they spread through the Italian trading cities, whilst those of Florence became so active that they conducted business in many parts of Europe.

In the fourteenth century, the Lombards (wealthy merchants from Florence, Venice and Genoa) began to settle in London. In 1318 they were given a grant of land in the area which came to be known as Lombard Street. They were mainly goldsmiths but brought with them a knowledge of banking practice (as well as many well-known commercial terms, e.g. *£.s.d.* = *lire*, *soldi*, *denarii*).

As distaste for usury weakened, so they built up a large trade as moneylenders and pawnbrokers.

3. Goldsmith to private banker. The reign of Elizabeth saw a great accumulation of wealth, but there existed no means of conserving it other than in hoards of plate and jewels. Paradoxically, wealthy men were frequently compelled to resort to pawnbrokers for ready cash.

Expanding commerce demanded more flexibility and some means of credit whereby merchants could finance their enterprises. This need the goldsmiths met by their willingness to advance money on valuables.

They also performed the service of accepting money and valuables for safekeeping. Realising it to be unlikely that all deposits would be demanded simultaneously, they shortly adopted the practice of utilising their clients' money to make loans and offered a rate of interest to attract more depositors. This inducement had the desired effect, e.g. Samuel Pepys was most agreeably surprised to discover that a £2,000 deposit yielded for him £35 after three months.

Until the end of the seventeenth century, the businesses of goldsmith, pawnbroker and banker were conducted side by side, but the growing needs of both foreign and domestic trade demanded more specialisation. The first to abandon the other activities in favour of banking was Francis Childs, who by the 1680s had acquired a considerable reputation. He made many innovations and is credited with introducing the first printed banknotes.

4. Paper money. The goldsmith bankers issued receipts to their depositors, and, as these acquired wide recognition, they soon passed as currency. With the great increase in business, there was much advantage in no longer having to make payments with large quantities of bullion.

Eventually, like Childs, many private banks came to issue their own printed banknotes.

5. Weakness of goldsmith bankers. Towards the end of the seventeenth century, the criticism grew that the needs of trade were not being adequately met. The individual goldsmith's scale of operations was too small and his interest charges too high for credit facilities to be satisfactory.

Out of this agitation sprang a demand for a large chartered institution which could command both greater resources and more public confidence.

6. Foundation of the Bank of England, 1694. Founded by royal charter and capitalised by public subscription, the Bank added to its privileges in 1708 by securing the sole right amongst banks with more than six partners to issue banknotes. Since this right was considered indispensable, no other joint stock banks were in fact founded until the monopoly was broken in 1826.

By its charter (which was periodically to be reviewed before renewal) it was authorised to:

(a) accept deposits and make loans;

(b) discount bills;

(c) issue notes.

In return for its privileged position, the Bank made a loan to the Government of £1,200,000 at 8 per cent plus a management fee of £4,000 per annum.

NOTE: From its birth, therefore, the Bank was closely associated with the Government, a connection which subsequently became more intimate as the Bank was allowed to extend its privileges in return for further loans. The natural culmination was nationalisation in 1946, when its central position as the Government's financial agent was recognised. Until that time there remained the anomaly of its ownership by private shareholders.

TRANSITION FROM PRIVATE TO JOINT STOCK BANKING

7. Eighteenth-century growth of private banks. With the Bank of England effectively barring the way to other joint stock banks, in private hands development was slow, especially in the provinces. By 1750 there were probably no more than a dozen banks outside London, and the Bank of England had not availed itself of the opportunity to set up branches.

The increase in commercial activity which accompanied the Industrial Revolution, in the second half of the century, saw a growth of banking, and by 1800 there were nearly 400 banks in the provinces and 68 in London.

By 1826 a Parliamentary return showed a total throughout the country of 554 private banks but no joint stock banks other than the Bank of England.

NOTE: A private bank was one owned by a sole proprietor or simple partnership and therefore had limited access to capital for expansion. A joint stock bank, on the other hand, was financed by a joint stock of shareholders' capital which could be increased by further subscription (*see* X, 1).

8. "Runs" on the private banks. Since the notes which each bank issued were in effect only receipts for gold coin, any loss of confidence might result in a run on the bank when all depositors simultaneously required their notes to be honoured. Until the mid-nineteenth century, this happened on a great many occasions and for a number of possible reasons, such as the following.

(*a*) During periods of economic or political instability, people wished to hold their savings in the safest possible form, namely gold. In 1797, in fear of French invasion, there was even a run on the Bank of England. The Government then authorised it to suspend gold payments and its notes remained inconvertible for more than twenty years.

(*b*) Isolated and independent banks were susceptible to local fluctuations in trade, e.g. a bad harvest or slackness in a local industry. This could mean difficulty in recovering loans in order to honour banknotes.

(*c*) Runs might be promoted by unscrupulous rivals.

For whatever reason it occurred, a "run" could spell ruin for a bank, no matter how well managed. Many banks, however, failed because they were not soundly administered (*see* below).

9. Evolution of banking principles. This formative period was one in which great industries were growing up and in which there was much investment both at home and abroad. Bankers had to keep pace with this development, learning their craft as they did so. It was not surprising that many mistakes were made, such as the following.

(*a*) Huge losses often resulted from unwise loans.

(*b*) Bankers sometimes engaged in speculative ventures which were not legitimately within the compass of banking.

(*c*) There were as yet no guiding principles for the allocation of resources between different classes of loan in order prudently to cover liabilities.

(*d*) Close co-operation between the many small banks could have been a source of strength, but it did not exist.

10. Extension of joint stock banking. By the 1820s there was much pressure for an end to the Bank of England's monopoly. It was felt that joint stock banks, which would have greater resources and more professional and prudent management, would not suffer the same reverses as the existing private banks.

Matters were brought to a head following a wave of speculation in 1825, when some sixty-three country banks failed. There followed in consequence a major landmark in banking history, the Country Bankers Act 1826 which permitted the formation of joint stock banks with the power to issue notes in any place outside a sixty-five-mile radius of London.

The Bank of England reacted to this threat by opening branches in eleven major provincial centres. Despite this opposition and in the face of bitter resentment from the private banks, new joint stock enterprises took root. By 1834, there were 47, while the number of private banks had shrunk to 416.

There was, however, a cleavage between the London and the provincial banks, each confining its business to its own domain. Since London was fast developing as the nation's financial centre, joint stock development was handicapped.

11. Joint stock banking in London. There existed some confusion in the terms of the Bank of England's charter. Clarification was called for to determine whether it had in fact an absolute monopoly in London joint stock banking.

(*a*) *An Act of 1833* specifically authorised the establishment of companies or partnerships of more than six members within the sixty-five-mile radius, provided that they did not issue their own notes. (The Act also established Bank of England notes as legal tender with which the promissory notes of all other banks could be redeemed. The Bank, however, had to redeem its own notes in gold.)

(*b*) *In 1834*, the promoters of the 1833 Act founded the London & Westminster Bank and there began the great movement in banking which culminated in the modern system.

The Westminster was followed by others, notably the London Joint Stock Bank (1836) and the London and Country Bank (1839).

12. Struggle for survival. In the face of the violent opposition of the Bank of England and the private banks, the London joint stock banks fought step by step to secure their existence.

(*a*) At first denied the right to sue as corporate bodies, they were freed of this disability in 1838.

(*b*) They were not permitted clearing house facilities until 1845 and, in the case of the Westminster, an account at the Bank of England until 1864.

(c) They were unable to issue their own notes but countered this disability by cultivating the cheque system.

13. The joint stock principle firmly established. Progress was temporarily checked in 1844 with an Act which regulated the joint stock banks so stringently that the movement was nearly destroyed. Only one new bank, the City Bank, was opened between 1845 and 1860.

(a) This Act was superseded by the Joint Stock Banking Companies Act 1857, which treated banking companies in the same way as other companies save for limited liability, which had been introduced for other forms of trading in 1855. This disability was removed in 1858.

(b) The great Companies Act 1862, under which most subsequent banks were constituted, codified the law and placed joint stock banks in the same position as any other class of trading company.

14. Amalgamations. The revolution in transport brought all parts of the country into close touch and emphasised the essentially national character of the economy. To meet its needs, a more comprehensive national banking system was required. This was accomplished as follows.

The security afforded by the limited liability principle encouraged the larger joint stock banks to make use of their resources by building up a network of branches and, where necessary, by absorbing the smaller joint stock and private banks.

The progressive Westminster Bank initiated the process of amalgamation in 1849. The National Provincial, which had been founded in 1833, concentrated at first on establishing branch offices. Lloyds was the first bank to pursue amalgamations on a large scale and did so continuously from 1866. The Midland Bank was the product of the movement which saw country banks establishing London offices while the London banks expanded into the country. The greatest amalgamation of all, in 1918, made it the largest of the banks. Barclays was the result of the gradual fusion from 1896 onwards of many private banks.

In this way British banking business was concentrated in the eleven banks who were the members of the London Clearing House. Further mergers during the 1960s reduced membership of the Committee of London Clearing Bankers to six: Barclays,

Lloyds, Natwest, Midland, Williams and Glyn's, Coutts. In 1975, the Co-operative Bank and the Central Trustee Savings Bank, while not joining the Committee, were allocated seats at the Clearing House.

THE BANK OF ENGLAND AND THE GOLD STANDARD

15. The nineteenth-century problem of the note issue. The failure of many banks in the early nineteenth century through their inability to redeem their notes in gold caused keen debate. There were the following two schools of thought.

(a) *The "convertibility" school*, which adhered rigidly to the belief that all notes should be readily redeemable. In this they were supported by contemporary economists, who taught that only through such a "gold standard" could international trade be satisfactorily regulated. (With an adverse balance of trade, gold flowed out of the country to pay the deficit. Notes would then be withdrawn and as a result of the reduced national purchasing power, prices would fall. Exports would improve and the balance be restored: *see* **25**.)

(b) *The "adequate means of payment" school*, which recognised the need of commerce for an increased supply of money to deal with the ever-expanding volume of transactions. Without this, they argued, business would be stifled and restricted.

Eventually a compromise, weighted heavily in favour of the first point of view, was translated into the Bank Charter Act.

16. The Bank Charter Act 1844. Its principal intention was to regulate the note issue and it effectively confirmed a gold standard in Britain which lasted (save for three suspensions of the Act, in 1847, 1857 and 1866) until 1931. The principal provisions were as follows.

(a) *Right of issue.* The intention was to vest the sole right of note issue in the Bank of England. No new banks or fresh amalgamations were to have this privilege (this intention was not finally realised until 1921, when the last private bank issue lapsed). Primarily as a means of advertising their identity, a number of Scottish banks were permitted to continue printing their own notes but only against the security of an equal holding of Bank of England notes.

(b) *Banking Department*. This department of the Bank of England would concern itself with everyday transactions.

(c) *Issue Department*. This would be quite distinct from the Banking Department. Responsible for the volume of currency, it held the securities with which the note issue was backed. In the first instance these consisted of £3 million of bullion and just over £11 million of securities, representing the Government debt. Apart from this fiduciary issue (taken on trust, since it was not fully covered by gold), any notes issued were to have an equivalent amount of bullion set against them in the reserves.

(d) *Existing private bank issues*. These were restricted to the average circulation over the twelve weeks ending 27th April 1844.

(e) *Increasing the fiduciary issue*. If a private bank issue lapsed, the Bank of England might increase its fiduciary issue against securities other than bullion by up to two-thirds of the lapsed issue (by 1921, the final sum was £19¾ million).

(f) *Convertibility*. All Bank of England notes were to be freely convertible at the Issue Department.

(g) *A weekly statement* was to be published, indicating the volume of the note issue and the securities held against it.

17. Evaluation of the Act.

(a) It confirmed the central position which the Bank of England was coming to occupy. It was the bankers' bank and managed the Government debt. Its notes were legal tender and now it was ultimately to achieve monopoly control of the note issue.

(b) The currency was tied rigidly to an automatic mechanism which controlled its volume. Gold was the master, and when there was insufficient to balance the needs of trade, lack of purchasing power caused a fall in the price level, and this carried the country into depression.

(c) Set against this, the world's confidence that the £ sterling was "as good as gold" played a significant part in establishing London as the world's financial centre. More and more, international trade came to be balanced in sterling.

DEPARTURE FROM THE GOLD STANDARD, 1914–31

18. Expansion of the note issue. Until 1914, gold and banknotes

circulated side by side. The smallest denomination note, however, was £5, so that coin was essential for all the smaller transactions. The state of emergency before the outbreak of war produced a minor run on the banks by people desiring liquid funds. The run was met in legal tender, Bank of England £5 notes.

To forestall the inevitable changing of these notes for gold at the Issue Department, the Government passed the Currency and Banknotes Act 1914. The Government printed £61.5 million of Treasury notes, in denominations of £1 and 10s. (50p), which were declared legal tender and convertible into gold. To support this convertibility, £56.25 million in banknotes and £5.25 million in gold were withdrawn from circulation and held as cover. Gold export, however, was prohibited.

The new Treasury notes had public confidence and no demand for gold developed. In this situation, the Bank was able gradually to withdraw gold coin from circulation, replacing it with Treasury notes.

As the war progressed, the circulation was greatly inflated to meet the huge increase in the volume of transactions. By 1918, it was well in excess of £300 million, about four-fifths of which were Treasury notes and in reality not backed by gold.

19. Attempts to restore a full gold standard. While nominally on the gold standard, the prohibition of gold export barred its most important function, the automatic balancing of foreign trade (*see* **15**). The result was that, immediately after the war, British prices remained high, since there was no close connection between the gold reserves and the enormous purchasing power represented by the inflated circulation (*see* XII, **20**). This factor, in conjunction with the general dislocation of world trade, created an adverse balance of payments and a continuing depreciation in the international value of the £ (e.g. the dollar exchange rate slumped from 4.76 to 3.22).

Since foreign currency was consequently dearer to buy, the price of imports of vital food and raw materials was adversely affected.

The remedy was thought to lie in deflating the currency (and therefore the price level) and freeing the export of gold, i.e. a return to the gold standard in its full sense.

Limited action was taken in the Gold Standard Act 1925. Gold could be withdrawn from the Bank of England to make foreign payments, but in minimum quantities of 400 troy ounces (about £1,700).

20. Results of deflation. The steady reduction in the note issue from 1920 and the free export of gold were at first successful in restoring the £ to its pre-war international value.

However, this stability was achieved at the expense of aggravating the problems of the depressed years of the 1920s. Falling prices meant low expectation of profit, curtailment of production and increased unemployment.

Moreover, the changed pattern of world trade, in which Britain figured much less prominently, caused gold to flow out continuously in order to support a £ which was over-valued. The implication was that export earnings were insufficient to meet the cost of imports, which were therefore subsidised from diminishing gold reserves.

Plainly, in these conditions a gold standard could not survive, and in 1931 it was abandoned. The use of gold to support the £ at a rigid international value ceased and the note issue remained inconvertible.

21. Currency and Banknotes Act 1928. This Act restored the whole note issue to the Bank of England. Banknotes were substituted for Treasury notes and, since a considerable number of the latter were fiduciary, this necessitated an increase in the Bank's fiduciary issue. From its 1929 level of £19.75 million, it was therefore raised to £260 million. All notes in excess were required to have gold cover.

22. The Exchange Equalisation Account, 1932. Since the value of the £ was not, after 1931, supported by the free export of gold, exchange rates fluctuated in accordance with variations in the volume of foreign trade.

To provide some stability, the Exchange Equalisation Account was set up to purchase sterling when the exchanges were adverse and to sell sterling when they were favourable.

The reasoning was that if the price of the £ was declining, owing to insufficient demand from foreign importers, it could be artificially supported by creating additional demand. Conversely if the £ were in short supply and its price rising then more would be made available from the Account.

The assumption was that over a period of time the losses and gains of the Account would balance. This did not prove to be the case, since the exchanges remained predominantly unfavourable.

The Account was steadily increased from £150 million in 1932 to £750 million in 1939 and at the outbreak of war it received most of the Bank's gold reserves.

23. Growth of the fiduciary issue, 1939–45. Since the Bank, in 1939, was left with scarcely any gold, authority had to be given for a corresponding increase in the fiduciary issue. The Currency and Bank Notes Act 1939 raised the amount to £580 million.

The enormous increase in the volume of business during the war called for an ever-expanding circulation. By the war's end, the fiduciary issue had more than doubled.

THE EVOLUTION OF CENTRAL BANKING

24. Functions of the central bank. Throughout its history the Bank of England had in piecemeal fashion acquired functions which distinguished it from all other banks.

(a) *National debt management.* From the date of its foundation the Bank continued to make direct loans to the Government. After 1844, it no longer did so but it retained the responsibility for all aspects of debt management, i.e. making new issues, interest payments, repayments of principal and all of the administrative work involved in maintaining a register of stockholders.

(b) *Government's accounts.* It was also the Bank which held the Exchequer Account and the accounts of government departments.

(c) *Note issue and monetary policy.* The 1844 Act made the Bank the central note-issuing authority and required it to back the currency with gold. To this end it had the responsibility of safeguarding the gold reserves and this it did through the application of a monetary policy whose instruments were a moving Bank Rate supported by open market operations.

25. Bank Rate. This was the minimum rate at which the Bank of England as lender of last resort would rediscount bills for the discount houses (*see* **27** below). It was the key interest rate to which all other rates were directly or indirectly related, e.g. bill rates, bank deposit rates, overdraft rates, mortgage rates.

It was argued that an outflow of gold consequent upon a payments imbalance could be checked first by raising interest rates which would increase the inducement to overseas holders of sterling. Secondly, the disincentive to domestic borrowers would cause a contraction of the volume of bank deposit money, i.e.

credit (*see* XII, **5**). Thirdly, this disinflationary policy would make British prices more internationally competitive. Exports would rise, imports decline and gold would flow back into the country.

26. Open market operations. Traditionally, open market operations in gilt edged securities were seen to be in support of Bank Rate. Thus a rise in Bank Rate would be accompanied by sales of securities to the general public. These would be paid for by cheques drawn in favour of the Bank of England and would result in an adverse balance for the clearing banks at the clearing house. The balance would be adjusted by a reduction of clearing bank deposits at the Bank of England. Since these deposits formed part of the cash reserves of the banks held to cover the possibility of withdrawals they would have to be made good by the realisation of the banks' most liquid assets, namely money lent at call to the London discount houses. The houses in turn would have to find cash and this they could only do by resorting to their unique borrowing facility at the Bank of England. They were obliged, however, to pay the penally high Bank Rate which was in this way made effective since bill rates and all other interest rates would now move up. When this sequence of events occurred it was said that the houses had been "forced into the Bank".

27. The London discount market. Prior to the development of the cheque and the overdraft, credit facilities were normally afforded through the bill of exchange. This is in effect a promise to pay at some future date, normally three months hence. Although the supplier might be prepared to accept such a bill he would naturally prefer cash and his bank would therefore discount it for him, i.e. pay him spot cash less an interest rate percentage.

(*a*) *The "running broker".* On occasion the single branch banks of the early nineteenth century had difficulty in coping with the volume of bills. There consequently emerged the "running broker" whose function was to find "good" bills at banks with cash shortages for banks in other areas with cash surpluses. For this service he took a commission.

(*b*) *Bill dealers.* After 1820, certain influential brokers such as Overend, Gurney and Co. acquired such sound reputations that they were able to borrow from the banks on their own behalf in order to finance their own portfolios. In 1829, the Bank of England also agreed to afford lending facilities to these embry-

onic discount houses. These developments were agreeable to the
banks, many of whom had only survived the 1825 crash
through the help of their major competitor, the Bank of England
(*see* **10**). From that time, they had determined to maintain a
more prudent level of reserves. However, to have increased their
cash holdings would have diminished profits since cash yields no
interest. They now had the alternative of a highly liquid asset,
money advanced to the discount houses repayable "at call or
short notice". Their ability to repay was guaranteed by the
Bank's willingness to act as "lender of last resort" to the discount houses.

(*c*) *Foreign trade bills*. By the last quarter of the nineteenth
century the volume of inland trade bills had declined and the
overdraft had become the principal means of providing trade
credit. However, the years 1870–1914 witnessed a huge expansion
of international trade, much of it financed by bills drawn on
London and discounted through the London discount market.
This period saw London emerge as the world's financial capital.

(*d*)) *Treasury bills*. With the outbreak of war in 1914, international trade collapsed and the stock in trade of the discount
market largely disappeared. However, the Government for the
first time now required to borrow vast sums at short-term repayment dates. This it did through the Treasury bill which now
became the principal instrument in which the market dealt.

(*e*) *Short bonds and other securities*. In the twentieth century
the discount houses widened the scope of their operations.
During the 1930s and again during the Second World War they
were active in the short-dated bond market and this remains a
major aspect of their business. The 1960s saw a revival of commercial paper and the development of strong markets in local
authority securities and certificates of deposit.

One characteristic is common to all of the various functions
which the discount market evolved. It will be seen that they all
relate to the provision of short-term credit. The houses are inter-
mediaries, borrowing from the banks in order to lend to a variety
of public and private sector borrowers. Moreover, since it retains
its unique borrowing facilities at the Bank of England it has still
a significant role in the application of monetary policy.

28. Bank, Treasury and monetary policy in the 1920s. Until 1914,
the Bank of England, a privately owned joint stock company,

applied monetary policy at its own discretion. During the 1920s
the influence of the Treasury became much more marked. Since
the Treasury bill was the principal instrument in which the
market dealt, it was in a strong position to influence short-term
interest rates by rationing the supply. In the capital market where
the Government bond was the main instrument, it could exert
similar pressure.

In the formulation of monetary policy there was consequently
evolved a close working relationship between Bank and
Treasury, a liaison which is today referred to rather vaguely as
"the monetary authorities".

29. Abandonment of an active monetary policy, 1931. In the prevailing economic depression no merit could be seen in interest
rates which rose as well as fell. Bank Rate was therefore reduced
to 2 per cent where it remained for the next twenty years save for
a short period in 1939.

During the 1930s it was argued that low interest rates helped
to reduce the burden of national debt servicing. Furthermore,
they might in due course provide the incentive to increased investment.

From 1939 to 1945, with a massive expansion of the national
debt, low interest rates were still thought to be desirable.

Similarly, after 1945 it was maintained that cheap money
would be conducive to the investment necessary for peacetime
reconstruction.

30. Nationalisation of the Bank, 1946. The close relationship
which had always existed between Government and Bank was
formally acknowledged in the Bank of England Act 1946. The
Government then bought out the existing stockholders.

It was clear that the Bank would have an important part to
play in an economy which for the first time was to have a large
measure of Government planning. In close liaison with the
Treasury it would be concerned with the following.

(*a*) *Domestic economic policy.* The formulation of an appropriate monetary policy.

(*b*) *External relations.* The safeguarding of sterling's external
value through the operation of the Exchange Equalisation
Account and the management of exchange controls. Additionally
the management of monetary relations with the sterling area,
foreign central banks and international institutions such as the
I.M.F.

31. Reactivation of monetary policy, 1951. Severe inflationary
pressures which had resulted in devaluation in 1949 continued
into the 1950s. To deal with this situation fresh economic thinking in 1951 led to the tentative revival by the Bank of an active
monetary policy. Bank Rate was raised from 2 per cent to 2½
per cent and thereafter the level of demand within the economy
was managed by a package of fiscal and monetary measures and
direct controls, e.g. incomes policies.

32. The Bank and monetary policy, 1951–71. The experience of
the 1950s did little to reinforce confidence in the effectiveness of
the traditional instruments of monetary policy. There seemed
little evidence that borrowing and spending were discouraged by
a high Bank Rate. Consequently, during the 1960s recourse was
made to direct instructions by the Bank to the clearing banks to
restrict their lending activities. By 1971 there had been a reaction
to this approach and in September of that year the Bank reverted
to the older methods of trying to influence credit creation
through freely moving interest rates.

33. Monetary policy 1971–8. The Bank of England Paper of
1971, *Competition and Credit Control*, placed more emphasis
upon market forces. A freely moving interest rate would harmonise the demand for and the supply of credit. The move in this
direction was supported in 1972 by the substitution of minimum
lending rate (M.L.R.) for the traditional Bank Rate. Whereas
movements in Bank Rate had previously determined market
rates, the latter now determined M.L.R.

This approach became progressively less satisfactory to the
Government, which was no longer able to apply monetary policy
through arbitrary movements of Bank Rate. Greater reliance was
now placed upon calls for special deposits which reduced the lending capacity of the banks and in 1973 a supplementary special
deposit scheme was introduced. The new scheme put banks under
penalty if they lent above prescribed levels.

This gradual drift back towards the 1960s, credit control by
Bank of England directive, was checked by the reinstatement of
Bank Rate in 1978. Although still described as minimum lending
rate, it was once again varied at the discretion of the Bank of
England with market rates being obliged to follow suit.

PROGRESS TEST 9

1. What forces retarded the development of banking in the

Middle Ages? **(1)**

2. What part did the Lombards play in the foundation of "the City"? **(2)**

3. Why were the moral objections to banking relaxed in the seventeenth century? **(1, 3)**

4. What was the nature of the first paper money? **(4)**

5. Account for the foundation of the Bank of England in 1694. **(5)**

6. In what two chief respects did the Bank of England differ from the other banks? **(6)**

7. What forces promoted the extension of joint stock banking in the 1820s? **(8–10)**

8. "In the first half of the nineteenth century, the natural growth of banking and commerce was retarded by the Bank of England's opposition to change." Comment on this view. **(10–13)**

9. "The growing sense of national unity induced by improved communications was reflected in the structure of banking." Explain. **(14)**

10. What is a gold standard? Why was early nineteenth-century opinion divided on its desirability? **(15)**

11. What was the principal result of the 1844 Bank Charter Act and why was it of such profound importance? **(16, 17)**

12. In what way did the First World War alter the nature of the note issue? **(18)**

13. What steps did the Government take to remedy Britain's weak competitive position after 1920? **(19)**

14. Were these measures effective? **(20)**

15. What methods were employed in the 1930s to achieve stability of foreign exchange rates? **(22)**

16. In what way since 1945 has the Bank of England acted as the Government's agent in regulating the national economy? **(25–27)**

17. What is meant by the expression "forced into the Bank"? **(26)**

18. How does the Bank of England seek to maintain the international value of sterling? **(30)**

19. How did M.L.R. differ from bank rate in the period 1971–8? **(33)**

20. Why did the Government dislike the 1971 form of monetary policy? **(33)**

CHAPTER X

Joint Stock Companies and the Stock Exchange

THE JOINT STOCK PRINCIPLE AND ITS EARLY DEVELOPMENT

1. Nature of the joint stock company. The limits to the scale of enterprise set by the restricted capital of a sole proprietor may be overcome by establishing a joint stock of capital. Subscriptions are invited privately from a prescribed number of shareholders (2–50 for a private company) or from the public at large (for a public company, which must have at least seven members). This method of financing enterprise offers certain advantages.

(*a*) The enterprise gains access to the small savings of the whole nation.

(*b*) Ownership and management are divorced, facilitating the growth of a professional managerial class.

(*c*) Investments may be quickly realised by the sale of shares on the stock exchange.

(*d*) The legal liability of shareholders may be limited to the extent of their investment (*see* **26–28**).

(*e*) Risk is diffused amongst a number of investors.

(*f*) Different types of share vary the degree of risk (and therefore profitability).

2. Origin. The trading partnership was common in the Middle Ages, as were corporate bodies such as the craft gilds and the ancient boroughs created by charter (*see* I, **14**). From the union of these two forms of organisation in the sixteenth century grew the modern joint stock company.

3. Sixteenth-century growth of overseas trade. Never before a seafaring or trading nation, in the sixteenth century England appreciated the advantage of her geographical position in a world growing larger through exploration. By Elizabethan times, she had secured control of her own overseas trade, previously in the hands of foreign merchants, and was competing in exploration and commerce with the maritime nations of Europe.

4. Early trading companies. In order to spread the great financial risks of foreign trade, many ventures were launched with a joint stock, such as the following.

(*a*) *The Russia Company, 1553*. The first, it had a capital of £6,000 subscribed in shares of £25, to finance a voyage in search of a China passage by way of north Russia. This was unsuccessful, but in 1555 the Company secured a charter granting it a monopoly of trade with Russia.

(*b*) *The East India Company, 1600*. By far the largest and most important, it was chartered to develop trade with India and the East Indies by way of the Cape of Good Hope.

(*c*) *Mineral and Battery Company, 1568*. Industry also made some use of joint stock finance. This company mined zinc ore and manufactured brass, iron and wire.

(*d*) *Colonising companies*. Many companies were formed in the early seventeenth century to colonise the Americas, e.g. Virginia (1606), Bermuda (1611), Guiana (1619) and New England (1620).

(*e*) *Public utilities*. From an early date this was also considered a suitable field for joint stock enterprise, e.g. the New River Company (1619) provided a water supply to London.

5. Limited liability, 1662. This was a landmark in company history when limited liability was granted to shareholders in three chartered companies, one of which was the East India Company.

6. Insurance companies. A speculative boom at the end of the seventeenth century brought a rash of new companies in manufacturing, trading and fire insurance.

By 1695, it is estimated that there were at least 140 joint stock companies, although many were unchartered and short-lived.

7. Share dealing. From the first, share transfers were effected by private negotiation, but only with the expansion of the 1690s did an organised market develop.

Dealings were in the hands of brokers from a great variety of trades, who gradually began to exclude their other commercial interests in order to concentrate upon:

(*a*) the transfer of shares in joint stock companies;

(b) dealings in the Government debt (see 12 below).

Transactions were at first carried out in the Royal Exchange, but from the 1690s most business was done in city coffee houses, particularly Jonathan's and Garroway's.

8. The South Sea Bubble. An ever present feature of early eighteenth-century company promotions was the "ingrafting" of Government debt into the company's capital. In effect, the Government granted a charter with certain monopoly rights in return for a loan on which they paid interest.

In 1720, the South Sea Company offered to convert the whole Government debt into their own stock. In the belief that the Company would make great profits, the market bid up its share prices to a quite unrealistic level.

The fever of speculation was transmitted to other dealings and innumerable companies, many fraudulent, were promoted. Vast sums were borrowed to purchase shares and inevitably a shortage of money resulted.

The South Sea Company, disliking the increased competition for investment funds, pressed for and secured the "Bubble Act".

9. The "Bubble Act" 1720. This was a drastic Act which:

(a) declared company promotion without a charter to be illegal;

(b) invalidated all dealings in the shares of illegal companies.

10. The joint stock principle discredited. The combined effects of money shortage and prosecutions under the Act pricked the "bubble" and share prices crashed. Few companies were able to weather the storm and for the rest of the century investors remained wary of new promotions.

11. Eighteenth-century share transactions. Business was confined chiefly to dealings in the stock of the Bank of England, the Royal Exchange and London assurance companies and the old-established trading companies.

Apart from the suspicions of investors and the restrictions of the "Bubble Act" there was little demand for new companies, since:

(a) *the scale of industry* was small and required only a fixed capital which could be provided by wealthy individuals or partnerships;

(*b*) *the domestic system* (*see* I, **21**) still prevailed in many industries and, in this case, the businessman made no investment in fixed capital;

(*c*) *the growth of banking* offered alternative sources of finance.

12. Dealings in Government securities. Recurring and increasingly costly wars caused a steady rise in the National Debt throughout the second half of the eighteenth century (*see* XXI, **4**).

The failure of the South Sea conversion virtually ended the policy of raising loans from trading companies, and appeal was made instead to the public.

There was therefore a brisk expansion in dealings in Government securities which, until 1815, when the war with France ended, dominated the business of the Stock Exchange.

NOTE: From this period emerged the "Consol" or Consolidated Bank Annuity (1751). The fusion of a number of earlier 3 per cent annuities, it later became the most popular medium for fresh loans.

13. Origin of the Stock Exchange. In 1762, 150 brokers formed a club which rented Jonathan's Coffee House for their exclusive use. Disagreement with the proprietor led them to purchase their own premises in Threadneedle Street (1773), the first stock exchange. Strangely, admission was not restricted to members. Anyone could transact business there upon payment of 6*d.* (2½p) a day.

In 1802, the Exchange moved to larger premises in Capel Court (its present site) and adopted a stricter constitution. The general public were excluded. Membership was to be by ballot and an annual subscription paid. Members could not deal on their own behalf and could not engage in brokerage in other trades.

NINETEENTH-CENTURY INVESTMENT

14. Its nature. Only in the last quarter of the century was there any major extension of joint stock organisation into industry and commerce. Although still of great importance, dealing in Government securities declined, since the National Debt was reduced from about £820 million in 1815 to under £650 million in 1914. The greatest expansion in business in the early part of the period was in public utilities, transport and overseas investment.

15. Overseas investment. In the period 1815–1914, Britain became the world's principal overseas investor. Capital flowed at first into Europe, especially during the railway boom of the 1840s, when French and Belgian companies were supported.

From the 1820s onward, numerous South and Central American Government loans were floated on the London market.

There was also extensive investment in United States railways and canals, while individual state governments obtained loans.

By the 1850s Britain's foreign investments totalled some £200 million. The following twenty years firmly established her as the world's financial centre. More than 150 loans for governments throughout the world were raised on the London market and huge sums were invested in companies operating overseas in railways, public utilities, docks, irrigation and drainage works, plantations and manufacturing. By 1876, investment abroad exceeded £1,000 million.

After a slight check, the flow continued in the 1880s, especially to the Empire, both in Government loans and in industrial and commercial investment.

The period 1905–14 was one of tremendous activity, bringing total British overseas investment to about £3,000 million.

16. Canal companies. The first major canal, the Worsley and Manchester, was completed in 1761 (*see* XIII, **17, 18**). While this was financed by the Duke of Bridgewater, others which followed were operated by joint stock companies, e.g. the Grand Junction, which cost over £1 million.

Where such large sums were involved, joint stock was essential. Moreover, little difficulty was experienced in attracting investors, since the early companies proved very profitable. By the 1790s, the Stock Exchange was doing a brisk business in their shares.

The last canal was built in 1840, by which time £12 million had been invested in sixty-two companies.

17. Dock companies. During the early nineteenth century, there was also some investment in docks. Until this time, the Port of London depended upon lighters which worked ships anchored in mid-stream.

In 1799, the West India Dock Company was incorporated by Act of Parliament and was followed by other companies which constructed the London Docks, Commercial Docks and East India Docks.

Later in the century, however, an increasing number of docks and harbours were run by public authorities.

18. Railway companies. By far the greatest part of transport investment was in railway companies (*see* XIV, **10–12**), and their securities accounted for a considerable proportion of stock exchange business.

(*a*) *1825–42.* Almost 100 Acts of Parliament incorporated railway companies, although some were short-lived. In 1842, the shares of sixty-six companies with a capital of £47 million were quoted on the stock exchange.

(*b*) *1842–53.* This was a further period of expansion, with 1845 a boom year in which no fewer than 1,398 companies were registered, although many came to nothing. Nevertheless, the share capital of quoted companies rose by 1853 to £200 million.

(*c*) *1853–1913.* The completion and improvement of the railway system required further vast investment, which brought total share capital to £1,200 million in 1913.

19. Public utilities.

(*a*) *Water.* A water company was amongst the first to operate with a joint stock (*see* **4**) but there was only relatively modest investment in this field (£10 million by the 1880s).

Increasingly, local authorities assumed the responsibility for water supply (*see* XVII, **9**).

(*b*) *Gas.* The Gas Light & Coke Company (1810) of London was first in the field and was followed by three others in the 1820s. Expansion was at first slow, with only £3½ million invested by mid-century. Progress was then rapid, with over £74 million of share capital quoted in 1913.

(*c*) *Electricity.* Following the invention of the Ediswan Lamp, there was a boom in electric lighting shares. In the following decade, dealings were stabilised at a high level.

Tramways also created a great demand for electricity and by 1913, £200 million had been invested in various electrical industries.

20. Industry and commerce. For most of the period, the dominant form of organisation was the family business. However, the limited liability laws (*see* **26–28**) led to a great increase in the number of company registrations. Many of these were small family firms which sought only legal protection, but in some industries the increasing scale of production was creating a demand for additional capital with the subscriber safeguarded by limited liability.

(*a*) *1856–80*. First in the field were coal, iron and steel, ship-building and heavy engineering, with a number of important companies (e.g. Ebbw Vale, Staveley Coal & Iron, John Brown & Co., Whitworth's, Nettlefold's).

(*b*) *1880–92*. This period brought to the market shipping (Cunard), chemicals (Brunner Mond & Co.), asphalt (Neuchatel), cotton (J. & P. Coates) and numerous breweries (e.g. Bass, Guinness, Ind Coope).

Share capital quoted on the Stock Exchange grew from £160 million to £358 million.

(*c*) *1892–1914*. This was a period of great activity. The low yield on Government securities during the 1890s turned the investor to industry and commerce. Many more companies were promoted in brewing (e.g. Watney, Coombe, Reid & Co., 1897) and textiles (e.g. Bradford Dyers and Fine Cotton Spinners, 1898; Calico Printers, 1899).

Rapid progress was made in the new cycle and car industries and in retail distribution, soap, tobacco, wallpaper and cement.

In banking and insurance, amalgamations led to many new companies and a tremendous growth of share capital (*see* IX, 14).

By 1914, companies with a total share capital of £1,527 million were quoted on the London Stock Exchange.

NINETEENTH-CENTURY STATUTORY CONTROLS

21. Unincorporated companies, 1720–1825. The "Bubble Act" prohibited operation as a company without a charter. Provided that there was no pretension to corporate status and there were no dealings in shares, there appeared to be no offence and many companies operated quite successfully without incorporation, e.g. the Sun Insurance Office. Nevertheless, they suffered the following two grave disadvantages.

(*a*) They could not take court action in the company's name since they were not corporate bodies.

(*b*) They could not claim limited liability.

Pressure for ameliorative legislation resulted at first in several Acts, commencing with that of 1825.

22. An Act of 1825. The restrictions of the "Bubble Act" were removed, leaving unchartered companies subject to no statutory controls whatsoever. The corporate status of such companies was, however, still in doubt and they certainly could not claim limited liability.

23. Trading Companies Act 1834. The Board of Trade was empowered to give companies the right to sue through their officers.

24. The "Letters Patent" Act 1837. This facilitated the granting of privileges and immunities (including limited liability) by letters patent.

25. Companies Act 1844. A milestone in company law, this Act attempted to clarify the status of trading companies.

(*a*) *A Joint Stock Companies Registration Office was established.*

(*b*) Provision was made for the registration of all new companies.

(*c*) Corporate status was secured by the signing of a deed of settlement by at least a quarter of the stock subscribers, and by registration.

The law in respect of limited liability continued to produce many anomalies. These were reduced by the Limited Liability Act 1855.

26. Limited Liability Act 1855. Any company could acquire limited liability provided that:

(*a*) it registered under the 1844 Act;

(*b*) 75 per cent of its nominal capital was subscribed;

(*c*) 15 per cent was paid up.

27. Joint Stock Companies Act 1856. This provided the basis of modern law. A minimum of seven people were permitted to form a limited company by lodging a memorandum which stated the company's aims and declared that it was limited.

28. Companies Act 1862. Preceding legislation was now codified and the lines upon which limited companies were to be constituted and administered were laid down.

Provision was made for winding up and for publicising a company's affairs.

EXPANSION OF THE STOCK MARKET
SINCE 1914

29. The character of investment. War, nationalisation and the changing world political pattern have brought radical changes in the distribution of investment. The markets in railways, canals, coal mines and utilities have disappeared and the volume of overseas investment has greatly diminished. This decrease in business has been more than compensated for by increased investment in industry and commerce.

30. Increased industrial and commercial investment. In 1913, if investment in financial institutions is excluded, home commercial and industrial securities amounted to £873 million, only 8 per cent of total investment. By 1939 this figure had risen to over £2,000 million and by 1962 to nearly £7,500 million—about a quarter of the nominal value of all quoted securities. The market value was much greater: about £21,000 million or 42 per cent of the market value of all securities.

Investment in banking and insurance accounted for a further £6,650 million market value, or 13 per cent.

31. Reasons for increased industrial and commercial investment.

(*a*) Technological progress has made possible economies of large-scale production in many more industries. Family businesses have had to become public companies in order to obtain sufficient capital for expansion.

(*b*) Competition between uneconomic small firms has led to the formation of amalgamated companies.

(*c*) The existence of the family business has been jeopardised by the need to sell assets in order to meet high death duties. Its continuity may be assured by forming a company.

32. Company promotions in the 1920s. The post-war boom brought many new share issues. Business slackened with depression, but from 1923 onwards there was a steady expansion, with many private firms—especially in textiles—becoming public companies.

The new motor and electrical industries also proved a profitable field for company flotation and Morris, Ford, English Electric, Pye and Thorn were founded.in this period.

This was also a period in which there was much unsound and even fraudulent company promotion. Unscrupulous promoters purchased private businesses, often at inflated prices, and by rigging the market were able to sell the shares of the companies they formed at even higher prices. The result was that the shareholder's investment bore little relationship to the earning capacity of the company and legislation was necessary to protect the public.

33. Companies Acts 1928 and 1929. House-to-house selling of shares was prohibited. If a direct approach was made to the public in writing, then information had to be given, similar to that required by the Stock Exchange when it granted permission for dealing in a security.

34. The market in the 1930s. Depression at the beginning of the decade caused a drop in the volume of transactions in existing shares and in new issues for commercial and industrial companies.

After 1934, there was a revival, and company finance became much more soundly based. In the 1920s there had been too much reliance upon preference shares and debentures, both of which yield a fixed rate of interest and which company earnings at that time often could not support. In the 1930s, fixed interest securities were increasingly displaced by ordinary shares whose yield varies with profits.

35. Post-1945 control of investment. The controls imposed during the war years were continued in the interest of directing national resources into the channels where they were most urgently required.

Permission to invite public subscription to a new share issue was granted by the Capital Issues Committee, subject to the directives of the Chancellor. Broadly, priority was given in the order: defence industries, export industries, home trade industries. The expansion plans of the latter were therefore made to conform to the Government's intention to diversify industry throughout the country (see III, 7 and 14).

Control was maintained with varying degrees of severity until 1959, when the restrictions upon new domestic issues were virtually removed. Foreign investment is still strictly regulated.

36. Company finance after 1945. Until 1959, restrictions curtailed the volume of new issues and compelled companies to depend for expansion much more heavily upon ploughing back profits, a policy which was encouraged by tax reliefs.

Relaxation of controls after 1959, together with easier credit conditions, led to a great increase in new issues and to increased borrowing from banks, while profit-financed expansion decreased.

By the 1970s the supply of fresh equity capital had been strangled. This position reflected declining company profitability which was concealed by the traditional method of historic cost accounting (see 37).

37. Company profitability and historic cost accounting. The whole of the post-1945 period has been one of continuing inflation. Throughout the period, historic cost accounting, which makes no allowance for inflation, was used to measure company profits. Demonstrably, these continued to be vastly overstated.

Taking into account the depreciation in the value of money when measuring profits, recent research has produced some striking conclusions for the period 1954–75.

(a) *Total company taxation.* The effective rate of taxation on true company earnings averaged 71 per cent and in three years exceeded 100 per cent.

(b) *Taxation of equity earnings.* The effective rate of taxation on true equity earnings averaged 83 per cent and in six years exceeded 100 per cent.

(c) *Dividends.* Distributions to shareholders exceeded true equity earnings in each of sixteen years, producing deficits which were financed by bank borrowings.

The illusion of profit was in part detected by the stock market and reflected in falling prices. Taking these prices into account, if a shareholder had invested in a portfolio in 1954 and sold it in 1977 his rate of return, having allowed for inflation and net of standard rate taxation, would have been a true 2.5 per cent.

If the period is divided into two, the return for 1954–64 would have averaged 6.8 per cent and for the period 1964–76 a negative 2.7 per cent.

The reason for the negative return is basically the enormous decline in the real value of equities since 1964. (The de Zoete Equity Index fell in real terms from 363 in April 1965 to 184 in January 1978, i.e. the true value of shareholdings was halved.)

Of more fundamental importance is the negative return in real terms to companies as a whole. For the period 1954–64 for manufacturing companies this averaged 5.9 per cent per annum but for 1965–76 a negative 1.5 per cent per annum.

The conclusion is that a more realistic accounting approach reveals the unprofitability of the private sector after 1964.

PROGRESS TEST 10

1. "In a private enterprise economy, the joint stock principle is the only feasible means of financing large-scale production." Explain this assertion. **(1)**

2. By what method were the early companies given a corporate existence? **(2)**

3. What inspired the development of joint stock companies in the sixteenth and seventeenth centuries? **(3, 4)**

4. To what extent had the joint stock principle been popularised by 1700? **(4–6)**

5. Account for eighteenth-century distrust of joint stock companies. **(8–10)**

6. Why was there only very slight economic pressure in the eighteenth century for the extension of joint stock organisation? **(11)**

7. What was the nature of eighteenth-century stock exchange business and where was it conducted? **(7, 12, 13)**

8. Describe the principal field of nineteenth-century investment and indicate its significance. **(15)**

9. "British transport facilities were created by private finance." Illustrate this statement with reference to nineteenth-century investment. **(16–18)**

10. How was the principle of *laissez-faire* demonstrated in the provision of public utilities? **(19)**

11. Nineteenth-century joint stock finance made only slow progress in industry. Illustrate and explain the reasons for this statement. **(20)**

12. What legal disabilities were suffered by many joint stock companies before 1825? **(21)**

13. How was their weakness subsequently remedied? **(22–28)**

14. Describe and account for the changed nature of twentieth-century investment. **(29–31)**

15. Why was company legislation made necessary in the 1920s? **(32, 33)**

16. In what respect was company finance sounder in the 1930s than it had been in the 1920s? **(32, 33)**

17. How was investment controlled after 1945 in order to influence the location of new industry? (35)

18. Why was stock exchange business stimulated in the 1960s? (36)

19. After 1964 the private sector of industry ceased to be profitable. Why was this not generally perceived to be the case? (37)

CHAPTER XI

Overseas Trade and Payments

THE AGE OF MERCANTILISM
(FIFTEENTH TO EIGHTEENTH CENTURIES)

1. Origins and growth of trade in 1760. Until the fourteenth century, English overseas trade was conducted almost entirely by foreigners. The growth of woollen manufacture in the fourteenth and fifteenth centuries led English merchants into foreign markets.

(*a*) *The merchant adventurers.* In accordance with prevailing mercantilist thought (*see* I, 30, 31), the State regulated trade by channelling it through associations of merchants. The merchant adventurers received royal charters granting certain monopoly privileges in trade to north Germany and the Baltic in 1404 and 1408. The privileges were extended by further charters in 1505 and 1564.

By the end of the sixteenth century this powerful association had wrested control of foreign trade from alien merchants.

(*b*) *Expansion of foreign markets.*

(*i*) In the seventeenth century, the export of manufactures—especially woollens—increased. In return, sugar and tobacco were obtained from the colonies in the West Indies and North America, and Eastern produce from India.

(*ii*) In the eighteenth century, colonial trade grew, until by 1760 its volume was one-third of the total. Impetus was then added by Clive's and Wolfe's victories, which opened up vast new markets in India and Canada respectively.

(*c*) *Government policy* (*see* I, 29–30). The consciousness of nationhood which was being experienced throughout Europe led British governments to safeguard markets by supervising trade strictly and, when necessary, by military action.

For a nation which did not have all its requirements within its own frontiers, overseas trade was vital. Markets and sources of supply had to be seized before competitors could monopolise them.

Exclusive privileges were granted to powerful trading companies (e.g. the East India and Hudson's Bay companies) and national support given when they came into conflict with European rivals.

2. Trade gathers momentum. The growth of overseas trade gave an impetus to manufacturing industry. In turn, eighteenth-century industrialisation led to lower prices, which further stimulated overseas trade, especially in Europe.

In earlier times, international trade had catered almost exclusively for the luxury requirements of the rich, e.g. silks and spices. Later there was a much wider market for cheap manufactured goods, especially woollen cloth.

NOTE: There was an important difference between eighteenth- and nineteenth-century trade. In the eighteenth century, insatiable markets stimulated industrial expansion. In the nineteenth century, ever-increasing industrial capacity made new markets essential.

3. Mercantilist restrictions of eighteenth-century trade. In the second half of the century, the main part of British trade lay with her colonies, upon whom the following severe restraints were imposed.

(a) Exports to foreign countries had to be shipped via Britain.

(b) Manufacturing in the colonies was prohibited.

(c) All imports had to be shipped from Britain.

(d) All trade had to be carried in British ships.

Restrictions (a) and (c) encouraged the growth of a great entrepôt trade in London.

4. The commodities of eighteenth-century foreign trade.

(a) *Imports.* From the Americas: tobacco, sugar, ginger, rice. From Europe: wines, fruit, timber, hemp, furs, hides. From the Orient: spices, silk, tea.

(b) *Exports.* Manufactures, particularly wool but increasingly cotton. The re-exports of the entrepôt trade included tea, sugar, timbers, tobacco and rice.

5. The wars with France, 1793–1815. Blockades by both sides retarded the natural growth of trade. Nevertheless, by running the blockade and by increasing trade in other directions (e.g. Russia), the volume of British overseas commerce was probably greater in 1815 than it had been in 1792.

The wars had the following important commercial consequences.

(*a*) *Destruction of European markets.* The Continental countries had been impoverished far more than Britain. Since these markets were now limited, for the following fifteen years attention was directed towards the colonies.

The growing cotton manufacture stimulated American cotton imports.

(*b*) *Destruction of European maritime power.* The full impact of American competition at sea had yet to be felt (*see* XV, **2**). Meanwhile, the destruction of French, Dutch and Spanish sea power left Britain unchallenged and with a monopoly in trade with the East and West Indies and India.

(*c*) *Elimination of potential industrial rivals.* By retarding European industry, the wars gave Britain a lead which she retained for the greater part of the century.

THE AGE OF FREE TRADE, 1823–1931

6. Pressures from expanding industry. The protective customs duties of mercantilism had carefully nurtured infant British industry. After 1815, supremely confident and with no rivals, industry sought to throw off the trade restrictions which held it back.

The application of steam power to manufacturing steadily increased output. The only safety valve lay in wider overseas markets.

7. Decline of mercantilist thought. With the home market assured, manufacturers argued that free trade would:

(*a*) lower wage costs by reducing imported food prices, thereby strengthening their competitive position;

(*b*) lower imported raw material costs;

(*c*) free them from the restraint of export duties;

(*d*) possibly induce foreigners to lower tariffs on British goods.

Between 1823 and mid-century, the transition to free trade was gradually accomplished by Huskisson, Peel and Gladstone (*see* XXI, **13–15**). Simultaneously, the annual value of exports trebled.

8. Pattern of the export trade, 1800–50.

(*a*) *Commodities.* In 1800, by far the most important export was woollen cloth. By 1816, it had been surpassed by cotton. In 1850, cotton and wool together accounted for two-thirds of the total, although metals were gradually gaining ground.

(*b*) *Markets.* Until 1830, Europe was virtually ignored in favour of America, Africa and Asia. In the 1830s and 1840s there was an especially brisk expansion of trade with China and India.

After 1830, European markets were exploited and, by 1850, accounted for about 50 per cent of the total of £71 million. The U.S.A. then absorbed about 24 per cent, Asia 22 per cent and Africa 4 per cent.

9. Years of rapid growth, 1850–70.
From the 1850s, the full effects of the Peel and Gladstone free-trade policies were seen in expanding trade figures, as follows.

Approximate value of exports (£ *millions*):	1850	1854	1860	1870
	71	97	135	250

NOTE: The figures tend to exaggerate the physical increase in exports since this was a period of rising prices (*see* XII, **15**). Whilst free trade was a prime cause of this prosperity, there were other important reasons (*see* **10**).

10. Supplementary causes of expansion, 1850–70.

(*a*) *Cheaper goods.* Allowing for changes in the value of money, relatively cheaper goods resulted from greater industrial efficiency and stimulated fresh markets.

(*b*) *Suez Canal, 1869.* The opening of the canal facilitated greater trade with the East.

(*c*) *American trans-continental railways.* The American interior was opened up to British trade.

(*d*) *Gold discoveries* in Australia and America, by increasing the world supply of money, stimulated demand.

(*e*) *Development of Australia* in mid-century provided new markets.

(*f*) *International specialisation.* Having embarked upon intensive specialisation in manufacturing, Britain was now compelled to export in order to live.

(*g*) *British overseas investment.* Trade surpluses were largely invested in developing the production capacity (and hence the potential demand for British goods) of overseas territories (*see* X, 15).

11. Pattern of the export trade, 1850–70.

(*a*) *Commodities.* Cotton goods still remained the most important item (about one-third of the total value) followed by woollens, but with machinery and iron manufactures closing up.

(*b*) *Markets.* The principal non-European markets were India and the U.S.A., while Australia and China increased their relative importance. Germany provided the main European outlet until 1860, when her place was taken by France, in consequence of the Cobden Commercial Treaty.

12. The Cobden Commercial Treaty, 1860.

As the exponents of free trade hoped, there was some emulation of Britain's example in lowering tariffs, e.g. by Holland, Portugal, Switzerland, Austria, Germany. However, the most beneficial event for Britain's trade was Richard Cobden's negotiation of a treaty with France, with whom relations had been strained since 1815.

(*a*) *France* reduced duties on flax and hemp manufactures, pig iron, coal, textile yarns, machinery.

(*b*) *Britain* abolished duties on manufactures and reduced them on wines and brandies.

(*c*) *"Most favoured nation" clause.* Any trade concession made by either nation to a third party would automatically be extended to the other nation. This clause brought many tariff remissions to Britain in the following decade.

Both import and export trade with France more than doubled, until in 1879 French protectionist interests forced the renunciation of the treaty.

13. Effects of the Great Depression, 1873–96.

This was a period of falling prices (*see* XII, 16), which were reflected in a fall in the annual *value* of exports. However, prices disguised continuing growth, since the physical exports of iron, steel and woollens fluctuated much less than is suggested by their earnings, whilst the export of cottons steadily increased although earning less. This apparent contradiction was the result of the two opposing forces.

(*a*) *Expanding world population.* Markets expanded and simultaneously more efficient production gave greater output at lower prices.

(*b*) *Rising foreign tariffs.* World depression led overseas manufacturers to shelter their new-born industries behind tariff walls which Britain could surmount only by cutting prices, e.g. Canada and Australia both protected their newly established industries. In 1880, Germany raised duties and was shortly followed by France. In 1890, the effects of the McKinley tariff in the U.S.A. were especially severe.

14. Rising world prices and foreign tariffs, 1896–1914.

Whilst, in every market, British exports increased absolutely both in volume and value, the most significant feature of the period was the decline in her relative share of world markets.

The industries of her competitors gathered strength in the lee of high protective duties (the Dingley Tariff of 1897 finally committed the U.S.A. to protection, and in 1902 Germany followed suit). The results were seen in the following.

(*a*) *Coal.* By 1900, British output had been exceeded by the U.S.A. and was being overhauled rapidly by Germany. Meanwhile, British exports to German manufacturing industry increased (*see* IV, **4**).

(*b*) *Iron and steel.* Britain's output was exceeded by America's in 1900 and by Germany's in 1913, by which date Germany's exports also exceeded Britain's (*see* V, **24**).

(*c*) *Textiles.* Despite growing opposition, Britain's supremacy was maintained (*see* VII, **17**, VIII, **11**).

(*d*) *Machinery.* There was a great increase in exports of equipment for foreign manufacturers, which at the time was much criticised (*see* VI, **14**).

In short, there was an increasing capacity in certain countries to meet their own industrial requirements and a growing willingness to compete with Britain for the markets of the non-industrial world.

15. Growing strength of Britain's competitors after 1870.

The revolution in industry and internal political stability had given Britain a head start, and until 1870 she virtually monopolised international trading.

Thereafter, her competitors narrowed the gap and in some spheres took the lead, favoured by circumstances other than protection, such as the following.

(*a*) *Political stability* was achieved in the U.S.A. after the Civil

War (1861–5) and in Germany after the unification of the several German states by Bismarck in 1871.

(b) *State support.* Both Germany and the U.S.A. assisted their economies by providing technical education, subsidising railways and shipping and, in the case of Germany, by developing a system of social security.

(c) *Natural resources.* In Germany and the U.S.A. these were greater in extent and more accessible than in Britain, e.g. by 1900, when surface reserves were exhausted, British coalmining became deeper and more expensive.

(d) *Large-scale production.* In many industries (e.g. iron and steel, chemicals) there were economies in large-scale production. In Germany and the U.S.A., the large-scale unit, financed by banks, was typical from the start. In Britain, the typical business unit remained the self-financed family firm (*see* X, **20**).

16. Pattern of trading, 1870–1914. The most significant feature was the increase in the quantity and variety of imports.

(a) *Imports.*

(i) Wines, spirits, tobacco: although these traditional imports increased absolutely, they declined in relative importance.

(ii) Foodstuffs: there was rapid expansion as the nation turned more and more to industry at the expense of agriculture, e.g. sugar and tea. With refrigerated shipping came meat from Australia, New Zealand and the Argentine. With canning came fruit and fish from North America. Wheat imports from the U.S.A. diminished when her own population grew but increased from Canada, Argentina and Russia.

(iii) Raw materials: Australian wool and Egyptian and American cotton all increased. The need for non-phosphoric ores (*see* V, **19**) led to new imports from Spain and Sweden.

(b) *Exports.* With the exception of the important trade in coal, manufactures (particularly textiles, machinery and ships) made up the bulk of British exports. Outside Europe, the U.S.A. had long been the principal market but by 1914 was displaced by India. In Europe, at the outbreak of war, Germany was Britain's best customer.

17. Growth of "invisible exports", 1870–1914. It became clear during the period that Britain's physical exports were not balancing her physical imports. The deficit fluctuated but was always present in the region of £100 million. Despite this, a balance of payments surplus was consistently achieved through the addition of "invisible exports", i.e. the earnings of the following.

(a) *Shipping*. By the last quarter of the century, a large proportion of world trade was carried in British ships (*see* XV, **11**).

(b) *Insurance*. London was the world's major insurance market and secured a great volume of foreign business.

(c) *Overseas investments*. Right into the twentieth century, Britain continued to be the world's principal overseas investor (*see* X, **15**). Investment income added to trade surpluses.

THE TREND AWAY FROM FREE TRADE,
1870–1939

18. Restricted overseas markets. Although Britain remained wedded to the ideal of free trade long after her competitors had taken refuge in protection, there was a growing awareness in commercial circles of the dangers of restricted overseas markets. Action was taken accordingly.

19. Expansion of colonial markets, 1880s. From the late eighteenth century, the colonies had been viewed unsympathetically as a source of defence and administrative expense, of military conflict (e.g. the American War of Independence) and, by nineteenth-century free traders, as being designed only to perpetuate trade restrictions.

After 1870, keen competition in world markets and foreign protectionist policies led to a revision of these ideas. Unless Britain secured her share of new markets, she would be excluded by her rivals. The scramble for a "place in the sun" in Africa and Asia began.

Companies were chartered to open up new territories, such as:

(a) the North Borneo Company, 1881;
(b) the Royal Niger Company, 1882;
(c) the British East African Company, 1888;
(d) the British South Africa Company (Cecil Rhodes), 1889.

Territorial rights were acquired by treaties negotiated by the companies. "The flag followed trade" and in due course the Government bought the treaty rights, thereby inheriting Nigeria, Rhodesia and East Africa.

20. Government supporting action, 1890s. The initiative had come in the 1880s from private enterprise, but in 1895 Joseph Chamberlain brought new life to the Colonial Office, previously a departmental backwater.

He made a number of important contributions to colonial development, amongst them the following.

(*a*) *Colonial Loans Act 1899.* This provided for substantial development loans. Chamberlain saw that a colony with an expanding economy would stimulate the demand for British goods.

(*b*) *Tropical medicine.* He supported medical research, which, in a short time, made the West African coast reasonably habitable for the first time.

Out of the movement towards greater colonial trade grew imperial preference.

21. Imperial and Commonwealth preference. From the Colonial Conference of 1897 sprang closer economic co-operation. By 1907, the Dominions were granting preferential treatment to British exports, and from that date conferences were held regularly to discuss matters of common economic and political interest. Of particular importance were the following.

(*a*) *The Imperial War Conference, 1917.* It was agreed that preferential treatment should be given by each part of the Empire to the produce of every other part.

(*b*) *The Ottawa Conference, 1932.* This was especially significant in drawing the Empire more closely together. Empire goods were exempted from Britain's new Import Duties Act 1932, while duties on certain foreign raw materials which competed with Empire produce were raised still higher.

In return, Empire countries extended preference to British manufacturers although not exempting them from duty totally (they were afraid that British competition might crush their own developing industries). Co-operation also took other forms: *see* below.

22. Empire economic co-operation. This was expressed in a number of ways, such as the following.

(*a*) *Pest control.* During the First World War, research institutes were set up to examine methods of controlling crop pests.

(*b*) *Imperial Department of Tropical Agriculture, 1989.* Experiments in improving crop yields and in introducing new crops were carried out in various parts of the Empire, e.g. American sea island cotton was introduced to the West Indies.

(c) *Trade Commissioners, 1908.* They were attached to the Dominions to investigate new avenues of trade and investment.

The relative importance of Empire trade grew steadily, especially after 1920, when there was an enormous contraction in the volume of world trade.

23. Economic nationalism, 1918–39. In the prevailing climate of political and economic instability, nations throughout the world sought self-sufficiency. Reverting to an earlier ideal, they believed that only in economic independence could national security be achieved.

In trade this desire was expressed in "beggar my neighbour" policies designed to build up domestic markets and productive capacity while "dumping" surpluses on international markets, e.g. German steel exported to Britain at prices below cost (*see* V, 29).

Moreover, four years of war had dislocated the traditional pattern of world trade. Old customers had found alternative suppliers or developed their own sources, e.g. Japan built up powerful textile and engineering industries which made deep inroads into British Far Eastern markets (*see* VII, 22).

These difficulties were aggravated by the little-understood problems of unemployment and the balance of payments. The cure for the former seemed to lie in the protection of markets, and, for the latter, in a return to a full gold standard (*see* IX, 19).

24. Bilateral trading, 1930s. The volume of international trade was further diminished by the slump in world markets of 1929–32. This was followed by numerous bilateral trade agreements which replaced the normal pattern of multilateral trade.

(a) *Multilateral trade.*

Direction of exports

Although Britain has an unfavourable balance with the U.S.A. of £50 million, this is met by her £50 million South American credit. Such trade would be restricted by bilateral agreements.

(*b*) *Bilateral trade agreements.* Each nation attempts to balance its payments separately with its trading partners. Thus imports from the U.S.A. would be cut by £50 million and exports to South America by £50 million.

Highly specialised industrial nations such as Britain, whose prosperity depended upon expanding world trade, were particularly hard-hit. Under mounting pressure from manufacturers, the British Government agreed to afford a modest degree of protection to the home market.

25. Import Duties Act 1932. A 10 per cent *ad valorem* duty was levied on all foreign goods not already taxed. An Import Duties Advisory Committee was set up and might recommend increases when protection was inadequate.

26. Declining overseas investment. The general decline throughout the world of overseas investment gave proof of economic stagnation. The productivity (and therefore the potentiality as customers) of the backward nations was no longer being developed.

INTERNATIONAL TRADE CO-OPERATION AFTER 1945

27. A new approach. In international economic relationships as in domestic affairs the Second World War provoked a radically new approach. It was seen that close co-operation would be necessary if a return to the stranglehold of economic nationalism was to be avoided.

It was now appreciated that pre-war attempts to "export" unemployment through policies of protection and the overseas dumping of production surpluses had only invited retaliation. There would now be a co-operative attempt to raise world living standards through the balanced expansion of international trade.

Instrumental to this aim were the following three subsidiary objectives.

(*a*) *The abolition of tariffs and quotas.* There would need to be close co-operation to reduce and finally abolish all tariffs and quotas (*see* **28–41**).

(*b*) *The improvement of the international financial system.* This called both for better international credit facilities (i.e. greater international liquidity) and for an improved exchange rate mechanism (*see* **42–48**).

(*c*) *Greater investment in the developing countries.* If the under-developed countries were to play a full part in the expansion of world trade their protective potential required active stimulation (*see* **49**).

Wartime planning produced the most immediate results in respect of finance and investment. Progress in world trade co-operation was more protracted.

28. The failure of the International Trade Organisation (I.T.O.). In March 1948, fifty-four countries signed a wide-ranging draft charter to found an International Trade Organisation which would have dealt not only with trade matters but also with co-operation in the fields of employment and economic development and policies in respect of monopolies and state trading. The activation of the charter depended upon the assent of the U.S.A. which had sufficient voting power to exercise a veto. Agreement was not forthcoming and the U.S. Congress refused to ratify the treaty in 1950.

29. The General Agreement on Tariffs and Trade (GATT). The attempt to secure global trade co-operation might well have foundered but for the almost accidental signing of a "General Agreement on Tariffs and Trade". When, in 1947, the draft charter for an I.T.O. had been first considered in Geneva, as a mark of good faith twenty-three countries simultaneously engaged in negotiations which resulted in commitments to reduce 45,000 different rates of duty within broad principles laid down in a temporary "General Agreement". This agreement was activated on the 1st January 1948.

In the event, what had originally been intended as a provisional and temporary arrangement remained as the principal apparatus through which world trade negotiations have been conducted.

The major achievement of GATT has been a series of six tariff conferences, the last completed being the "Kennedy Round" which continued from May 1964 until June 1967. These conferences have succeeded in reducing or abolishing rates of duty on more than 60,000 items covering more than half the world's trade.

In September 1973, a ministerial meeting of GATT was held in Tokyo and attended by eighty-three contracting nations. The meeting launched a fresh series of international negotiations designed to produce further tariff cuts. The persisting exchange rate instability of the 1970s inhibited real progress (*see* **48**).

Although dramatic by comparison with the absence of co-operation between the wars, progress was much slower than had originally been anticipated and negotiations became tougher and more protracted. That this would be the case had been apparent as early as 1948. Faced with Soviet expansionism, attention was then concentrated upon promoting as rapidly as possible European reconstruction and economic co-operation as the surest means of countering this threat.

30. The Organisation for European Economic Co-operation (O.E.E.C.). The O.E.E.C. was established in 1948 with the initial task of administering Marshall Aid (American Assistance to Europe) in the Joint European Recovery Programme.

It then developed into an organisation for general economic co-operation whose major achievement was to bring about the progressive removal of quota barriers to trade. This was accomplished with the aid of a system of multilateral payments (cf. **24** above) provided by the European Payments Union.

Certain members of the O.E.E.C. wished to progress more rapidly towards complete economic integration and this gave rise to the E.C.S.C.

31. The European Coal and Steel Community (E.C.S.C.). In 1952, Belgium, the Netherlands, Luxembourg, France, Germany and Italy abolished all restrictions on trade in coal and steel amongst themselves while agreeing a common tariff policy for countries outside the group.

In 1955, they decided to enlarge the scope of the agreement to cover the whole of their economies. This led to the establishment of the E.E.C.

32. The European Economic Community (E.E.C.). The Treaty of Rome which established the E.E.C. was signed on the 25th March 1957. Its 200 articles are aimed progressively to achieve the following objectives.

(*a*) *The creation of a full customs union.* A customs union has two aspects. Firstly, the abolition of all internal restraints upon trade and secondly, the adoption of a common external tariff and commercial policy.

The Treaty envisaged a transitional period of twelve to fifteen years but by July 1968 tariff and quota restrictions (other than in exceptional circumstances) had been abolished.

(*b*) *The creation of a common market in labour, enterprise and capital.* In order that the factors of production may move with complete freedom the harmonisation of social legislation, labour and company law are necessary. This process was begun in the 1960s.

(*c*) *The integration of national economies.* Beyond the creation of a formal customs union lies the integration of many aspects of the social and economic life of the combining countries, e.g. common policies in respect of fiscal and monetary matters, transportation and energy, monopolies and mergers, education and pensions.

(*d*) *Political union.* The ultimate goal is political union but little progress has been made in this direction since there exist conflicting views on the form which such a union should take.

THE U.K. AND EUROPE

33. The U.K. and the E.E.C. in the 1950s. In the mid-1950s the U.K. was unprepared to accept many aspects of the Treaty of Rome, particularly with regard to the loss of sovereignty implicit in full political and economic union. Moreover, historically her trade had been global rather than centred upon Europe and the common external tariff seemed to threaten these relationships, especially with the Commonwealth and the U.S.A.

Attention was therefore concentrated upon negotiations to broaden the O.E.E.C. into a loose free-trading area of which the E.E.C. would be a part. These negotiations failed and from 1958 to 1960 discussions were continued with countries outside the E.E.C. Agreement was finally reached in the Stockholm Convention which set up the European Free Trade Area (EFTA) comprising Norway, Sweden, Denmark, Portugal, Switzerland, Austria and the U.K. The aim was the abolition of tariff and quota restrictions but each member remained free to establish its own external tariff in respect of its trade with the rest of the world.

34. The U.K.'s applications for E.E.C. membership. In the early 1960s it became apparent that despite the obstacle of the Community's rising tariff this was the segment of U.K. trade which was expanding most rapidly. Moreover, the dramatic economic progress of the Community could be observed and this vast and affluent market seemed increasingly attractive.

Therefore in 1961 the U.K. followed by other members of EFTA, opened negotiations with a view to signing the Treaty of Rome. France, however, was suspicious of the effect which Anglo-Saxon influence would have upon her own concept of a united and independent Europe and also of the challenge to her own aspirations to emerge as the European leader. Therefore in 1963 the French unilaterally vetoed the U.K. application.

In May 1967 the U.K. lodged a second application for full membership but in the absence of unanimous agreement by the Community's Council of Ministers a decision was deferred for two years. Finally, negotiations were opened in 1969 which led to the U.K.'s accession to the Treaty of Rome in 1972.

35. The Treaty of Accession 1972. The Treaty was signed by the original six members and the four new applicants, the U.K., Eire, Denmark and Norway. (Subsequently, however, Norway did not ratify and therefore did not become a member.) The U.K. then published enabling legislation (*see* **36**).

The Treaty provided for entry into the E.E.C. and Euratom while accession to the E.C.S.C. was effected by a decision of the Council of Ministers. The terms provided for:

(*a*) the progressive removal of tariffs and quotas between the original and the new members;

(*b*) the progressive adoption by the new members of the Common Agricultural Policy and the Common External Tariff;

(*c*) gradual liberalisation of capital movements;

(*d*) certain preferential treatment for some Commonwealth countries.

A five-year transitional period would be allowed for the full implementation of the Treaty, which was given effect by the ratifying nations on the 1st January 1973.

36. The European Communities Act 1972. Domestic enabling legislation gave the force of law in the U.K. to present and future Community law as it affected member states under the Treaty of Accession. Subordinate legislation repealed or amended existing statutes to permit the U.K. to meet its Community obligations.

37. Paris summit, 1972. A meeting of the nine heads of state of the enlarged Community outlined an ambitious programme of development for the rest of the decade. Progress would be made in stages towards the establishment of full economic and monetary union (E.M.U.). They intended "to transform before the end of the present decade the whole complex of their relations into a European Union".

38. Renegotiation. The incoming Labour Government of 1974 considered the terms of U.K. membership to be inequitable and had undertaken in its election manifesto to renegotiate and put the whole issue to the British people. There were the following four areas of complaint.

(*a*) *Community budget.* The system of financing was considered unfair resulting in a net transfer of resources from the U.K.

(*b*) *Common Agricultural Policy.* Changes would be sought in the C.A.P. which would reduce its cost, make it more flexible and avoid its development into "an instrument of excessive protectionism".

(*c*) *Trade and aid.* Improved access for Commonwealth agricultural produce together with a more balanced distribution of aid to the developing world.

(*d*) *Regional and industrial policies.* The U.K. should not be inhibited in dealing with its own particular problems.

These matters were discussed with the other members of the E.E.C. during 1974 and 1975.

39. Results. Renegotiation was completed at a meeting of heads of government in Dublin in March 1975. Some progress had been achieved.

(*a*) *Financing the Community budget.* Details were agreed on a mechanism for refunding excessive contributions.

(*b*) *C.A.P.* The economic problems raised by the oil crisis of 1974 led to a more flexible operation of the C.A.P. Moreover, the Community agriculture ministers agreed to a full review of its operation.

(*c*) *Convention of Lomé, 1975.* This agreement established new trade and aid links with forty-six developing countries, twenty-two of them from the Commonwealth. This went some way to meeting the U.K.'s objections.

40. Referendum, 1975. Although in British political history there was no precedent for a referendum, it was argued that the whole

issue of E.E.C. membership was of such constitutional importance that it should be put directly to the British people. In the
light of its renegotiation the Government recommendation was in
favour of continued membership. In a free vote the House of
Commons endorsed this view.

The referendum was held in June, producing a 65 per cent
return from those eligible to vote. Of this number, 67.2 per cent
voted in favour of continued membership and 32.8 per cent
against. This majority was far greater than that achieved in any
parliamentary general election.

41. E.E.C. and EFTA. Upon conclusion of negotiation for entry
to the E.E.C. the U.K. withdrew from EFTA. The remaining
EFTA members, Austria, Iceland, Portugal, Switzerland and
Sweden, and associated member, Finland, continued the Stock-
holm Convention and undertook trade negotiations with the
E.E.C.

In July 1972 agreements were concluded between the E.E.C.
and EFTA for free trade, with some safeguards, in industrial
goods and the harmonious development of trade in agricultural
products. Norway signed similar agreements in 1973.

A five-year transitional period was allowed at the end of which
emerged a free trade area of sixteen nations and about 300 million people.

INTERNATIONAL FINANCIAL CO-OPERATION AFTER 1945

42. International Monetary Fund (I.M.F.). The most immediate
consequence of wartime planning was the I.M.F., the product of
an international conference at Bretton Woods, New Hampshire,
in 1944.

Its objectives were twofold.

(*a*) *A system of multilateral payments.* Exchange controls,
which restricted international trade as effectively as tariffs, would
be abolished. With currencies freely convertible, payments on
current account could be balanced multilaterally, e.g. a U.K.
debt invoiced in francs might be settled in dollars which could be
freely converted to francs (*see* **43**).

(*b*) *Short-term credit.* Members would contribute to the Fund
in gold and in their own currencies. In return they would enjoy
short-term credit facilities (i.e. drawing or borrowing rights)

which would enable them to remedy a temporary payments imbalance without resorting to trade restrictions (*see* **44**).

43. The abolition of exchange controls. Restrictions upon the convertibility of currencies were first practised by many governments during the First World War as a means of safeguarding vital imports. Controls were abandoned after the war until the 1931 financial crisis obliged many countries to reimpose them. The U.K., however, reacted to the crsis first by abandoning the gold standard and allowing sterling to depreciate and then, in 1932, by stabilising the exchange rate at a lower parity with the aid of the Exchange Equalisation Account.

Upon the outbreak of war in 1939, *all* countries imposed stringent exchange controls. In 1945, it was hoped that these could be rapidly dismantled. However, there existed a massive trade imbalance between North America and the rest of the world, i.e. a persistent dollar shortage. For more than ten years redress was found only in the continuation of exchange controls in order to "ration" the supply of dollars between the most vital American imports.

In 1958, the U.S. economy moved into a trade and payments deficit which has persisted to the present time. The dollar shortage having been eliminated it was then possible for all the major trading nations one by one to restore full convertibility of their currencies for current account payments.

44. The availability of short-term credits. The intention was that the Fund should make available to its members those currencies which they found temporarily to be in short supply. It could not of course go on supplying a currency for which there was a continuing and chronic shortage. It was therefore not until the disappearance of the dollar shortage after 1958 that the Fund began to function in the way which had been intended.

45. The inflexibility of exchange rates. The Bretton Woods intention was an exchange rate system which gave short-term stability combined with long-term flexibility. In the event stability was achieved at the expense of an almost total inflexibility. For a variety of reasons governments were reluctant to vary the parity rates of exchange which they declared upon joining the Fund, e.g. in the case of the U.K. it was only with great reluctance and under extreme pressure that devaluations were made in 1949 and 1967, despite the fact that on each occasion sterling had been clearly over-valued for some years. It was argued that a devaluation would both dishonour the U.K.'s moral obligations to overseas sterling holders and would also raise the cost of imports. Germany on the other hand resisted the revaluation of the mark on a number of occasions on the grounds that her export trade would be adversely affected. Most significantly the U.S. resisted any movement away from the pre-war mint parity of $35 per fine ounce.

46. Dollar surplus and exchange rate crises. It has been observed that after 1958 the dollar shortage was gradually transformed to a dollar surplus. Initially this was no bad thing for world trade. The dollar was the key currency in the world financial system and was itself freely convertible to gold at the fixed rate of $35 per fine ounce. However, such was the world's confidence that far from being converted to gold these "surplus dollars" were readily accepted by the trading nations in settlement of debt between themselves. By the middle 1960s the generation of still more surplus dollars began to weaken this confidence. There was a corresponding increased rate of conversion to gold and a depletion of the U.S. gold reserves. The first major crack in the system appeared in 1968 when the U.S.A. restricted convertibility at the official rate of $35 to central banks only. For a time this move stemmed the drain on the reserves.

In August 1971 a fresh crisis developed when large conversions of dollars by European central banks produced such a strain on the U.S. reserves that convertibility was entirely suspended. Pressure on the dollar exchange rate then caused the emergency closure of foreign exchange markets throughout the world. When they reopened, the dollar had fallen substantially but in varying degrees away from its previous ratios to other currencies. Since the dollar was the central currency to which all others had been linked at fixed exchange ratios it followed that these currencies equally had varied in relation to each other. In short, the stable and orderly Bretton Woods system was on the verge of collapse.

47. The Smithsonian agreement and after. During 1971, international exchange rates fluctuated and fears were expressed over the detrimental effects that this instability might have on world trade.

In December 1971, at the Smithsonian Institution, Washington, the finance ministers of the ten major trading nations arrived at a temporary solution to which the I.M.F. gave its support. The U.S.A. agreed to devalue to $38 per fine ounce while the other members of the Group of Ten revalued their currencies by varying amounts. In this way occurred the first major realignment of currency values since the end of the war and a new stable rate system appeared to have been re-established.

However, the weakness of the dollar persisted and a further crisis of confidence in February 1972 necessitated another re-alignment between a number of currencies (notably the dollar, the mark and the yen) and the abandonment by other countries of any attempt to maintain fixed parities. The search then continued for means by which confidence and stability could be restored.

48. Floating exchange rates. There subsequently emerged an international exchange rate system in which two blocs of countries related their currencies at fairly stable rates to the U.S. dollar and the German mark. A third group including Britain, France and Italy floated their currencies against both. The result has been much more violent exchange rate movements with a destabilising effect upon international trade and payments.

The arrangement centred upon the mark was known as "the snake in the tunnel". The participating countries, which have included West Germany, Benelux, Norway, Sweden and Denmark, limited the range within which their exchange rates varied against each other to a much narrower band than that permitted by the Smithsonian agreement. They then floated in unison against the currencies of the rest of the world.

At a meeting in Bremen in July 1978 it was agreed in principle that with the backing of a new fund with resources far in excess of those of the I.M.F. this approach should be improved and adopted by the whole of the E.E.C. The agreement was viewed as a major step along the path to European Monetary Union (*see* 37). The scheme was given partial implementation with the creation of the European Monetary System (E.M.S.) in March 1979.

49. International investment by the World Bank Group. The World Bank Group has been concerned to promote investment by the developed countries in the underdeveloped countries in order that the latter may play a fuller part in an expanding world economy.

(*a*) *International Bank for Reconstruction and Development* (*I.B.R.D.*). The I.B.R.D. or "World Bank" was founded by the leading trading nations with a capital of $9 billion to be used for guaranteeing loans raised on the world's capital markets. These loans are for approved projects up to thirty-five years at an interest rate of $5\frac{1}{2}$ per cent.

(b) *International Finance Corporation* (*I.F.C.*). The I.F.C. was founded in 1956 as an offshoot of the I.B.R.D. It has similar aims but does not make loans to governments. Along with private investors it participates in private industrial enterprises.

(c) *International Development Association* (*I.D.A.*). Financed by the governments of the developed countries, it provides support for those projects which do not qualify for I.B.R.D. assistance and does so on much more liberal loan terms.

PROGRESS TEST 11

1. What was the State's interest in overseas trade and how was it demonstrated during the eighteenth century? (1)

2. Distinguish the stimulus of eighteenth-century trade from that of the nineteenth century. (2)

3. To what extent did the Napoleonic wars benefit Britain's overseas trade? (5)

4. What inspired the free trade movement and with what results? (6, 7, 9)

5. To what extent were these results favoured by other considerations? (10)

6. Why did France become Britain's chief European customer in the 1860s? (12)

7. "The Great Depression" of 1873–96 is not a completely accurate description of its effects upon industry and trade. Explain this statement. (13)

8. What evidence is there to suggest that the prosperous period 1896–1914 was ominous for Britain? (14)

9. Britain's economic supremacy reached a climax in 1870. What factors then favoured her rivals? (15)

10. What were the effects of improved shipping services upon British imports after 1870? (16)

11. What compensated for the excess of imports over exports after 1870? (17)

12. Account for "the scramble for Africa" in the 1880s. (9)

13. To what extent did the Government encourage the movement away from free trade at the turn of the century? (20–22)

14. Explain the reasons for the economic nationalism of 1920–39. (23)

15. Why did bilateral trading tend to diminish the volume of world trade? **(24)**

16. At what point did Britain finally abandon free trade? **(25)**

17. In what ways did the post-1945 world see international co-operation to be essential to prosperity? **(27)**

18. What world-wide agencies have sprung from the desire for co-operation? **(29, 32)**

19. Distinguish between the constitutions of the E.E.C. and EFTA. **(32–33)**

20. What were the provisions of the Treaty of Accession, 1972? **(35)**

21. Why did the U.K. Government subsequently seek to re-negotiate the Treaty? **(38)**

22. What was the Convention of Lomé? **(39(c))**

23. What was the response of EFTA to the enlargement of the E.E.C.? **(41)**

24. What were the results for the Bretton Woods agreement of the dollar crisis of 1971? **(46, 47)**

25. What progress, if any, has been made towards E.M.U.? **(48)**

CHAPTER XII

Price Trends

ECONOMIC THEORY

1. The determination of price. The English classical economists of
the early nineteenth century were concerned to discover the principles by which price or "value-in-exchange" was determined.
Attention was at first focused upon the influence of cost of production and it was suggested that since nature provided land free
and capital was simply the product of earlier labour, then labour
itself was the sole source and determinant of value. This explanation simultaneously disposed of the further problem of establishing a constant measure of value. A day's labour was the same
regardless of when it was performed, but money on the other
hand was an unsatisfactory measure since its own value varied
from time to time with movements of the general price level.

This simplistic view was developed in mid-century into a wider
cost of production theory. It was seen that the true nature of cost
was an "opportunity cost", i.e. alternatives which were forgone.
Thus the cost of producing 50 kg of carrots could be seen as the
50 kg of potatoes which could no longer be produced. On this
view, not only labour but also land and capital had a cost of
production. The cost of all three had to be calculated in order to
arrive at price.

However, towards the end of the century it became apparent
that there was not a single cost of production but many, depending upon the scale of output. Since output was determined by the
intensity of demand it followed that any valid theory of price
must take account not only of supply and the factors which influenced it but equally of demand. Price then was the product of the
interaction of demand and supply.

2. Demand and quantity of money. It was long accepted that there
existed a close relationship between the level of demand and the
quantity of money. This relationship was expressed in the quantity theory of money which in its simplest form says that the

general price level is a ratio between the amount of money in circulation, multiplied by the number of times it changes hands, and the flow of goods on to the market. If any one of these factors varies then the general price level changes, i.e. if the quantity of money is doubled but the other factors remain the same then we should expect the price level to double. The implication is that the price level can be controlled through the regulation of the money supply and that there exists therefore a direct link between the quantity of money and the level of demand.

3. Evaluation of the quantity theory. The validity of the theory rests upon the assumption that any change in the quantity of money is immediately followed by a corresponding change in expenditure.

But if, following an increase in the quantity of money, expenditure remains the same while people simply store or "hoard" more, the price level will not change.

Equally, if the quantity of money remains constant but people decide to spend more and store less, the price level will rise.

Viewed from another standpoint the halving of the money supply may be offset by the doubling of the velocity of circulation, i.e. the number of times money changes hands. Equally, if the quantity of money is doubled the velocity of circulation may be halved.

These considerations led during the 1930s to scepticism as to the validity of the quantity theory and to the view expressed by John Maynard Keynes that the ultimate determinant of the level of demand was the interaction of the rate of saving and the rate of investment. Variations in the level of demand could be effected not by varying the money supply but by direct Government intervention to regulate the rate of investment.

4. The counter-revolution in monetary theory. During the 1960s the controversy was revived when the Chicago school of monetary economists led by Professor Milton Friedman put forward a more sophisticated version of the quantity theory. The monetarists argue that the initial effect of a change in the money supply is not upon incomes and expenditure but upon the price of existing assets such as bonds, equities, houses and other physical capital. When, for example, the money supply is increased cash balances grow relative to other assets. The holders of excess cash attempt to adjust their position by purchasing other assets but since one man's purchase is another man's sale total liquidity is unaltered.

However, the higher turnover of assets pushes up their capital value and reduces interest rates. At lower rates, borrowing and spending on current goods and services are stimulated and the general price level is given an upward tilt.

In this way, they establish a regular relationship between money supply, the level of demand and the general price level. If prices are to be stabilised they therefore recommend that the rate of growth of the money supply should be carefully regulated. (*See* Appendix I for a summary of the Keynesian monetarist controversy.)

5. The quantity of money and the gold standard. So long as metal coinage alone was current the quantity of money was clearly restricted to the supply of precious metals. The first paper money was also closely linked to the stock of these metals and, following the 1844 Bank Charter Act, a strict relationship was maintained until 1913 between the gold reserves and the note issue (*see* IX, **16, 17**). During this period the money supply would therefore have remained wholly inflexible but for the development of the cheque in conjunction with the overdraft.

The significance of this development is that when a bank grants a £100 overdraft facility to a customer who then writes out a cheque for £100 the bank in the first instance acquires a new interest-yielding asset. However, when the cheque is paid into the payee's account there appears a corresponding deposit liability, figures on the ledger which are new money in the fullest sense of the word. The banks through their lending activities are thus able to increase the supply of "bank deposit money", limited only by the need to maintain a minimum ratio between assets in the form of cash and securities which can be readily converted to cash, and their deposit liabilities. This is of course a matter of prudence in order that they meet all foreseeable demand for withdrawals over the counter.

Although it is true that the cheque gave some flexibility to the money supply the whole edifice was nevertheless based upon the gold reserves. When, due to a foreign payments imbalance, gold flowed out of the country, the banking system was obliged to restrict its lending in order to maintain the ratio between cash and deposit liabilities. In recalling a loan it cancelled out both the asset and the corresponding liability. In short, the total money supply defined as notes, coin and bank deposits was linked firmly to the gold reserves.

The effective link with gold was broken in 1913 and the gold standard formally abandoned in 1931. Thereafter the note issue was increased at the discretion of the Bank of England and the Treasury and it is doubtful whether the supply of cash exerted any braking effect upon the power of the banking system to create credit.

6. Conclusions on the quantity theory of money. Certain conclusions may be drawn from the foregoing discussion.

(a) *The controversy continues.* This remains a controversial area of economic thought (*see* Appendix I). There is no agreement on the relationship, if any, between the money supply and the price level and therefore there has been no continuing attempt in Britain to counter the post-1945 problem of inflation by manipulating this variable.

(b) *The restrictiveness of the gold standard.* With the passage of time bank deposit money assumed an ever larger proportion of the total money supply. Today, notes and coin account for only about one-fifth. While Britain adhered to a gold standard the supply of bank deposit money was as much restricted as the supply of notes and coin. Subsequently the total money supply was limited only by the monetary policy of the authorities (*see* IX, 24–32).

(c) *Agreement on the effect of large-scale variations in the money supply.* Although there remains controversy on the precise relationship between prices and the quantity of money, there has always been general agreement that any sudden and large-scale variation in the ratio between the quantity of money and the flow of production would produce inflation or deflation. This conclusion is verified by reference to the price movements which will be examined later in this chapter.

7. Inflation and deflation. It is of prime importance that the price level should not be subject to violent upheavals since both inflation and deflation bring hardship and social injustice.

(a) *Inflation.* Rising prices, i.e. depreciation in the value of money, affects most severely those with fixed or relatively unresponsive incomes, e.g. pensioners and salaried workers. It favours the debtor at the expense of the creditor—since repayment will be made in depreciated money—and hence it is thought to be conducive to business expansion.

(b) *Deflation.* At first, those with fixed incomes may appear to benefit since their purchasing power is increased. Conversely, wage earners may find their earnings depressed. The debtor has now to repay in money whose value has appreciated, while the creditor appears to benefit.

In the long run, however, everyone is likely to be worse off. Falling prices and profits cause pessimism, contracting business and unemployment.

After 1945, when the Government assumed responsibility for the overall supervision of the economy, the aim was to stabilise prices and when necessary to encourage business expansion by giving them a slight inflationary tilt. However, by the late 1960s this approach had become counter-productive. Business confidence and the rate of investment were then adversely affected by the instability of the £.

Subsequently the position deteriorated still further. Attempts to stimulate the economy were at the expense of accelerating inflation, particularly in the period 1972–5. Business confidence continued to diminish and the economy stagnated. In a society in which there had been fostered a belief in an annual entitlement to a *real* wage increase the resulting pressures for a larger share of a static national income produced a considerable redistribution from the unorganised to the highly organised sections of the community. This occurred despite the restraining influence of incomes policies.

8. Index numbers. These provide a means for comparing prices at different times. A large representative selection of goods is taken and prices computed. The process is repeated at regular intervals and to one calculation is attached the base number of 100. Movements above or below 100 will indicate the behaviour of the general price level, i.e. the purchasing power of money.

The index number was not invented until 1798 and only entered into common use in the second half of the nineteenth century. It is therefore difficult to make completely accurate conclusions about early price movements.

Even when index numbers are available, it should be remembered that they are not wholly reliable in comparing widely separated periods of history, since the goods and services which enter into trade vary from one period to the next.

Nevertheless, they give a general indication of price tendencies and when necessary may be weighted to allow for changing circumstances.

EARLY PRICE MOVEMENTS

9. Stability in the Middle Ages. With both the volume of money and the flow of production static, medieval prices were characteristically stable.

10. Sixteenth-century rising prices. The influx to Europe of Spanish gold from the Americas was very great in relation to the existing stock of money. Linked with the debasement of the coinage by Edward IV and Henry VIII, it caused a steep rise in prices throughout the century.

11. Eighteenth-century falling prices. With world gold production levelling off and population and the volume of trade increasing, prices fell, for a limited quantity of money had now to perform a greater amount of work.

Moreover, the countries of Asia—particularly India—steadily drained the world's bullion supplies, since gold and silver were valued for hoarding and ornamentation rather than for trade. Europe tended to pay for Oriental imports in bullion, which was then lost to circulation.

Prices continued to fall until the 1780s for all save agricultural products. Owing to the great increase in population, foodstuffs were relatively scarce and prices rose.

12. 1793–1819: rising prices. This was a period of almost continuous warfare in which Britain had to depend far more upon her native resources. Short-term prices, therefore, tended to fluctuate violently in response to good or bad corn harvests, since the price of bread, the staple foodstuff of the workman, was a basic production cost.

In the long term, there was great inflation and by 1819 the general price level had almost doubled. This was explained by the following factors.

(a) *Quantity of money.* Between 1797 and 1819 the Bank of England suspended gold payments. This meant that the note issue was inconvertible and no longer restricted by the extent of the gold reserves. During this time, the paper currency was considerably inflated. The quantity of money was further increased after 1815 by the renewed importance of bullion.

(b) *Flow of production.* The diversion of men and materials to war production restricted the volume of consumer goods.

PRICE MOVEMENTS ON THE GOLD STANDARD, 1820–1914

13. Index numbers and price trends, 1820–1914.

WHOLESALE PRICE INDEX (1900 = 100)

Period 1, beginning	1820:	172	(falling prices)
Period 2,	„	1849:	107	(rising prices)
Period 3,	„	1873:	148	(falling prices)
Period 4,	„	1896:	81	(steeply rising prices)
		1914:	113	

14. Period 1: falling prices, 1820–49.

(a) *Quantity of money*. This was diminished owing to the following:

(i) Resumption of gold payments by the Bank of England in 1819 and the consequent reduction of the Bank's paper circulation.

(ii) Bank failures: a number of private banks failed in 1825, following which the remainder maintained a closer relationship between their note issues and their gold reserves.

(iii) The revolt of the Spanish American colonies during the Napoleonic wars had cut off fresh supplies of gold.

(iv) The Bank Charter Act 1844 strictly limited the note issue (*see* IX, **16, 17**).

The effects were moderated slightly by the increasing use of cheques and, in the 1840s, by the gradual influx of gold from a fresh source, Russia.

(b) *Flow of production*. By 1830, the full effects of mechanisation were seen in the steady expansion of industrial output at diminishing cost.

Moreover, the tax reforms of Huskisson and Peel (*see* XXI, **13, 14**) and improvements in communications were lowering costs still further. In a competitive world, lower prices were the necessary accompaniment.

(c) *Real wages* (i.e. the real purchasing powers of nominal or money wages). This was a period of great distress. Although production and the demand for labour were growing, the population was growing even faster. Employers, anxious to conserve their capital for further expansion, drove hard bargains and nominal wages fell. Though prices fell too, the decline was least in the staple foods of the poor.

15. Period 2: rising prices, 1849–73. The rise was not consistent. In the years 1849–54 and 1870–3 prices climbed steeply, while in the intervening years they were relatively steady.

(*a*) *Quantity of money*. In the five years from 1849, the world's stock of gold was multiplied sixfold in consequence of the discovery of new deposits in California (1849) and Australia (1851). In the course of trade, much of it found its way to the Bank of England and to the joint stock banks. With their reserves increased, they were able to lower interest rates and lend more.

Apart from the increased domestic circulation, the pressure of demand from the goldfields for British goods tended to draw off home production and force prices still higher.

In 1870, a wave of speculation in Germany and the U.S.A. was eventually transmitted to Britain. While not increasing the absolute quantity of money, it did greatly increase the velocity of circulation and therefore had the same effect.

(*b*) *Flow of production*. This was a boom period, encouraged by:

(*i*) liberalisation of trade under Gladstone;

(*ii*) completion of an outline railway network;

(*iii*) technical advances, particularly in the metal trades;

(*iv*) low interest rates.

Although the flow of production accelerated rapidly, the quantity of money increased even more rapidly. Prices therefore rose.

16. Period 3: falling prices, 1873–96. The general price level was almost halved, yet the economy continued to expand. For this reason, the traditional description of the period as the "Great Depression" is not strictly accurate, although it remains true for conditions in agriculture.

In the short term, there were fluctuations. Prices fell sharply during the period 1874–9 but recovered in 1880–2. A further sharp fall then occurred until 1886, after which prices steadied until 1890. They then fell steeply until 1894.

The long-term decline may be explained by the following.

(*a*) *Quantity of money*. There was an acute shortage of gold, owing to the following.

(*i*) Germany's adoption in 1873 of a gold standard, having previously employed both gold and silver.

(*ii*) Convertibility of the U.S. dollar was restored after 1878. More gold was now required to honour notes printed during the Civil War, when gold payments had been suspended. Europe was therefore denied fresh supplies from California.

(*iii*) France, having hitherto employed both gold and silver, now virtually adopted a gold standard.

(*iv*) By 1874, the great expansion in world gold output had levelled off.

(*v*) Gold continued to drain to the East.

In these circumstances Britain was unable to increase her gold reserves, and there was insufficient to meet the following needs.

(*b*) *The flow of production.* Throughout the world, there was a great increase in industrial, mining and agricultural output.

(*i*) Industry and mining: the Gilchrist-Thomas process (*see* V, **19**) gave a tremendous impetus to iron and steel, while world coal output was greatly augmented by Germany and America. Great strides were also being made in shipbuilding, engineering and textiles.

(*ii*) Agriculture: improved communications by land and sea brought a dramatic expansion in trade in agricultural products. British markets were flooded by North American wheat, Australasian and South American meat, Indian tea, as well as sugar, cotton, wool, dairy produce, rice and potatoes (*see* XI, **16**).

(*c*) *Real wages.* Under the pressure of falling prices, efforts were made to streamline production costs. Men worked short time or were dismissed, and money wages fell. Paradoxically, real wages advanced, since prices declined more steeply.

Evidence of this is found in the increasing consumption of tobacco, sugar, tea and meat, while the consumption of bread varied little.

17. Period 4: rising prices, 1896–1914. Once more, the rise was not uniform. In the short term, prices rose in 1896–1900, fell slightly to 1903, rose steeply until the boom year of 1907, fell and rose again briefly before levelling off in 1912–14. The long-term rise of about 39 per cent was again explained by the following.

(*a*) *Quantity of money.* The exploitation of new goldfields in the Yukon and on the Rand, together with a new process for refining low-grade ore, greatly increased world gold stocks. In Britain it amounted to a 43 per cent expansion of reserves by 1910.

(*b*) *Flow of production.* There was a slight divergence between industry and agriculture, as follows.

(*i*) Industry continued to expand, but not so rapidly as the quantity of money. Moreover, a modifying factor was the appearance in Britain of the combination movement. Concentration of an industry in the hands of a few firms could lead to deliberate restrictions of output in order to maintain prices.

(*ii*) Agriculture: the cultivation of new areas of the world, refrigeration, canning and other methods of preserving food, together with low freight rates and better communications, supported a high rate of growth. Food prices therefore rose less markedly.

(*c*) *Real wages.* Money wages rose, but not so quickly as prices. Allowing for the tempering effect of the relatively small advance in food prices, it has been established that real wages fell by about 10 per cent between 1896 and 1914. This occurred despite the general commercial prosperity and is explained by the following factors.

(*i*) The legal difficulties encountered by the trade unions in the 1900s made them less militant (*see* XIX, **30**).

(*ii*) Increasing foreign competition made British manufacturers resistant to cost-increasing wage demands.

18. The trade cycle. It has been noted that in the nineteenth century there were long-term alternations between rising and falling prices.

Within each period, however, there were short-term fluctuations, accompanied by expanding or contracting trade. The economist Stanley Jevons (1835–82) observed that these movements approximated to a ten year cycle.

(*a*) *Rising prices* (boom). Trade improved and credit expanded, based partly on increased willingness of the banks to lend and partly upon the greater confidence of businessmen in borrowing.

(*b*) *Crisis.* At the peak of the boom, some event would shake confidence in credit. Bankers and businessmen alike would fear that more money had been advanced than was warranted by the prospects of profit.

(*c*) *Depression* (slump). Loans would then be recalled, business contracted, with consequent unemployment, and a downward spiral of prices began.

(*d*) *Recovery* would follow the renewal of business confidence, which in turn depended upon the realisation that capital's earning capacity was underexploited and therefore that more borrowing and lending were justifiable.

19. Nineteenth-century trade crises.

(a) *1816.* After the peace with France, goods were exported to America and Europe on an unprecedented scale without regard to whether those markets could absorb them. Failures caused the contraction of credit and a slump.

(b) *1825.* For similar reasons, a collapse followed speculation in South American markets.

(c) *1839 and 1866.* On these occasions, the primary cause of collapse was the failure of banks to maintain a safe reserve ratio (i.e. the proportion of deposits kept in reserve to meet current withdrawals). The realisation that more money had been loaned than was prudent led to crises.

(d) *1847.* This crisis was associated especially with "railway mania", i.e. excessive investment in railways whose profitability was currently overestimated.

(e) *1875 and 1883.* These were low points in the Great Depression, whose primary cause was the maladjustment of increasing productivity and a restricted demand.

TWENTIETH-CENTURY PRICE MOVEMENTS

20. Inflation, 1914–18. The war brought an unparalleled rise in prices of 196 per cent, despite Government attempts to restrain them with controls and subsidies.

(a) *Quantity of money.* While the country still adhered nominally to the gold standard, the Currency and Banknotes Act in effect broke the link. Vast sums in Treasury notes were circulated, largely in consequence of the expansion of credit. The Government borrowed from the Bank of England; as the money was spent, so private deposits and therefore joint stock bank reserves expanded; the latter could now increase their own lending activities.

By 1918, currency notes and "bank money" (i.e. deposits) had more than doubled.

(b) *Flow of production.* Diversion to war production caused an acute shortage of consumer goods, which were, in any case, no longer produced in the competitive conditions which restrained price.

(c) *Real wages.* Nominal wages soared in response to the necessity of attracting sufficient labour to the war industries, but they failed to keep pace with rising prices. Real wages therefore tended to decline although the picture is confused by rationing and wartime shortages.

21. Deflation and depression, 1920–39. The origins of depression were complex (*see* XI, **23**) but deflation of the price level was both a cause and a symptom.

In 1920–2, wholesale prices fell by a third and then drifted slowly downward until 1929. The crisis of that year swept round the world, and by 1932 the price level in Britain had dropped by a further 40 per cent. There was then a gradual recovery, with prices tending upwards until 1939, when they stood at somewhat less than half the 1920 level.

(*a*) *Quantity of money.* In an attempt to restore a full gold standard, between 1920 and 1924, £70 million in Treasury notes were withdrawn from circulation. In 1925, a degree of convertibility was restored to the currency but it could not be maintained and in 1931 the gold standard was formally abandoned. From that time the currency enjoyed a greater elasticity (*see* IX, **19**, **20**).

(*b*) *Flow of production.* The fall in prices was most acute in primary products, world production of which was expanding most rapidly (e.g. in 1929–33 the price of rubber fell by 80 per cent, wool, cotton and tea by 60 per cent, and wheat by 50 per cent). Reorganisation and improved techniques also led to increased productivity in the manufacturing industries.

(*c*) *Real wages.* The significant feature was the effective resistance of the trade unions to wage cuts and the complementary increase in unemployment. This contrasted with the nineteenth century, when unemployment in depression tended to be eliminated by reabsorbing the whole labour force at lower wage levels.

Apart from the years 1920–4 and 1929–33, money wages therefore declined very little; in fact after 1933 they inclined upward. Since prices—especially of agricultural products—fell so steeply, there was a corresponding increase in real wages, even after prices recovered in 1934.

22. Wartime inflation, 1939–45. Prices were kept much more firmly in check than in 1914–18, the cost of living rising by only about 31 per cent. This was accomplished by:

(*a*) much more stringent rationing;

(*b*) food subsidies;

(*c*) American aid.

23. The wage–price spiral since 1945. During the period 1945–57, prices and wages rose unchecked. A period of relative stability followed, but since 1967 the upward spiral has continued. This may be explained by the following.

(*a*) *Excessive purchasing power.* In their efforts to exercise a supervisory control over the whole economy, post-war governments have sought to regulate effective demand in accordance with the analysis of J. M. Keynes (*see* Appendix I).

To secure full employment and uninterrupted economic expansion, national purchasing power has been sustained by redistributive taxation, credit expansion and direct Government expenditure. When excessive demand has provoked inflation sufficient to cause balance of payments difficulties, it has been cut by taxation and credit restrictions. Since such deflationary measures are unpopular and apparently endanger employment, the tendency has been to err on the side of inflation.

(*b*) *Scarcity of labour.* Full employment policies and industrial expansion created a scarcity which has caused many industries to hoard labour and to offer little resistance to wage demands. The reflection of these demands in prices has given rise to yet a further round of wage increases.

(*c*) *Combination amongst primary producers.* The agricultural nations have been much better organised than in the 1930s and have, in general, been able to maintain prices at higher levels. In this, they have been assisted by the demands of a rapidly expanding world population.

(*d*) *Subsidies for domestic agriculture.* The necessity for expansion in order to relieve the balance of payments has guaranteed prices and removed competitive pressures.

An upward twist was given to the prices of many agricultural products with the application of the Common Agricultural Policy upon Britain's entry to the E.E.C. In effect this policy guarantees high prices to European farmers by subsidising them and protecting them from overseas competition.

(*e*) *"Adaptive expectations".* Some economists argue that after a prolonged period of inflation a psychological readjustment occurs in which expectations are adapted to the certainty that prices will continue to increase. Therefore in formulating wage claims trade unions will allow for this expectation. In estimating future costs producers will make similar allowances. The result is to make wholly certain that the anticipated price rise does in fact occur.

(*f*) *A falling exchange rate.* A currency whose purchasing power is depreciating more rapidly than that of currencies against which it is exchanged will be subjected to pressures in foreign exchange markets which may be relieved by devaluation as in 1949 and 1967 or by floating the exchange rate as Britain did in 1972. In each case the external purchasing power of the pound was diminished. Since imports cost more there was further upward pressure on prices.

24. Prices and incomes policy. In an attempt to deal with the problem of inflation without impeding full employment and economic growth policies, the Government has on six occasions instituted prices and incomes policies.

(*a*) *1948.* A balance of payments crisis in 1947 persuaded the Government to apply its remaining wartime powers to halt price rises. At the same time the trade unions were invited to postpone wage claims. After some initial success, the 1949 devaluation brought external inflationary pressure to bear which caused the policy to be abandoned.

(*b*) *1956.* A Conservative Government was unsuccessful in securing trade union co-operation when it called for a voluntary and temporary "wage pause". At the same time there was set up a Council on Productivity, Prices and Incomes which was to act in a purely advisory capacity. It had little success.

(*c*) *1961.* A "pay pause" was introduced and in 1962 the National Incomes Commission was established to review pay claims. This body also met with little success.

(*d*) *1965.* With a measure of trade union co-operation the Labour Government set up the National Board for Prices and Incomes whose function was to review proposed price and pay increases and to make recommendations. It enjoyed some success but following the inflationary pressures induced by the 1967 devaluation it became less influential and was disbanded by the incoming 1970 Conservative Government.

(*e*) *1972.* Despite its ideological objections to interference with the working of a free market, an unparallelled rate of inflation in 1971 and 1972 persuaded the Government to reintroduce a prices and incomes policy in three phases.

(*i*) Phase I: a total freeze on wages and prices was imposed for a period of six months.

(*ii*) Phase II: wage increases were limited to £1 per week plus

4 per cent with a ceiling of £250 per annum. Price increases were also subject to severe scrutiny.

(*iii*) Phase III: from the autumn of 1973 more flexibility was to be given to collective bargaining.

(*f*) *1975*. The 1974 Labour Government abandoned the apparatus of the preceding formal incomes policy in favour of an informal agreement with the T.U.C. which was referred to as the "Social Contract". The two parties to the agreement determined the broad outlines of the social and economic policies to be pursued. In return the T.U.C. supported limits on wage increases of £6 per week with no increases for those earning in excess of £8,500 per annum. Stage II was based upon a flat-rate increase of £4 per week. Stage III emerged as a general indication that increases should not exceed 10 per cent per annum, a guideline which in practice was treated as a 10 per cent norm.

In 1978, in the belief that incomes policy would of necessity be a permanent feature of economic life, the Government was seeking some formula which would be supported by the T.U.C.

On every occasion that a prices and incomes policy has been attempted more success has been achieved in restraining incomes than in holding down prices. Its effectiveness would seem to depend upon the correctness of the assumption that rising wage costs are the principal element in inflation, (*see* Appendix I, 5–7).

25. The retail price index from 1947. The constitution and weighting of the retail price index has been changed on four occasions, 1952, 1956, 1962 and 1974. Taking 17th June 1947 as the first base date, the index rose from 100 to 123 by 15th January 1952. Taking that date as the next base, there was then a rise from 100 to 153.4 by the 17th January 1956. From then until the 16th January 1962, the index rose from 100 to 117.5. Between January 1962 and the 15th January 1974, the rise was from 100 to 208. Taking the last date as the next base, during 1974 the index rose to 108.

Index of retail prices 1962–76
(16th Jan. 1962 = 100; 15th Jan. 1974 = 100)

Monthly average

1962	101.6	1970	140.2
1963	103.6	1971	153.4
1964	107.0	1972	164.3
1965	112.1	1973	179.4
1966	116.5	1974	208.2

1967	119.4	1974	108.5
1968	125.0	1975	134.8
1969	131.8	1976	157.1

Source: Annual Abstract of Statistics.

It should be noted that the rate of inflation accelerated throughout the period and that by the close of 1978 the index had again exceeded 200.

PROGRESS TEST 12

1. If the volume of money is increasing faster than the flow of production, what would you expect of the price level? **(2)**

2. If the flow of production, the velocity of circulation and the volume of money all remain static but the rate of saving increases, what would you expect of the price level? **(3)**

3. For what reason were gold movements after 1844 largely able to determine the price level? **(5)**

4. Why may inflation be preferable to deflation? **(7)**

5. What accounts for the declining prices of the eighteenth century? **(11)**

6. Distinguish between the short- and long-term effects upon prices of the wars with France, 1793–1815. **(12)**

7. What factors contributed to a decline in the quantity of money and hence the price level in the period 1820–49? **(14)**

8. Between 1849 and 1873, prices rose despite the great increase in production. Explain. **(15)**

9. In the period 1873–96, the flow of production outstripped world purchasing power. Elaborate. **(16)**

10. What were the consequences for the working class of the rise in prices from 1896–1914? **(17)**

11. Explain the nature of the trade cycle and give examples of its occurrence in the nineteenth century. **(18, 19)**

12. How did the First World War affect the price level? **(20)**

13. To what extent may the Government be held responsible for the depression of the 1920s? **(21)**

14. What efforts has the Government made to control the general level of prices since 1945 and why? **(23, 24, 25)**

15. What do statistics tell us of inflationary trends after 1945? **(25)**

PART FIVE

TRANSPORT

CHAPTER XIII

Roads and Canals

CONSTRUCTION OF A ROAD SYSTEM

1. Condition of roads before the eighteenth century. England, as late as the seventeenth century, had no serviceable inland communications. Much reliance was placed upon coastal shipping, river navigation and, where roads could not be avoided, pack-horses rather than wheeled vehicles.

Road maintenance was nobody's responsibility until it became the concern of the parish by an Act of 1555. Two surveyors were to be appointed by each parish and every parishioner with land worth £50 was required to provide material, tools and six days' labour a year.

The Act was never rigidly enforced. In any case, repair work was unscientific and slipshod. Consequently, early eighteenth-century England had roads which were rutted, pot-holed and virtually impassable in wet weather.

2. The need for improvement. There were three main motives for improvement.

(*a*) *Growing industry and commerce.* Industrial expansion in the north depended upon closer contact with London, the commercial hub of nation, and with adjacent markets and sources of food and raw materials.

(*b*) *Expanding agriculture.* The growth of population set the spur to arable farming (*see* II, **2**) but access to wider markets was the first essential.

(*c*) *Political and military requirements.* Strong central government could only survive with adequate internal communications.

The danger was most apparent in the 1745 rebellion, when the Government had difficulty in moving troops to meet the Pretender marching from the north. In making improvements, two problems had to be faced: (*i*) administrative, (*ii*) engineering.

3. The administrative problems. The question of responsibility for improvements was answered in the eighteenth-century *laissez-faire* fashion by private enterprise. Prominent local citizens secured private Acts of Parliament in order to found turnpike trusts. Monopoly rights were granted to maintain given stretches of road and to charge tolls for their use.

The first Turnpike Act was passed in 1663 but they did not become common until after the 1745 rebellion, when the military significance of roads and their importance to industrialisation were finally grasped.

There were then very many (between 1760 and 1774, well over 400) and by the end of the century stage-coaches could run between many of the principal towns.

Since the stretches of road operated by individual trusts were relatively short, there was a lack of uniform quality. An attempt was made to remedy this by amalgamation.

4. Consolidation of turnpike trusts. After 1815, many trusts amalgamated. The larger authorities had access to greater funds. They appointed better surveyors who, in the light of new engineering techniques, made further progress, e.g. in 1827 the North London trusts amalgamated and appointed John Macadam surveyor-general.

It then appeared that the nation might be served by a system of trunk routes provided by the trusts and fed by local roads maintained by the parish.

Despite these promising developments, the total length of turnpike roads was still comparatively short by the 1840s, when the force of railway competition was felt. Thereafter, the trusts declined.

5. Reasons for the decline of the turnpike trusts.

(*a*) *Division of responsibility.* Amalgamation did not go far enough because of vested local interests. Some trusts were more progressive than others, with consequent variations in the quality of their roads.

Beyond this, bridges were the responsibility of the country rate, whilst many miles of road were maintained inefficiently by the parish with statute labour.

(b) *Inadequate funds*. Many trusts were small and with insufficient toll revenue.

(c) *Promotion expenses*. Funds which would have been better directed to construction work were devoted to buying off opposition and promoting private parliamentary Bills. (This obstacle was slightly mitigated by a General Turnpike Act 1773, which reduced promotion costs.)

(d) *Archaic legislation*. Road traffic was hindered by much outworn legislation restricting the weight of loads and the type of vehicle. Designed to protect inadequate surfaces, it was not relevant to the newly engineered roads. Only in 1835 were vehicle regulations abolished, along with statute labour.

(e) *Railway competition*. The success of the railways sealed the fate of the turnpikes and postponed any large-scale attempts at road improvements.

6. Disappearance of turnpike trusts, 1865–95. Faced with railway competition, revenue declined and maintenance difficulties were experienced. By 1850, there was a growing demand for the abolition of tolls, never popular, and after 1864 Parliament began to dissolve the trusts, transferring their power to Highway District Boards. The last tolls were abolished in 1895.

7. New administrative bodies. In 1888, the newly formed county councils were made responsible for the main county roads while borough councils attended to local requirements.

In 1909–10, national revenue was raised for the first time for road constructions. A Road Improvements Board was to administer funds raised by a road fund tax.

8. The road engineers. The technique of road building was revolutionised by the efforts of three men. In place of dirt roads mended haphazardly with unbroken stones, they engineered roads with good foundations and surface and with due regard for drainage and gradient.

(a) *John Metcalfe* (1717–1810). "Blind Jack" of Knaresborough, despite his physical handicap, constructed 290 km of turnpike in the north of England. His road through the Pennines made a vital link between the growing industrial regions of Lancashire and Yorkshire. His great technical prowess lay in minimising gradient and in construction across soft ground.

(b) *Thomas Telford* (1757–1834). The first President of the In-

stitution of Civil Engineers, he was concerned in the construction
of canals, bridges and harbours as well as roads (perhaps his
most elegant work was the Menai suspension bridge).

As a road engineer, he was concerned mainly with foundations. On well-drained soil, he carefully laid selected stones in a
shape neither too flat for drainage nor too convex to prevent the
use of the side of the road. There resulted a road which was
proof against floods.

(c) *John Macadam* (1756–1836). Appointed Surveyor-General
for Bristol in 1815, he worked mainly on old roads. His contribution lay in providing them with an impervious surface which
would support any weight. This was accomplished with fine chip-
pings covered with a thin layer of mud, which bound together
under the weight of traffic.

9. The twentieth-century problem. The ever-increasing volume of
motor traffic has made apparent the deficiencies of a road network which, like its railway and canal counterparts, was never
conceived as a national system.

Since 1945, much attention has been given to the creation of
such a system, which would complement rather than compete
with the other forms of transport. This has involved an ever-
expanding road building programme, financed largely by central
Government. In the 1960s a national motorway system began to
take shape.

THE ROAD NETWORK
IN THE 1970s

10. Government policy. The principal purpose of the Government's programme in England is the completion of a 4,990 km
trunk road network linking the main industrial cities with each
other and with the ports. Besides benefiting industry, it will relieve towns and villages of heavy through traffic.

By the mid-1970s about 3,200 km were in use, the remainder to
be completed by the 1980s.

In Wales the priority is the improvement of the links between
the southern ports while in Scotland the programme centres on
oil-related developments.

11. Motorways. Several major motorways have been completed
including the 322 km London to Leeds M1; the 370 km Cat-
thorpe to Carlisle M6; the 175 km M62 from Liverpool to Hull

which dramatically improved communications between the east and west coasts; the 253 km M5 between Birmingham and Exeter and the 224 km M4 between London and South Wales (Newport). A major scheme in progress is the M25 London orbital motorway, the first sections of which were opened in 1976.

12. Bridges and tunnels. Major improvements in coastal communications have been achieved with the Forth and Severn road bridges completed in the mid-1960s and the Humber bridge completed in 1978.

A second Mersey tunnel was opened in 1971 linking Liverpool with the Cheshire motorway system.

13. Transport planning in towns. With the exception of trunk roads, for which central Government is responsible, local authorities undertake general traffic planning. Following the development of medium-term transport studies a local authority adopts a strategy within which short-term traffic management is conducted.

In consequence many cities have abandoned urban motorway schemes in favour of an integrated transport policy the limitation of traffic access, the development of public transport and the improvement of traffic flow through better control systems. The first computerised control system was opened in Leicester in 1974.

Following local government reorganisation in 1972 passenger transport authorities were established to co-ordinate different forms of transport in the new metropolitan counties of Merseyside, Greater Manchester, West Midlands, Tyne and Wear, South Yorkshire and West Yorkshire.

14. Road research. Research is carried out at the Transport and Road Research Laboratory which is sponsored jointly by the Department of Transport and the Department of the Environment. Advice on planning, design, construction and maintenance of roads, bridges and tunnels is provided to the Government together with recommendations on road safety and the efficient movement of people and goods in different types of road layout and the evaluation of existing freight and passenger systems.

THE AGE OF CANAL PROSPERITY, 1760–1800

15. The need for canals. Eighteenth-century road improvements were insufficient to carry the new heavy industrial traffic. There

was, therefore, greater recourse to the rivers, which had long
been arteries of commerce. These "inland navigations" were
improved, e.g. cuts were made through the loops in the Mersey
and Irwell, thus improving Liverpool–Manchester communications. However, charges were so high that there was an incentive
to canal construction. In addition:

(a) there was an especial need in the north and Midlands to
move coal cheaply and easily from pit-head to industry;

(b) in the same area, there was a need for better facilities to
distribute agricultural produce amongst a rapidly growing industrial population whose demands outstripped local farming capacity.

16. Obstacles to construction.

(a) *Physical.* Construction made most progress in the plain of
south Lanchashire, Cheshire and the Midlands, but further
north, high land called for many costly locks and pumping stations.

(b) *Vested interests.* Like the turnpike trusts and the railway
companies, canal companies were promoted by private Acts of
Parliament, which were made expensive by the opposition of
vested interest, i.e.:

(i) turnpike trusts;

(ii) landowners who feared the loss of agricultural water
supplies and the dissection of their estates;

(iii) mill-owners who feared the loss of water power.

17. Construction of a canal network.

(a) *Bridgewater Canal*, 1761. The first canal was completed by
James Brindley in 1761 to link Manchester with the Duke of
Bridgewater's colliery at Worsley. It was a complete success and
coal sales were greatly increased. It was therefore extended from
Manchester to the Mersey at Runcorn, thus facilitating commu-
nications with Liverpool.

(b) *Trent and Mersey Canal*, 1777. The Staffordshire potters,
Birmingham hardware manufacturers and Cheshire salt producers combined to promote the Trent–Mersey canal, which then
linked Birmingham with Liverpool and Hull. A local network
subsequently developed around Birmingham.

(c) *Leeds–Liverpool Canal*, 1777, linked the Yorkshire woollen
district with Liverpool.

(d) *"Canal mania"*, 1790s. The success of the early canals accelerated the rate of construction, and a peak was reached in 1792–3. Investors were led to believe that any canal would be successful and share prices soared. However, many schemes were illconceived and never prospered; in 1973 there was a financial collapse.

Construction continued into the nineteenth century but never again with the same optimism.

18. Finance. Like the roads and railways, the canal network was the product of private enterprise in an atmosphere of *laissez-faire*.

Apart from the Bridgewater and the Trent and Mersey, which were aimed at improving the coal and manufacturing properties of those who promoted them, subsequent canals were speculative investments intended to exploit local needs. There was therefore no co-ordination and canals lacked uniformity in width, depth, height of bridges and lock construction. Through traffic was therefore difficult.

As with the turnpikes and the railways, there was a network but never a system.

19. Benefits from the canals.

(*a*) *Cheap transport*. The canals opened up the interior to heavy industrial traffic (e.g. clay, coal, iron ore and building materials for factories and towns) at relatively low freight rates. This was a prerequisite to industrial and commercial expansion.

(*b*) *Dissemination of industry*. Congestion in the existing towns was relieved by the spread of industry over a wider area.

(*c*) *Expanded agricultural market*. The industrial north was able to draw upon the agricultural south. More elastic food supplies helped to stabilise prices.

(*d*) *Road traffic reduced*. The canals relieved the strain on a road network which was still in its infancy.

DECLINE OF THE CANALS

20. Cause of the decline. The advent of the railways in the 1830s spelled disaster for the canals. Their decline synchronised with railway expansion, since, for a number of reasons, they were unable to compete effectively.

(*a*) *Complacency*. In the earlier absence of competition there had been little incentive for improvement. It was now attempted, but belatedly.

(b) *Difficulties of through traffic.* Lack of a uniform gauge necessitated frequent loading and unloading (*see* **18** above).

(c) *Inefficient service.* The canal companies provided only the waterway and were not authorised to carry until 1845. Meanwhile, the large number of independent carriers made no attempt to co-ordinate their services, either with each other or with shipping in the ports. Delivery was therefore unpredictable.

(d) *Uneconomic routes.* Earlier opposition had denied to many canals the most direct and economical routes.

(e) *Lack of speed.* By its nature, canal transport was much slower than rail.

(f) *Railway aggressiveness.* The railway line frequently paralleled the canal routes and undercut rates in order to force the sale of the canal. Having acquired control of what was possibly a strategic link, they let it fall into disrepair or charged prohibitive rates. Such action worked against co-ordination of services and through traffic.

NOTE: The railways ultimately controlled about half the canals. In 1888, further absorption was prohibited. At this stage, complete control might well have produced the unification necessary to efficient working.

(g) *Steamship competition.* The coastal trade, captured from the sailing ship, was recaptured by the steamship.

21. Manchester Ship Canal, 1894. Despite the opposition of the port of Liverpool and the railway companies affected, a Bill was forced through Parliament.

The Canal, constructed by Sir E. Leader Williams, was a major engineering feat which linked Salford with the Mersey estuary. It proved immensely successful and has made Salford a major port.

22. Government intervention. The success of the Manchester Ship Canal inspired new interest, and in 1906 a Royal Commission was appointed to inquire into the state of the whole canal network.

(a) *Royal Commission report, 1909.* The recommendations were:

(i) the unification of management in a Waterways Board which would acquire control from the companies;

(ii) improvement of the basic system centring on Birmingham with trunk routes radiating to the Severn, Mersey, Humber and Thames.

An accurate estimate of cost proved impossible but the report hinted that the Government should be prepared to shoulder the burden.

No action was taken in a period which saw heavy financial demands for social services followed by the First World War and trade depression in the 1920s.

(b) *Royal Commission on Transport, 1930.* A rejuvenated canal system was seen as an integral part of a national transport system.

(c) *Transport Act 1947.* With the exception of the Bridgewater Canal and the Manchester Ship Canal, all inland waterways were brought into public ownership.

That they play only a relatively minor part in national communications is due not only to their inherent disadvantages against other forms of transport but also to the astronomical sums which would be involved in modernising them at this late date. Nevertheless, in recent years there has been some revival of interest for freight and particularly leisure purposes.

23. British Waterways Board. (*See also* XIV, 39(d).) In Britain there are today some 4,800 km of canal and river navigations of which about 3,200 km are in public ownership. A further 800 km are managed by regional water authorities and the remainder are under the control of local authorities, charitable trusts and independent commissioners.

(a) *Freight.* Some 550 km of the Board's waterways are in commercial use for freight movements, in particular the river navigations and broad canals of the Yorkshire–Humberside area. In this connection the Board operates docks, warehouses and inland freight terminals and a freight carrying fleet. However, most of the 4 million tonnes handled annually is carried by independent operators.

(b) *Leisure.* The rapid growth of the leisure industry in the 1960s and 1970s led to considerable interest in the development of inland waterways for recreational purposes. Among the most popular navigations are the River Thames, the Norfolk Broads, and the Shropshire Union, Oxford and Leeds and Liverpool Canals.

In the mid-1970s the Board had an annual turnover in excess of £8 million.

PROGRESS TEST 13

1. To what extent were the roads maintained before the eighteenth century? **(1)**

2. What was the driving force behind the improvements of the eighteenth century? **(2)**

3. How did road improvements exemplify current *laissez-faire* philosophy? **(3)**

4. Account for the decline of the turnpike trust. **(4, 5)**

5. How did road engineers contribute to the revolution in transport? **(8)**

6. Identify the major improvements in road communications that have occurred since the 1960s. **(10, 11)**

7. Would you say that the canals reinforced or competed with the turnpikes? **(15, 16)**

8. Explain the phrase "Canal Mania". **(17)**

9. How did the canals contribute to the Industrial Revolution? **(19)**

10. "The spirit of *laissez-faire* which gave rise to the canal network also accounted for its destruction." Evaluate this statement. **(20)**

11. What interest has the State shown in canals in the twentieth century? **(22, 23)**

CHAPTER XIV

Railways

ECONOMIC AND SOCIAL SIGNIFICANCE OF RAILWAYS IN THE NINETEENTH CENTURY

1. Communications before the eighteenth century. The Romans had provided England's first road system. In the centuries which followed their departure, little attempt was made to extend the existing roads, which, owing to lack of effective maintenance, fell into disrepair (*see* XIII, 1).

A long inland journey in the seventeenth century was a protracted and hazardous experience and many areas of the country were completely inaccessible to wheeled vehicles. Communications by sea were often speedier and more reliable but could serve only limited coastal areas. Relatively few people travelled outside their own locality and high transport costs restricted the natural expansion of industry and trade.

The remedy began with the eighteenth-century construction of canals and turnpike roads but it was not until the creation of the railway network in the nineteenth century that the whole country enjoyed the benefits of fast, reliable and economical communications.

2. The impact of railways upon the economy. The development of cheap and efficient communications was a prerequisite to the success of the Industrial Revolution. The canals, the turnpike roads, but most of all the railways, fostered the following.

(*a*) *Keener competition.* Prior to the eighteenth century, manufacturing industry had been scattered throughout the country with little regard to the suitability of local conditions. Inefficient producers were protected from competition by the barrier of transportation costs. Improved communications stimulated competition, at first regionally and then nationally.

(*b*) *Regional specialisation.* Increasing competition meant that only the most efficient firms could survive and certain industries began to gravitate to areas where conditions favoured low costs, e.g. the woollen industry declined in formerly active areas such as

East Anglia and Hampshire and concentrated in the West Riding of Yorkshire (*see* III, **2**).

(*c*) *Expansion of the scale of production.* The localisation of an industry implied that it had now to serve a very much broader market, and in order to meet demand it would have greatly to increase the scale of production. In this way, the door was opened to the greater use of capital in production, since it was only the large firm which could justify the installation of expensive machinery.

3. The impact of railways upon society. The social consequences were many and varied.

(*a*) *Greater mobility.* The common people now enjoyed a mobility previously denied to them. Vast numbers availed themselves of the opportunity to travel and towns like Blackpool, Margate, Brighton and Bournemouth began to develop as popular holiday resorts.

(*b*) *Newspapers.* Railways facilitated distribution and the subsequent growth of the national daily. They also assisted the collection of news, since the construction of railways and the electric telegraph went hand in hand.

(*c*) *Mails.* The Post Office was quick to realise the possibilities of the railways and as early as 1830 mails were despatched on the Liverpool & Manchester line.

(*d*) *Greenwich time.* In 1840, the timetables of the G.W.R. made Greenwich time standard for all their lines. Until the completion of the main telegraph lines in 1852, this decision was not fully effective, since there was no way for time in the provinces to be verified. After 1852, all the railway companies adopted London time, a practice which spread rapidly into the areas adjacent to the stations.

(*e*) *Remote areas absorbed into the nation.* For the first time many remote areas were brought into close contact with the rest of the country.

In knitting together more closely the thought, the fashions and the customs of different parts of the country, the railways fostered a greater sense of national identity.

CONSTRUCTION OF THE RAILWAY SYSTEM

4. Two lines of technical development converge.

(*a*) *The permanent way.* Wagonways were a familiar feature of

Tyneside and Wearside from the seventeenth century. Tubs of coal were drawn by horses or men along wooden plates (hence the term "platelayer") with flanges to guide the wheels. These plateways led from the pit-head to the loading staithes on the river.

The wooden plate was superseded by the iron plate from 1783, and in 1767, with the invention of the flanged wheel by William Jessup, cast iron rails began to replace the plate.

By the end of the eighteenth century, short lines existed in many parts of the country and experiments were being made to provide motive power with steam driven drums and cables.

(b) *Steam locomotion.* The steam engine had been developed by Newcomen in the eighteenth century in response to the demand for a means of pumping mine shafts dry. In its application to transport, early ideas centred upon steam coaches for use on the roads.

The union of steam locomotive and permanent way was first accomplished in 1804 by Richard Trevithick, in the Penydarren tramroad, South Wales. Other engineers made significant advances but it was left to George Stephenson to utilise and perfect their ideas.

As a mechanical engineer George Stephenson was not original. It is in his tenacity and his far-seeing conception of a railway as a working entity that his importance lies.

In 1814, he built a locomotive, the *Blucher*, which was defective in many ways. By 1825, he had improved the design and in the same year the Stockton & Darlington Railway was opened. This was not a railway in the fullest sense of the word, since horse-drawn coaches as well as steam locomotion were used.

In 1830, largely owing to the drive and civil engineering skill of Stephenson, the Liverpool & Manchester Railway was completed and his locomotive design, the *Rocket*, was accepted for service. The age of railways had begun.

5. Rapid expansion, 1830–50.

(a) *Construction.* This was the great age of construction which reached its zenith in the 1840s, when much money was invested both wisely and foolishly.

By the end of 1850, 9,600 km of track had been built and London was connected to the Midlands and Lancashire by the London & North Western from Euston. A line continued to

Scotland via the west coast and at Rugby the Midland line branched to Yorkshire and the north-east. A direct route from London to the north-east had already reached Peterborough. In the south, several points on the coast were connected to London, and, in the west, Bristol was linked to Plymouth, Gloucester and London. Three lines crossed the Pennines; the South Wales Railway was open and in Scotland, the traveller could reach Glasgow, Edinburgh and Aberdeen. In short, Britain already had a fairly comprehensive national railway network.

(b) *The companies.* Continuing the precedent established by the canal companies, the railway companies were incorporated by Act of Parliament and given powers of compulsory land purchase. From the outset, three companies dominated the rest and forced the pace of amalgamation. These were the L.N.W.R., G.W.R. and the Midland Railway.

(c) *The Railway Clearing House.* The companies, by agreement, permitted through running of passengers and freight, revenue being apportioned through a clearing house established in 1842.

(d) *Evaluation of the importance of this period.* The early capitalist railway promoters (e.g. George Hudson, who was associated with many companies which were later amalgamated to form the Midland, the Great Eastern and the North Eastern) have been frequently criticised in providing a network of railways not planned on a national basis and built at such high cost that interest payments proved a lasting burden.

Against this view, it must be remembered that the tremendous energy of the railway pioneers, in creating the world's first railway network, placed Britain out of reach of her commercial and manufacturing competitors.

6. The second phase of construction, 1850–70. In the 1850s, the pace of expansion levelled off, as investment funds were not so readily available. However, amalgamations progressed and the North Eastern, the Great Eastern and a larger Great Western made their appearance.

In 1864–6, with investment capital now eagerly seeking an outlet, there followed a second boom in construction. In this period, railways were carried to the outermost corners of Britain.

By 1870, there were 21,600 km of track, which provided the outline of the system which has survived into the twentieth century.

7. The third phase of construction, 1870–96. This period was largely devoted to filling in the detail of the railway map and many country lines were built to the ultimate margin of profitability.

8. Light railways, 1896–1914. Acts of Parliament of 1864 and 1868 had been designed to encourage the building of light railways to serve local interests. Little advantage was taken of these measures, and in 1896 the Light Railways Commission was established to develop construction in inadequately served areas. There was some activity in narrow gauges and lighter standards with standard gauge, but the results were disappointing, for the following two reasons.

(*a*) Railways are not suitable transport for sparse traffic, since overheads are high.

(*b*) Changes of gauge meant that rolling stock could not run through from the main lines.

By 1914, the period of expansion was complete and Great Britain possessed more than 32,000 km of permanent way.

9. Twentieth-century construction. Development in this century has been characterised by a continuous reduction in track length in favour of intensive use of the more profitable routes. This has taken the form of better planned and situated terminals, improved signalling, improved track, flying junctions and electrification.

THE PROVISION OF CAPITAL

10. 1830–50. The normal method of financing railway schemes was to call upon local support, often through public meetings, and to appoint a local agent who would work to build up subscriptions. The directors would attempt to make up the balance by borrowing from the banks. In periods of boom, however, an advertisement in a newspaper would bring applications from all over the country.

11. 1850–70. Except in the case of local lines, two fresh sources of capital were now employed to finance new projects.

(*a*) *The existing railway companies.* In order to exercise some control over the potential competition of a new neighbour, they were sometimes prepared to extend financial assistance.

(*b*) *The big contractors* such as Peto, Brassey, Sarin. Frequently they were paid for their constructional work in shares at a considerable price discount. The system worked well in times of boom, but when share prices sagged its weakness was exposed and in 1866, following the second great boom, a number of contractors went bankrupt.

12. 1870 onwards. Almost all fresh capital was now raised through the companies by private placing with existing shareholders and not by public issue.

In contrast to many other countries, Britain's railway system was entirely the product of private enterprise. No financial help was given by the State. Capital was subscribed by people of means who saw in the railways a profitable field of investment and who expected a quick return on their money. A railway was built in response to demand and not (except in parts of Scotland and Ireland) as a means of opening up a country, as was the case in North America and elsewhere.

Private investment was adequate to the task, since in the early days of the Industrial Revolution many people had made fortunes which were seeking investment outlets. In sparsely populated countries such as South Africa or backward countries such as Russia and India, private capital was insufficient and the State had to take the initiative in building the railways.

PUBLIC CONTROL, 1830–1914

13. Fear of monopoly. In an age which had embraced the principle of *laissez-faire*, the nineteenth-century railway companies were unique in being, from the moment of their incorporation, subjected to a measure of public control.

Fearful of the monopolies which it was creating, Parliament envisaged three possible remedies: competition, nationalisation and State regulation.

14. Competition. The ideal remedy for monopoly was universally considered to be competition, but Parliament was undecided on how it should be made effective. Two questions had to be answered.

(*a*) Were new competing lines to be sanctioned despite uneconomic duplication of services?

(*b*) Were amalgamations to be permitted?

In the main, Parliament's reactions were inconsistent. Competitive lines were sometimes sanctioned but, despite a show of parliamentary disapproval, amalgamations progressed with few setbacks and were finally endorsed in 1921 with the formation of the "Big Four" (L.M.S., L.N.E.R., G.W.R. and S.R.).

The result was that at no time did competition provide a satisfactory check upon monopoly.

15. Nationalisation. As early as the 1830s, the view was advanced that after a period sufficient to allow for the repayment of capital with interest, new companies should revert to the State.

In the face of company opposition, this opinion was accepted by Parliament in the Regulation of Railways Act 1844. The Act provided for the State purchase of all future companies after an interval of twenty-one years from their incorporation.

Not surprisingly, the issue became topical in the 1860s and many influential writers and economists pressed for nationalisation. The exclusion of the 2,300 miles (3,700 km) of track sanctioned before 1844 (substantially, the main trunk lines) made acquisition impracticable and the purchase clauses of the Act were never given effect.

Nevertheless, agitation from traders who hoped for lower freight rates continued throughout the rest of the century. In the twentieth century, the cause was taken up by socialists and trade unionists, who pressed for nationalisation in the interest of social justice and economic efficiency.

16. State regulation, 1830–1914. Public control was extended through the Board of Trade in four spheres.

(*a*) *Safety of construction.* Public opinion was not well disposed to the first railways, since their safety was suspect, and at an early date the Government took the following regulatory powers.

(*i*) In 1840 the Board of Trade was empowered to inspect all lines prior to their opening.

(*ii*) In 1842 the Board of Trade could delay the opening of a new line if dissatisfied with the standard of construction. It could also inquire into accidents.

(*b*) *Accounting.* The Act of Parliament which incorporated the Stockton & Darlington Railway (1830) required the Company to keep a proper record of its transactions. The intention was to make the Company accountable to the public and to the shareholders. The instruction was too vaguely phrased to be effective, but with the development of railway accounting practice this weakness was remedied.

From 1844 onwards, all Acts of incorporation included accountancy clauses which stated precisely the form in which the accounts were to be published. By making the companies' affairs public, some check upon monopoly power was provided.

(c) *Rates and fares.* The original conception of a railway was a highway which would be open to the public upon payment of a toll. The user would provide his own vehicle, as on the roads. The parliamentary Acts of incorporation by which all the companies were founded included maximum toll rates.

In the event, the railways became the carriers as well as the toll takers and, since carrying charges were not controlled, the restrictions were not effective. Slowly, legislation blocked this loophole.

(i) In 1844 the Regulation of Railways Act (the "Cheap Trains Act") made compulsory, on every line, a daily train in each direction at a fare not exceeding 1d. a mile (1p = 2.4d.)

(ii) In 1845, Parliament consolidated the separate charges for various services rendered in the shipping of freight and imposed a maximum rate.

(iii) In 1854, "Cardwell's Act" followed a Royal Commission under the chairmanship of a Mr Cardwell. It made the railway companies public carriers and forbade "preferences". The preference system permitted discrimination in the rates levied upon individual railway users, and resulted in much corruption. For many years, however, preferences persisted, and the Act remained ineffective.

By the 1870s, Parliament recognised that some measure of systematic control of the whole railway system was necessary and it enacted:

(iv) the Regulation of the Railways Act 1873. The Railway and Canal Commission was established. Its functions were:

1. to enforce the law concerning preferences;
2. to adjudicate on the reasonableness of rates;
3. to compel the keeping of rate books for public inspection at all stations;
4. to examine proposed amalgamations.

Evaluation of the Act. The Commission did not at first enjoy the success which it had later. It did not command public confidence and many cases were never brought before it. Moreover, its judgments were often flouted, without penalty to the company concerned. It did exercise a moderating influence, however, since the companies did not wish to focus public attention upon themselves by too flagrant abuse of their monopoly powers.

(*v*) The Railway and Canal Traffic Act 1888 marked a further extension of public control. An effort was made to solve the unending dispute between the companies and commercial users on the subject of freight charges.

The Act made provision for the settlement and publication of rates and this task occupied the companies for a number of years. The basis finally agreed was a goods classification scaled to value and not to bulk or weight.

The new schedule naturally implied an increase in some rates and a decrease in others. They were confirmed by Parliament and were to become law in 1893, but there was such an outcry from those who had to pay more that the companies reverted to the old rates plus 5 per cent.

The protests continued and the Railway and Canal Commission instituted another inquiry which resulted in a further Act (*see vi*).

(*vi*) The Railway and Canal Traffic Act 1894: the effect of this Act was to enforce the decreases and prohibit the increases. *Evaluation of the Act*. The railways were the losers and were so in a period in which competition was becoming more intense. Rates now being standardised by law, the companies vied with each other in the services they offered.

Between 1890 and 1914 were introduced corridor coaches, workmen's tickets, contract and excursion rates (these fare innovations were not covered by legislation), saloons and buffet cars, Pullmans and sleepers, bigger and more expensive locomotives, more elaborate signalling equipment and safety devices. To these extra costs was added a rising wage bill, the result of effective trade union action.

In a period in which charges were restrained by legislation, the profitability of railway investment diminished considerably. Some relief was afforded to the companies in 1913.

(*vii*) The Railway and Canal Traffic Act 1913 permitted an increase in freight rates and some fares to compensate the railways for their rising costs.

(*d*) *Wages and hours.* The extension of public control in the nineteenth century was completed in the 1890s with the State's intervention on wages and hours.

STATE REGULATION TO STATE OWNERSHIP, 1914–47

17. First World War, 1914–18. While the idea of private or public monopoly was foreign to the English mind and suggestions of nationalisation had been steadfastly resisted, it was considered perfectly proper that the State should assume control in an emergency. Provision for this had been made in the Regulation of the Forces Act (1871), and in 1914 the Railway Executive Committee, a Government agency, took over the administration of the whole system.

For the next four years, the general condition of the railways deteriorated, for three main reasons.

(*a*) There was a great loss of personnel to the Armed Forces.

(*b*) Much equipment was shipped to France for railway construction and operation in support of the Expeditionary Force.

(*c*) Railway works had undertaken the making of arms and munitions and maintenance work was neglected.

Financial arrangements were made for the compensation of the companies but these were inadequate to the task of making good the decay of the war years.

18. The 1921 grouping. The co-ordination of services practised during the war had demonstrated many advantages, and legislation was enacted to safeguard this progress.

(*a*) *The Railways Act 1921.* This most important Act promoted the amalgamation of 121 of the railways of Britain into four great companies (L.M.S., L.N.E.R., G.W.R., S.R.). It was expected that the subsequent economies would give rise to a new era of railway prosperity.

(*b*) *A Railway Rates Tribunal* was established whose duty was to fix rates and fares to such a level as would provide the companies with a standard revenue (the revenue which the Government thought it proper that the companies should enjoy). The figures were finalised at L.M.S., £20 million per annum; L.N.E.R., £15 million per annum; G.W.R., £8 million per annum; S.R., £7 million per annum.

(*c*) *Evaluation of the Act.* In so far as the Act was intended to eliminate wasteful competition, it was not entirely successful, since there remained considerable duplication of services. Competition continued for both goods and passenger traffic but, since charges were standardised by the Railway Rates Tribunal, it took the form of heavy advertising and better services.

The Act achieved no more success in restoring prosperity and, in fact, none of the companies ever succeeded in achieving the standard revenue. Their freedom of action was severely curtailed in a period when commercial conditions were distinctly unfavourable to them.

19. Decline in railway profitability. In the period between the wars, costs rose and revenue declined for the following three main reasons.

(*a*) *The general depression in trade.*

(*b*) *Labour troubles.* While the unions were reluctant to strike, on occasions their claims had to be met.

(*c*) *The ever increasing competition from motor transport,* which was by far the most important reason. The merits of the motor vehicle had been proved in the war and in peacetime its numbers multiplied.

As personal transport, the motor car had the advantages of privacy and convenience. With freight, the road haulage companies were able to be selective, taking only the traffic that paid the highest rates. They had, moreover, the great advantage of much lower fixed costs (no permanent way to maintain) and, from the shippers' point of view, the ability to carry direct from door to door. Railway traffic usually began and finished its journey by road.

20. Relief for the companies.

(*a*) *1937.* Some relief was afforded to the railway companies when the Railway Rates Tribunal authorised a 5 per cent increase in charges, but it was by no means certain that this would remedy the situation. More traffic might be redirected to the roads.

(*b*) *1938.* The four railway companies addressed an appeal for a "Square Deal" to the Minister of Transport. They gave assurances that they would continue to provide a comprehensive service but asked for the same liberty to charge economic prices as was enjoyed by road hauliers.

(*c*) *1939.* The Minister referred the appeal to the Transport Advisory Council, which recommended that, subject to certain safeguards, the companies be permitted to make what charges they thought proper.

21. Second World War, 1939–45. The railways did not have the opportunity to test the validity of their new economic freedom.

With the outbreak of war, the Government assumed control, although management was left in the hands of the existing operators.

As in the First World War, financial arrangements were made to compensate the companies. In effect, the Government agreed to pay a rental of £43 million per annum in addition to 50 per cent of all war damage.

Once again, the physical condition of the railways deteriorated greatly through lack of maintenance, lack of replacements and bomb damage. It was plain that reconstruction would prove a tremendous task.

22. Nationalisation. The Labour Government of 1945 envisaged a co-ordinated national transport system under State ownership. In this system, the railways had a vital part to play. Moreover, the whole history of their amalgamation pointed to monopoly, and whether this should be private or public was not in question. The railway companies therefore ranked high in the list of industries for nationalisation.

By the Transport Act 1947:

(*a*) the British Transport Commission was established to acquire control of the railways and their subsidiary undertakings, the harbours and inland waterways, and road haulage;

(*b*) the Railway Rates Tribunal and the Railway and Canal Commission were replaced by a new Transport Tribunal whose approval of rates and fares had to be obtained;

(*c*) the B.T.C. was required to balance its budget.

On the 1st January 1948 the four great railway companies ceased to exist and 31,966 km of track, staffed by more than 700,000 people, passed into public ownership.

BRITISH RAILWAYS SINCE 1948

23. Reconstruction. The first years of operation of the nationalised industry were concerned largely with restoring war damage and bringing the system back to its pre-war level of efficiency. It was appreciated, however, that a real advance depended upon new thinking.

24. 1955: a fifteen year modernisation plan. The plan involved the investment over the period of £1,240 million, to be borrowed on the money market against Treasury guarantee. The resulting

improvements, it was estimated, would effect economies amounting to £85 million annually. They would include the following.

(*a*) *Improvements.*

(*i*) Safer, quicker and more easily operated track and signalling.

(*ii*) The substitution of electric and diesel traction for steam.

(*iii*) Improved terminal facilities and streamlined freight services.

(*b*) *Management.* The cumbersome management structure
would be decentralised and replaced by six Area Boards, each
with a high degree of autonomy.

25. The results. There was no immediate success. In 1955, there
were railway strikes which added greatly to the costs for the year.
At the same time, the Government announced a credit
"squeeze" and the railways had to cut back their capital investment plans, upon which modernisation depended. The financial
position deteriorated further in 1956 and gave rise to another
reappraisal in 1957.

26. 1957: B.T.C. memorandum. The Transport Commission outlined the financial position in a memorandum and expressed the
view that the rehabilitation of the railways was "a matter not of
rescuing a moribund concern from ruin, but of enabling an
undertaking with a sound future to pass through a difficult
period without being thrown into hopeless disarray". The Commission's current rate of deficit was £45 million annually (mostly
on the railways' account) and was rising. To depend upon an
annual subsidy to balance the budget would, it was thought, be
disastrous to morale and efficiency.

It based its remedy upon four points:

(*a*) modernisation;

(*b*) elimination of redundant services;

(*c*) greater productivity based upon work study and mechanisation;

(*d*) greater freedom in fixing fares and freight rates.

The Government agreed to these proposals and made available
a maximum of £250 million to cover working deficits until 1961 or
1962, by which time it was expected that the railways would be in
a position to pay their way.

27. 1958: the B.T.C.'s annual report. The report showed the
highest loss recorded, chiefly on railways' account and due prim-

arily to a decline in certain types of traffic. The Minister of Transport ordered another review of the modernisation programme to take account of likely traffic changes in the future. He stressed that the railways should "break even" at the earliest possible moment.

28. 1959–60: the Guillebaud report. The economies urged by the Minister led to labour troubles and an interim wage increase was granted pending the publication of the Guillebaud report. The Government accepted the report's wage recommendations but emphasised that corresponding obligations should be accepted in accordance with the conclusions of a new Planning Board to be established. This was formed in April 1960 and made regular reports to the Government and the B.T.C.

29. 1960: White Paper on the Reorganisation of the Nationalised Transport Undertakings. A White Paper, published in December, accepted that railways would form a vital part of the transport network for as long as could be foreseen, but it was equally clear that competition from other forms of transport was increasing. The standard by which society should gauge the railways' usefulness and whether or not to abandon any portion of them was how far the user was prepared to pay economic prices. This would determine the final size and pattern of the system. Moreover, besides modernising operating techniques, a radical reorganisation of management was essential. There were three main proposals.

(*a*) *Management structure.* Each of the main activities of the B.T.C. was to be given its own board of management, responsible only to the Minister.

NOTE: The British Railways Board would concern itself only with national policy, e.g. wages. The Regional Boards (which replaced the Area Boards) would in all other respects be autonomous.

(*b*) *Financial reconstruction.* The Treasury would assume the railways' debt, thereby relieving the enormous burden of interest payments (about £75 million annually). The railways should aim first at covering operating costs and then move into a position where they could meet interest charges on new borrowing on capital account.

(*c*) *Commercial freedom.* Relaxation of statutory restrictions, particularly on fares and charges, with a corresponding diminution of the functions of the Transport Tribunal.

The main provisions of the White Paper were embodied in the Transport Act (August 1962) and the British Railways Board was created under the chairmanship of Dr. Richard Beeching.

30. Other transport boards. Apart from setting up the British Railways Board, the 1962 Act completed the process of decentralising the old British Transport Commission by forming a number of other boards.

(*a*) *London Transport Board.*

(*b*) *British Waterways Board.*

(*c*) *British Transport Docks Board.*

(*d*) *Transport Holding Company.* This Board inherited B.T.C.'s interests in road haulage, buses, travel and tourism, shipping and manufacturing.

31. Reshaping of British Railways, March 1963. The new B.R.B. published its proposals for reconstructing railway operations in March 1963. After analysing the statistics and financial results of various categories and rail traffic recommended the pruning of about one-third of the total route distance and the closure of over 2,000 passenger stations and the concentration of freight upon major routes in conjunction with more efficient handling methods.

To improve the competitiveness and efficiency of railways it proposed the following.

(*a*) *Passenger services and stations.* The discontinuance of many passenger stopping services and the consequent closure of small stations but the selective development of inter-city routes.

(*b*) *Liner trains.* The development of a network of "liner train" services to carry flows of traffic which though dense were composed of consignments too small in themselves to justify through train operations.

(*c*) *Traction.* The continued replacement of steam by diesel and electric locomotives for main line traction.

(*d*) *Co-ordination of local transport.* The co-ordination of local train and bus services and charges in co-operation with local authorities.

It was estimated that these proposals would produce savings of between £125 million and £147 million per annum.

32. The development of the major railway trunk routes, February 1965. During the following two years progress was made with the

implementation of the Beeching proposals despite substantial
opposition to closures. In February 1965, further proposals
were published which, although they made no specific reference
to closures, indicated the Board's plans to concentrate traffic
upon a comparatively small number of routes. It was intended
to reduce total trunk distance from 12,000 to 4,800 km by
1984.

33. British Railways Board Annual Report for 1964 (May 1965).
The Report showed that the operating deficit had fallen from
£81,556,000 in 1963 to £67,475,000 in 1964 despite increases in costs
of £18,000,000.

Since the beginning of 1962, manpower had fallen from 502,000
to 399,000 while traffic had remained virtually unchanged. This
indicated a productivity increase of more than 26 per cent which
had been matched by a parallel increase in wages. Thus, in a
period of severe wage inflation the Board had managed to stabilise the total wage bill.

34. British Rail Annual Report for 1965. The difficulties experienced during the year were attributed to a 9 per cent wage increase, to the decline in coal traffic receipts and to a decline in
the rate of closure of uneconomic lines.

"Economies in working expenses were harder to obtain than in
previous years, savings from the more obvious and easier sources
having already been obtained. . . . The railways can never become
wholly viable without further action to relieve them of social bur-
dens which, if they must be met, should be financed from sources
other than railway revenue."

The Report in this way crystallised the principal dilemma of
the 1960s. Were railways to be operated wholly on commercial
principles or were they to be seen as in part providing a vital if
uneconomic social service which could be deemed a legitimate
burden for the taxpayer?

Nevertheless, the Report continued, rationalisation had continued to produce solid results. Staff had been reduced by a further 33,000 while over the preceding three years the number of
goods depots had fallen from 2,833 to 1,934, total route distance
from 28,000 to 24,000 km and stations from 6,800 to 4,300.

NOTE: The new title "British Rail" was introduced by Dr.
Beeching at an exhibition, "The New Face of British Railways" in January 1965.

35. British Rail Annual Report for 1966. Concern was again expressed that until there was a change in the 1962 Transport Act's principle of commercial accountability British Rail would have to continue to support uneconomic services.

On the credit side, liner trains had made rapid progress since their introduction in April 1965, while "motorail" was currently the fastest passenger growth point.

Completion of the London Midland electrification had produced a 50 per cent increase in passenger receipts. However, the major sources of economies in operating expenses, in particular the conversion from steam to diesel and electric traction, were now almost exhausted and under its present terms of reference British Rail would continue to show a deficit.

36. British Rail Annual Report for 1967. The operating deficit had now reached £153 million, £18 million more than in 1966. This was attributed primarily to the depressed state of the economy and in particular to the low output of coal, iron and steel. Additionally, because of the current price freeze, it had not been possible to raise fares and freight charges. This seemed to highlight the perennial problem of fares and charges lagging continuously behind costs.

37. Queen's Speech, 1967. The first major modification of transport policy since 1962 was heralded in the 1967 Queen's Speech. It was indicated that legislation would be enacted to achieve a "better integration of rail and road transport within a reorganised framework of public control".

The Transport Act 1968 and the Transport (London) Act 1969 were based on a series of White Papers on Transport Policy (July 1966); British Waterways (September 1967); Transport of Freight (November 1967); Railway Policy (November 1967); Public Transport and Traffic (December 1967).

38. Railway Policy White Paper, November 1967. It was argued that a substantial railway network would be required for a long time to come. To give the public the service they needed, to give confidence to the industry's employees and to enable the Board to break even by 1971, the following proposals were made.

(*a*) *Financial reconstruction.* The interest burden currently running at about £60 million per annum on a capital debt of about £912 million would be reduced by writing down the valuation of

capital assets to a degree which would give British Rail a reasonable prospect of breaking even.

(b) *Ending of deficit grant.* To reinforce British Rail's internal
financial discipline the practice of making an annual £60 million
deficit grant would be discontinued. This measure was expected
to lead to a major reappraisal of British Rail's investment programme.

(c) *Direct grants for social services.* Of 300 passenger services
currently losing money (about half of the total) it was recognised
that many would never pay their way. Those which could be
shown to be of vital importance to the community would now
qualify for assistance of between £50 million and £55 million.

(d) *Surplus track.* A further £15 million grant in 1969 reducing
by stages to nil in 1974 would be devoted to the elimination of
surplus track.

(e) *Management structure.* The existing nineteen-member
board was to be reduced to thirteen members who would concentrate upon policy, planning and financial control. The Chair-
man's responsibility for day-to-day operations was passed to the
Chief General Manager and the Regional Boards were to be abolished.

39. Transport Act, October 1968. The Act marked a major reorganisation of the nationalised transport undertakings.

(a) *National Freight Corporation.* A new corporation was
founded to ensure the proper integration of road and rail freight
services and to ensure that goods were carried by rail whenever economic. The Corporation took over the Transport Holding Company's road and sea freight interests, British Rail's
Roadrailer and Tartan Arrow services and its National Carriers
Ltd.

(b) *Freight Integration Council.* This body was formed to help
co-ordinate the activities of British Rail and the National Freight
Corporation.

(c) *National Bus Company.* This new organisation took over
the Transport Holding Company's road passenger interests and
operates through locally based subsidiaries.

(d) *British Waterways Board.* Separate divisions were now set
up within the Board to supervise the operation and development
of:

(i) commercially viable canals and river navigations,
(ii) cruising waterways.

(e) *The commencing capital debt of the various boards*. The £705 million capital debt of British Rail which had been suspended under the 1962 Act was now extinguished together with a further £557 million of its original commencing capital debt.

The British Waterways capital debt of £19.25 million was reduced to £3.75 million.

(f) *Passenger transport authorities*. Any area might be designated a Passenger Transport Area for the purpose of setting up authorities to integrate local road and rail services. The first four authorities were set up on the 1st April 1969 to cover Merseyside, Tyneside, West Midlands, S.E. Lancs. and N.E. Cheshire.

(g) *Grants and subsidies*. Effect was given to the proposals made in the 1967 Railway Policy White Paper (*see* **38** above).

40. Policy review, 1973. The British Railways Board and the Government completed a comprehensive policy review in 1973. The over-all conclusion was that a railway network of the current size and quality could only be maintained through continuing substantial financial support from public funds.

Since 1975, therefore, the rail passenger network has been operated on this basis with Government compensation for the net annual loss. In the first year total railway receipts amounted to £774 million which then required the support of £409.6 million for current operations alone. Of this sum, £66.3 million was a special grant to meet the deficit on freight operations and £324.1 million was in respect of public obligations for passenger services. Despite this massive aid the Board made a loss of £60.8 million having allowed for interest payments of £32.5 million.

41. Technical development. In the 1970s the most important developments have been the improvement of inter-city passenger services and the increase of freight traffic through higher speeds and greater mechanisation in the handling of bulk commodities and containers. Track and signalling have been improved to permit higher running speeds.

(a) *Passenger traffic*. High-speed inter-city connections and commuter services are the two aspects of this traffic. The Board has had considerable success in the first area following the completion in 1968 of the programme to replace steam with diesel and electric traction. In 1976, the world's fastest diesel service, Inter-city 125, was introduced on the London to Bristol and South Wales route. The new production high-speed trains

(H.S.T.s) travel at maximum sustained speeds of 125 m.p.h. (201 k.p.h.) and are now in operation throughout the western region. Higher speeds will follow the introduction into service of the advanced passenger train (A.P.T.) capable of speeds up to 155 m.p.h. (250 k.p.h.).

Commuter services on the other hand have continued to experience problems of overcrowding, derelict rolling stock and poor timekeeping.

(b) *Freight traffic.* In the mid-1970s the most important traffic comprised coal and coke, iron and steel with increasing attention directed towards petroleum products, construction materials, cars and containers. Operation has been improved through the introduction of larger-capacity, higher-speed wagons and the concentration of traffic in fewer, better-equipped terminals. The installation of a computer-based operations system has permitted more intensive use of rolling stock with a corresponding reduction in running costs.

42. The continuing problem of railway finance. Despite world-leading technical advances and modernisation programmes accomplished at the expense of massive public investment, British railways continue to present a major financial problem.

In the first place it may be questioned whether today's track length of 18,118 km with its heavy maintenance costs is excessive. Secondly, despite the reduction in staff from over 700,000 in 1948 to 250,000 in the mid-1970s, railways remain overmanned. As in other industries there is resistance to further cuts particularly amongst the skilled grades. Thirdly, in respect of the heavily subsidised commuter services it is debateable whether or not the repeated fare increases of the mid-1970s have in the long run reduced potential revenue by diverting passengers to alternative transportation.

PROGRESS TEST 14

1. Explain how railway construction proved vital to nineteenth-century industrialisation. (2)

2. How far may railways be said to have promoted the idea of "being British"? (3)

3. "From a technical point of view, the evolution of the idea of a railway was a happy accident." Explain. (4)

4. To what extent did the first period of railway construction (1830–50) open up the interior of Britain? (5)

5. What was the function of the Railway Clearing House? **(5)**

6. How were the railways financed? **(10–12)**

7. "The progressive restriction of the railways' commercial freedom accounts for their subsequent difficulties in the twentieth century." How much credence can be given to this point of view? **(16)**

8. Assess the extent to which the 1921 Act both assisted and retarded the railways' recovery. **(18)**

9. What adverse circumstances militated against railway prosperity between the wars? **(19)**

10. What was the broad intention of the nationalisation Act? **(22)**

11. How successful was the 1955 modernisation plan? **(24–28)**

12. To what extent was there inaugurated in 1960 a more drastic policy towards the railways? **(29)**

13. What technical progress has been made in the 1970s? **(41)**

14. Identify the principal problems of modern railway management. **(42)**

CHAPTER XV

Shipping

SAIL AND STEAM, 1800–60

1. Stagnation in naval architecture before 1800. For almost two centuries, very little progress was made in the design and performance of ships. Their average size increased from 80 to only 100 tons (1 ton = 1.016 tonnes) while the established proportion of 4:1 in length to beam (a factor vital to increased speed) remained unchanged. This conservatism may be explained by the following.

(*a*) *The system of overseas trade* in which chartered companies held monopolies (*see* XI, 1). That their freight costs were uneconomical did not matter, since they were able to pass them on to the customer without fear of competition.

(*b*) *The navigation laws* (there were a number, the first in 1381) made it illegal for British trade to be carried in other than British ships. This protection in a period of expanding world trade fostered Britain's maritime supremacy in the seventeenth and eighteenth centuries but left her in a weak competitive position in the early part of the nineteenth, when new and unprotected markets were opened.

2. Growth of American competition. By 1800, the only prospect for independent British shipowners lay in the Atlantic trade. Europe was closed by war, whilst trade with much of the rest of the world was closed by monopoly. In the Atlantic they met increasing competition.

(*a*) *Improved design.* The newly independent Americans, with their dynamism, their unlimited natural resources and their freedom from obsolete legislation, were the first fully to appreciate the potential of the sailing ship. Instead of relying upon heavy armaments to safeguard a passage, they developed fast clippers which could outrun any attacker and which had far greater cargo and passenger capacity. From 1815 to 1840 they built up a fleet of ships for the Atlantic trade which steadily increased in size from 500 to 1,200 tons, and which secured most of the growing volume of emigrant traffic.

(b) *The liner*. Commercially, too, the Americans had advanced ideas, and in 1816 the Black Ball Line began the first service between two ports (New York and Liverpool) with regular sailings irrespective of weather, and loaded or empty. Other lines, notably the Red Star and the Swallow Tail, followed in quick succession.

That British shipping was able ultimately to stave off the challenge was due to the engineer rather than the shipowner.

3. Impact of the steam engine. The steam engine eventually revolutionised ship design and operation. Between the first steam ferry service in 1807 and the first British steamship line, the Peninsular & Oriental in 1840, the battle for survival was fought and won. Although a long struggle still lay ahead, steam navigation had come to stay. Shipowners, particularly Americans, continued to resist steam for many years more. By their refusal to recognise the newcomer, the Americans undermined their commanding position and Britain's maritime supremacy was assured.

4. Development of early steamship services.

(a) *William Symington*. In 1798, Symington built a vessel which steamed at 7 m.p.h. (11 k.p.h) on the Forth and Clyde Canal. In 1802, he built an improved version, the paddle-wheeler *Charlotte Dundas*, but it was never employed commercially.

(b) *Robert Fulton*. It is suggested that Fulton may have pirated Symington's design, for in 1807 he began to operate a similar vessel (the *Clermont*) on the Hudson river, New York. This ferry was the world's first commercial steamship service.

(c) *Henry Bell*. The first British steamship service was provided by Bell's *Comet* on the Clyde in 1812. Its success led to others on the Mersey and the Thames, but while independence of winds was seen to be an advantage in rivers and tidal waters, steam was not thought to be a challenger in the open sea.

(d) *Messrs. Langtry of Belfast*. In 1819, the first coastal trader, the *Waterloo*, was provided for the Liverpool–Belfast service.

(e) *The City of Dublin Steam Packet Company and the General Steam Navigation Company*. Founded in 1824, these were two of the most successful companies. By this time, steamships were firmly established in coastal trade.

(*f*) *American developments*. Meanwhile, in America, river and coastal services had made progress similar to that in Britain. In 1819, the Americans even despatched the first steamship (the *Savannah*) across the Atlantic, but this appears to have been a curious experiment rather than a serious commercial venture.

(*g*) *Peninsular & Oriental Steam Navigation Company*. Only in Britain were serious attempts made to extend steam navigation to ocean trading. In 1826, City of Dublin and General Steam opened trade with the Spanish peninsula. In 1837, the firm of Willcox & Anderson secured the first private contract for the carriage of mails by sea. To this was added a contract for mails to Alexandria in 1840 and in the same year the company was chartered under the name of Peninsular & Oriental Steam Navigation Company, the first of the modern ocean shipping companies.

5. The steam packet companies, 1840–60. For ten years from 1837, the British Government remained the only one to contract sea mails to private companies. This policy proved of paramount importance, giving to British steam navigation a lead which it retained for the rest of the century.

Early steamships were handicapped by low boiler efficiency which meant devoting far more space to machinery and coal than to cargo. Only with the subsidy of a mail contract could a profit be shown and the steam packet companies with such contracts were the ones which survived.

(*a*) *Cunard Line*. In the face of competition from the G.W.R. whose *Great Western* steamship had just made a spectacular Atlantic crossing, a Nova Scotian shipowner, Samuel Cunard, secured an Atlantic mail contract in 1838. The service was inaugurated by the *Britannia* in 1840.

(*b*) *Pacific Steam Navigation Company*. An American, William Wheelwright, came to Liverpool, England to obtain capital and a mail contract for the Pacific coast of South America. In 1841, his company was established in Liverpool.

(*c*) *Royal Mail Steam Packet Company*. The most ambitious project, it secured the mail contract for the whole of the Caribbean area.

(*d*) *Wilson Line*. This was granted a mail contract for Baltic ports.

(*e*) *African Steamship Company*. In 1852, this company gained a contract for the West African coast.

(*f*) *Union Steamship Company* (later, the Union Castle). In 1857, this company obtained a contract for South Africa.

By this time, commercial steamship services encircled the world, almost all the companies being British.

6. American and European opposition. The ocean-going steamship seemed to operate under such tremendous handicaps that American owners were at first in no way perturbed by their competition.

The 1840s proved, in fact, the most notable period of American sailing ship construction. The brilliant designer Donald McKay increased their size, speed and elegance so that they often outran steam rivals and provided far more comfort and cargo space.

Only in 1850 did American shipowners appreciate the danger. The Collins Line was founded with a subsidy from Congress but mismanagement led to the company's collapse in 1857.

In Europe, political upheavals in 1848 precluded any serious attempts to participate in the Atlantic trade. Only in the Mediterranean were there efforts which paralleled those of Britain. A number of companies resulted, the most notable being Austrian Lloyd (1836) and Messageries Maritimes (1851). Steam navigation remained virtually a British monopoly.

NOTE: Despite the progress that was made in this field, it must be remembered that the steam packet companies survived only through Government mail contracts. They had yet to prove themselves able to compete freely with the sailing ship in general trade.

Meanwhile the general standard of British shipbuilding, management and seamanship began steadily to improve, largely in consequence of the repeal of the navigation laws (*see* **8**).

AN IMPROVED SHIPPING INDUSTRY, 1849–70

7. Condition of the industry before 1849. Save for those who were pioneering steam navigation, British shipowners remained extremely conservative. In the first half of the century, tonnage increased by only 8 per cent and little attempt was made to improve standards of service or of professional competence.

Sheltered by the navigation laws, owners had little desire to compete with the more efficient Americans, who were securing the greatest share in the new Atlantic trade.

Moreover, the great increase in coastal traffic had absorbed the best British seamen. There was little to attract them to deep-sea service. Ocean-going vessels were therefore manned by ill-disciplined and poorly trained crews with incompetent officers.

8. Repeal of the navigation laws, 1849. This event was probably the most important single cause of later progress. Exposed to the full force of foreign competition, British shipowners were now compelled to put their house in order. The "amateur" shipowner who speculated in shipping as one of many interests was eliminated, and the foundations of a professional mercantile marine were laid.

9. British clippers and the Australian trade. The American maritime lead would probably not have been narrowed in the 1850s but for the opening of a new trade. The discovery of gold in Australia led to a great increase in emigrant traffic. London and Liverpool shipowners responded, the former building ships in Britain, while the latter bought secondhand and new in America.

British shipbuilders, faced with the loss of domestic orders, accepted the challenge and a new breed of ships (admittedly based on American design) was born.

10. The triumph of steam. The difficulties of providing a bunkering service excluded steamships from the Australian trade, since none could carry sufficient coal to complete the last leg from the Cape to Melbourne. In the Atlantic, the steamship's precarious hold was safeguarded throughout the 1850s only by the mail contracts.

The turning-point came in 1862, when Alfred Holt fitted improved compound engines to three new ships destined for the China trade.

NOTE: The first compound engine was developed by John Elder in the 1850s. It aimed to increase the power output of coal. Steam was admitted to a small cylinder, where it expanded partially and drove one piston. Expansion was completed in a larger cylinder, where a second piston was driven.

Holt's ships made such economies in fuel that they had a cargo capacity of well over 3,000 tonnes for the trip from Foochow. This they completed in sixty-five days, while the fastest tea clipper took ninety.

11. Britain's lead in 1870. The improved operating standards of the post-navigation law period were therefore reinforced by the achievements of British marine engineering. No other country had a comparable industry, and even when foreign steamships were built, British engines were installed. Often the ships themselves were constructed in British yards, e.g. the ships of the only rivals of any consequence: the Hamburg–America and North German Lloyd lines and the Netherlands Steamship Company.

By the 1860s, British shipowners had appreciated that the future lay in the steamship, and in 1865 more steamers than sailers were built. Moreover, they were constantly improved, e.g. (*i*) the propeller screw had by now displaced the paddle; (*ii*) by 1870, five-sixths of the new tonnage was constructed entirely of iron plates; (*iii*) the compound engine was constantly improved.

Britain's pre-eminence in 1870 is indicated by her tonnage of about 5.5 millions against a total tonnage for the rest of the major maritime nations of about 7.5 millions.

BRITISH MARITIME SUPREMACY, 1870–1914

12. Creation of a mercantile marine. From the commanding position in which British engineers had placed them, shipowners, shipbuilders and seamen created a mercantile marine which dominated world trade.

(*a*) In 1914, more than two-fifths of total world tonnage was British.

(*b*) These ships were carrying more than half the world's seaborne traffic.

(*c*) British shipyards built not only British ships but also the majority of those which were in foreign service.

(*d*) British seamen charted the world's oceans and built up a body of seafaring practices which were imitated everywhere.

This success may be attributed to a number of factors: *see* below.

13. Natural advantages in shipbuilding. With the use of first iron and then steel plates, Britain had the great advantage of a growing iron and steel industry in proximity to both coal and navigable waterways, e.g. the Clyde and the Tyne.

14. Growth in world trade. The steamship did for the world what the steam train did for the nation. Distances were reduced and an

expanding market opened to British industry. International specialisation was furthered and Britain was confirmed as a nation
which imported foodstuffs and raw materials and supplied the
world with manufactures.

The process was cumulative, since greater specialisation in turn
produced a greater demand for merchant shipping, while further
impetus was provided by diminishing freight rates. This was due
to the following.

(a) *The proportional reduction in operating costs* which resulted
from the increasing size of steamships. (N.B. This factor caused
the final elimination of the sailing ship, the size of which was
limited by the need to carry unwieldy amounts of canvas.)

(b) *Britan's great export trade in coal*, which enabled tramp
steamers to sail outward with coal instead of in ballast and
inward with grain or ores.

(c) *The laying of submarine cables* during the 1880s, which
made it possible for owners to maintain close contact with tramp
steamers. Instead of depending upon chance cargoes between
foreign ports, concrete information could be provided to captains
about where work was to be found. In short, British ships seldom
sailed without full loads.

(d) *The opening of the Suez Canal* in 1869 cut costs on routes
to the Orient.

15. Prudent management. The cargo liners which sailed scheduled
services (distinct from tramp steamers, which found work wherever
and whenever they could) were the direct descendants of the clippers and the steam packets.

They were developed by companies such as Holt, Booth,
Brocklebank, Bibby and Harrison—solid family concerns which
understood the shipping business and financed it soundly. In
avoiding speculative risks, they contrasted with many of their
predecessors who had failed. That their growth throughout the
period was financed largely from revenue is proof of their success.

16. State regulation. In mid-century, Britain was alone among
maritime nations in having no means of testing the competence
of ships' officers and crews. Nor were vessels subject to any test
of seaworthiness or to loading limits.

The progressive liner companies steadily raised their standards.
In the case of the smaller and less responsible firms, pressure was
exerted by the Board of Trade. There were many measures which

ultimately brought every aspect of shipping under supervision. The principal enactments were as follows.

(a) *1850:* An Act for improving the condition of masters, mates and seamen and maintaining discipline in the merchant service. Certification of ships' officers was begun. Minimum standards of feeding and accommodation were established for seamen and penalties imposed for insubordination and desertion.

(b) *1875, 1876:* Merchant Shipping Acts. Standards of seaworthiness were established, namely deck loads which caused instability were restricted. A maximum load-line was set (commonly known as the Plimsoll line, because of the propaganda work of an M.P., Samuel Plimsoll).

(c) *1894:* Merchant Shipping Act. All preceding safety regulations were codified and requirements were established for rescue equipment, e.g. lifebuoys, lifebelts, lifeboats.

17. Foreign competition. British supremacy was not achieved without opposition. It did not come from America, whose high tariff policy reduced her foreign trade. Coupled with her belated acceptance of the steamship, this policy destroyed her mercantile marine. In 1830, America carried about 90 per cent of her own foreign trade. In 1914, she carried practically none.

In the 1890s, the threat came from the recently united German empire, whose industry and commerce were rapidly expanding. Within thirty years, her export trade had more than doubled.

At first the ships employed were either British-owned or built. In 1886, however, the German Reichstag decided to follow the British example of fifty years previously and grant mail contracts.

The Imperial Far East Mail Line was founded and employed only German-built ships. This company was not so successful as the Hamburg-America Line which, in twelve years, created the largest company fleet in the world.

By 1914, with strong Government backing, German tonnage was 10 per cent of the world total and one-quarter that of Britain's.

DEPRESSED TRADE AND EXCESS TONNAGE, 1920–39

18. Increase in world tonnage, 1914–20.

(a) *Great Britain.* Since one-third of her merchant fleet had been sunk and much of the remainder was obsolete, 1918–20 were boom years as owners made replacements in the expectation of resuming their pre-war trade.

(b) *Germany.* With their shipping confiscated and sold to the shipowners of the victorious nations, German owners made good their losses with new modern ships.

(c) *Holland, Norway, Japan.* Having increased their fleets during the war to carry trade normally enjoyed by the belligerents, they expanded further in the hope of still greater profits in peace time.

(d) *U.S.A.* By far the greatest increase was American. In 1914, with scarcely any merchant ships, the U.S.A. had to embark upon a huge building programme to provide ships for trade with the neutrals. Upon entry into the war, the pace of construction was increased.

(e) *The Dominions, Poland, Russia, Italy, etc.* Many other countries which had never previously owned merchant fleets now built them as as matter of prestige.

19. Depressed trade. The war had dislocated the traditional patterns of world trade. Old-established markets had been lost and this called for readjustments in the economies of the trading nations. Unable to appreciate the nature of the problem, they retired into the shell of economic nationalism, imposing tariffs and subsidising domestic industry in order to soften the blow (*see* XI, 23).

The consequent reduction in the volume of international trade, allied to the tremendous growth in tonnage, had a devastating effect upon world shipping.

20. Foreign shipping subsidies. Determined that their national trade should be carried in their own ships, almost all the maritime nations, with the exception of Britain, subsidised their merchant fleets heavily, e.g. between 1920 and 1937 the U.S. Congress spent more than $900 million upon a merchant fleet which consistently operated at a loss.

21. Effects upon British shipping. The first to suffer were the "tramps". whose bulk cargoes the liners now sought in order to complete their loads. Up and down the country, hundreds of tramp steamers were laid up. The hard-pressed liner companies themselves only managed to survive at the expense of the reserves which they had built up during the pre-war years of prosperity..

In this situation, the Government was forced to render assistance.

22. British Shipping (Assistance) Act 1935. This was viewed only as a temporary measure, to be renewed annually and applied only to tramp steamers. A standard rate for various routes was established and subsidies granted for voyages undertaken at lower rates.

23. Revival. In 1936 and 1937, there was some recovery, following an increase in the world trade, and the 1935 Act was allowed to lapse. However, British ships, especially passenger liners, continued to suffer from the competition of heavily subsidised rivals. Despite these difficulties, in 1939 Britain still owned more than one-third of the world's ocean-going vessels.

EXPANSION AND COMPETITION SINCE 1945

24. 1945–56, shipping boom. Post-war reconstruction called for brisk international trade and the replacement of sunk shipping in order to carry it. The world's shipbuilding industries, with the exception of those of the U.S.A. and Britain, had been largely destroyed, and in 1946 about half the world's shipbuilding was in British yards. The problem at this time was to find sufficient steel plates and labour to meet demand.

Expansion was levelling off in 1949, when further demands were imposed by the Korean war, which lasted until 1952. The subsequent contraction was reversed by the closure of the Suez Canal in 1956, during the British military expedition, when the need for more ships was acute.

The result of this artificially sustained demand was to induce a degree of complacency. Shipping is essentially an international and competitive industry and after 1956 competition became more intense.

25. The nature of competition. British shipping has been faced by fierce competition from State-aided foreign rivals. This aid has taken the form of the following.

(a) *Discrimination against the shipping of particular nations,* e.g. the extreme case is the U.S.A., which reserves for its own ships all trade between American ports. Moreover, 50 per cent of all aid cargoes must be carried in American ships. In contrast, British coastal trade is open to all comers.

(*b*) Bilateral trade treaties with restrictive shipping clauses
which tend to reserve carriage to the ships of the nations concerned. Almost all the world's maritime nations have such agreements.

(*c*) *Operating subsidies.* Financial assistance is given to shipping in the U.S.A., France Germany, Japan, Italy, Sweden,
Denmark, Greece and other lesser seafaring countries.

(*d*) *Building subsidies,* e.g. the U.S. Government pays approxi-
mately half the cost of a new ship and makes it possible for the
owner to borrow the remainder at low interest rates.

(*e*) *Preferential taxation.* Foreign companies are often
favoured by minimal taxation or by permission to transfer their
ships to flags of convenience, e.g. Liberia and Panama, where
they can escape taxation.

In Britain, some allowance is made for depreciation but, in
general, this is inadequate in the face of soaring ship-building
costs. Existing fleets are not permitted to transfer to flags of convenience.

(*f*) *Aircraft.* Competition on many passenger routes has been
increased by expanding air services, often State-subsidised.

British ships which are international, not purely national carriers, find that the many restrictions upon free trade are a severe
handicap.

26. Expansion in the 1970s. Despite these disadvantages and although the proportion of the world's tonnage registered under the
British flag declined from 27 per cent in 1948 to some 10 per cent
in 1977, the total tonnage increased very gradually during the
1960s and dramatically after 1968. Britain now has the world's
third largest tanker fleet, the fourth largest bulk carrier fleet, the
second largest container ship fleet and the largest fleet of liquefied gas carriers. This expansion was made possible by the huge
increase in world traffic in bulk cargoes which continued into the
1970s. It has then to be recognised that world recession after
1973 led to much of this tonnage lying idle or underutilised.

27. Changing structure of the merchant fleet. Today a growing
proportion of the fleet is accounted for by tankers, bulk carriers
and container ships while both the number and tonnage of cargo
liners providing scheduled services has declined.

Moreover, rapid technological change is reflected in the age
and size of ships. Vessels become obsolete over a shorter period

and are replaced with larger ships with lower building costs per
tonne and lower operational costs per unit carried.
Computerisation, greater speeds and faster turn-round facilities
are all serving to stabilise operational costs.

Crude oil is by far the most important commodity carried by
sea. Tanker size has increased from a maximum of 20,000 deadweight tonnes in the 1950s to 500,000 deadweight tonnes today
(1 ton = 1.016 tonnes).

A large part of the dry cargoes formerly carried in tramp steamers is now transported in large bulk carriers or in the recently
introduced combined carriers, either O.B.O. (oil, bulk, ore) or
ore/oil.

Specially insulated tankers are employed to carry the increasing trade in liquefied natural gas.

Container ships have largely replaced conventional cargo vessels, some of them with refrigerated cargo space. Substantial
sums have been invested in ships, terminals and containers.

On short sea routes, ferry vessels include roll-on/roll-off ships
designed to carry road vehicles complete with cargo, thus reducing handling, delivery times and time spent in port.

28. Ownership. The greater part of the merchant fleet is in private ownership. Some companies operate a range of vessels while
others specialise in particular types.

About two-thirds of the tanker fleet belongs to the oil companies, in particular British Petroleum Co. Ltd. and Shell
Tankers (U.K.) Ltd. There are additionally a number of independent operators.

A small number of groups, some of which also have interests
in bulk carries, dominate the liner market. The leading company,
Peninsular & Oriental Steam Navigation Company (P & O) has a
fleet of over 200 including all the main types of ship. Other important operators are the Furness Withy Group, British and
Commonwealth Shipping and Ocean Transport and Trading
Ltd.

A number of companies participate in consortia particularly
for the operation of bulk carriers and container ships, e.g. the
liner companies mentioned above formed Overseas Containers
Ltd. (O.C.L.) in 1965. Associated Container Transportation Ltd.
(A.C.T.) was formed in 1966 as a consortium of five lines, Blue
Star, Ben, Cunard, Harrison and Ellerman. There are also a
number of independent container services.

Consortia have also been formed to deal with the heavy capital investment involved in bulk carriers, e.g. Seabridge Shipping Ltd., Associated Bulk Carriers Ltd. and Panocean Shipping and Terminals Ltd.

29. Conferences. Since the 1890s British shipping companies have subscribed to "conferences" in an attempt to avoid the wasteful duplication of services and unfair competition in freight rates. The modern conference seeks standardisation of rates and regularity of services.

There are about 100 conferences dealing with trade to and from Britain. In 1971 a code of practice was agreed for conferences by the then Committee of European National Shipowners Associations. In 1974 a Convention on a Code of Conduct for Liner Conferences was adopted under the auspices of the United Nations Conference on Trade and Development (U.N.C.T.A.D.).

30. European Community. With the U.K. is accession to the Community the size of the combined fleets of E.E.C. members was doubled to 65 million gross tonnes. For the time being sea and air transport lie outside of the Community's Common Transport Policy but provision is made in the Treaty of Rome for their eventual inclusion.

31. Government policy. In principle the Government believes in freedom from regulation in this industry apart from matters of safety and employment. The regulations of the various Merchant Shipping Acts are administered by the Department of Trade through the Marine Survey and Mercantile Marine Offices at ports. There is also a Registrar General of Shipping and Seamen at Cardiff.

The Government has not adopted discriminatory measures against foreign shipping since the middle of the nineteenth century. However, the Merchant Shipping Act 1974 affords contingency powers to retaliate where British shipping is subject to foreign discrimination.

32. Trade and earnings. Nearly all goods which make up Britain's external trade are carried by sea. In recent years almost one-half by value of these cargoes has been carried in British registered ships, the rest in foreign vessels. The proportion has declined largely because of the importance of tanker cargo of which a relatively small share, about one-third by value, is carried under the British flag. The foreign ships which sail to Britain are mainly from Liberia, Norway and the Federal Republic of Germany.

The balance of payments accounts reflect this position, When overseas earnings in cross trade between third countries are included, shipping proves to be one of the biggest credit items. However, taken over a period of years, earnings have been offset by expenditure on foreign shipping, some years in fact showing a debit balance.

PROGRESS TEST 15

1. What factors retarded technical progress in shipping before the nineteenth century? (1)

2. Why did this weakness then prove commercially dangerous? (2)

3. Outline the events which led up to the use of the steam packet in ocean service. (4)

4. How were the steam packet companies commercially handicapped and what important factor contributed to their survival? (5)

5. Assess the strength of the opposition to British steam navigation in the mid-nineteenth century. (6)

6. What were the two principal causes of greater operational efficiency in British shipping companies after 1849? (8, 9)

7. What technical advance finally established the steamship in open competition with the sailing ship and why? (10)

8. How did the steamship confirm Britain's specialisation in industry at the expense of her agriculture? (14)

9. What interest did the State show in the efficiency of British shipping during the nineteenth century? (16)

10. Assess the effects of the First World War and the following trade depression upon the prosperity of the shipping industry. (18–21)

11. What measure of assistance did the Government provide? (22)

12. Why may British shipowners consider foreign competition to be unfair? (25)

13. How has the composition of the merchant fleet changed in modern times? (27)

14. What response has there been to the problem of financing ships of large tonnage? **(28)**

15. What is the Government view of subsidising shipping operations? **(31)**

16. How significant are the earnings of shipping to the balance of payments? **(32)**

PART SIX

SOCIAL DEVELOPMENTS

CHAPTER XVI

The Relief of Poverty and Unemployment

GROWTH OF PAUPERISM TO 1760

1. Pauperism in the Middle Ages. In the modern sense of destitution, pauperism did not exist. Poverty there was, since the national wealth was much less than today and even more unequally distributed. However, the English peasantry were still closely tied to the land which supported them and the only major catastrophe that might overtake them was the failure of a harvest.

Beyond this, there still lived a strong spirit of collective responsibility. The lord of the manor may have appeared a despotic figure but the nature of the feudal system obliged him to care for those who were dependent upon him.

In the towns, the gilds assisted members who fell upon hard times and, throughout the country, the Church and the great lords extended charity, a Christian virtue, to all who needed it.

2. Pauperism becomes a national problem. The pressure of economic forces in the sixteenth century made pauperism a national problem. The growth of pasture farming (*see* I, 26) was separating the peasantry from the land. They drifted into the towns or wandered about the countryside as vagrants and robbers.

The prosperity of the gilds was in decline and they were no longer able to assist. In any case, the magnitude of the problem was becoming too great for the traditional sources of charity. It was now a matter for action by the State.

3. The 1601 poor law. The Tudor monarchs (1485–1603) in-

239

herited the problem and also a paternal view of their subjects handed down from a previous age. Successive enactments showed an increasing understanding that the problem was economic; that punitive measures were insufficient to cure it and that society had the duty to accept responsibility for its less fortunate members. Their legislation culminated in the great Poor Law of 1601, which, with amendments, remained the basis of poor relief until 1948. The provisions of the Act were as follows.

(*a*) The parish would be the administrative unit for poor relief.

(*b*) The sick and maimed would be cared for.

(*c*) Work would be provided for the able-bodied.

(*d*) Pauper children would be apprenticed.

(*e*) Vagrants would go to "houses of correction".

(*f*) Relief would be financed by a rate levied on householders.

4. Application of the law. For half a century, the law was rigorously applied throughout the country. The Civil War, however, destroyed the absolute power of monarchy and its ability to impose a nationally uniform system of relief (*see* 1, 32, 33).

This change coincided with the growth of *laissez-faire* and of Puritan morality. There was now an insistence that the prime cause of poverty was idleness. To cure it, men should be made to bear the responsibility of their own maintenance and so relief should not be generous.

That a poor law survived at all during the eighteenth and nineteenth centuries in a climate of opinion often hostile to it was due to:

(*a*) its flexibility, which made it possible to vary its operation at different times and in different localities;

(*b*) the realisation by the governing classes that even a minimal relief of poverty checked social upheaval and revolution.

5. Results of the 1601 Act. There were two important indirect consequences.

(*a*) Until the last quarter of the century, pressure from the central Government ensured the vigorous administration of the Act. Thereafter, with the diminished authority of the Crown, a lack of supervision led to considerable discrepancies in the law's application. Many parishes were eager to avoid the responsibility of maintaining a pauper if he could be persuaded to migrate elsewhere.

(b) *The Law of Settlement 1662.* A newcomer to a parish could be returned to his last place of settlement if he was unable to provide some surety that he would not become a charge upon the parish.

The effect of the 1662 Act was to aggravate the problem of unemployment and pauperism, since it restricted movement in search of work. Not until 1795 was the law relaxed to the extent that the newcomer would not be expelled until such time as he in fact became a charge upon parish funds.

6. The Workhouse Act 1722. As a means of reducing the burden of the poor rate, the parishes were empowered to erect workhouses to which the poor could be consigned. If the poor refused to go to the workhouse, they received no relief.

The task of operating the workhouse was often given to a contractor at a fixed price. It followed that if he kept his operating costs low, his profits increased. The inmates suffered accordingly.

THE EFFECTS OF EIGHTEENTH-CENTURY INDUSTRIALISATION

7. The problem intensified. The growth of an industrial proletariat, completely separated from agriculture, intensified the problem in the towns. Industrialisation meant production for an uncertain market. If this failed, unemployment resulted.

Moreover, population was expanding and the increased pressure of demand upon foodstuffs raised prices. The inability of the workhouses to meet the problem may be explained partly by:

(a) the lack of central direction and the discrepancies in practice between parishes;

(b) the smallness of the parish as a unit of administration and finance;

(c) the indiscriminate use of the workhouse as a depository for all types of pauper—young, old, mad, sick and able-bodied.

8. Gilbert's Act 1782. Its provisions were as follows.

(a) Parishes were permitted to combine for more efficient administration.

(b) Separation of the able-bodied and the infirm. Only the latter might be sent to the workhouse.

(c) Work to be found for the able-bodied. If necessary, wages might be supplemented from the poor rate. If no work was available, then out-relief could be granted.

(d) "Guardians" of the poor might be appointed to administer relief.

This was a permissive Act but within a short time was widely accepted.

The intentions of the Act marked a step forward. Unfortunately it had repercussions which adversely affected the humanity of poor relief and retarded a proper understanding of the problem throughout the greater part of the nineteenth century.

9. The "Speenhamland system". There occurred in the 1790s a steep rise in prices due to the war with Revolutionary France. This was accompanied by a series of bad harvests. The resulting disturbances caused alarm lest revolution should spread across the Channel.

Accordingly, the Berkshire justices at Speenhamland, in 1795, decided to supplement wages (as they were so empowered by "Gilbert's Act") on a sliding scale geared to the price of bread and the size of a man's family.

Under the threat of starvation of the people or of possible revolution, the "Speenhamland system" was widely adopted, especially in the south of England.

10. Consequences of the Speenhamland system.

(a) *It provided an immediate remedy* for serious circumstances.

(b) *Wages remained unnaturally low*, since employers availed themselves of the situation to have them supplemented from the poor rate.

(c) *Men remained tied to the land* even though real employment opportunities in agriculture were shrinking while in industry they were expanding.

(d) *The morale of the labourer was undermined.* If his wage increased, his poor relief supplement diminished. He therefore had little incentive to support himself and made maximum use of relief.

(e) *The stringency* with which relief had been hitherto administered disappeared.

(*f*) *The burden of the poor rate steadily rose.* (In 1776, it had been £1.25 million annually. This figure rose to £4.25 million in 1802 and in 1832 was £7 million, despite the over-all fall in prices since the end of the war with France.)

In different parts of the country, variations on this form of relief were practised, but until the 1830s the "allowance system" described remained the principal method.

THE POOR LAW IN THE NINETEENTH CENTURY

11. Pressures for reform. These resulted from the following.

(*a*) *The growing burden* of the poor rate.

(*b*) *The "Labourers' revolt"* of 1830. Violence and destruction were particularly acute in the counties where the allowance system was most deeply entrenched. This pointed to the inadequacy of the system.

(*c*) *Changing public attitudes* influenced by writers and thinkers, such as the following.

(*i*) Jeremy Bentham, was the founder of the philosophy of utilitarianism, which preached "the greatest good of the greatest number". An individualist, he believed that this would be achieved by men pursuing their own self-interest but that it was not inconsistent that the Government should intervene in spheres which could not be left safely to individual action, e.g. poor relief, education, public health. Implied was the substitution of central for local government supervision.

(*ii*) Thomas Robert Malthus's *Essay on population* taught that, without a voluntary willingness by the working man to restrict the size of his family, population would continue to expand, thereby preventing any rise in the standard of living above subsistence level. To give poor relief unsparingly encouraged the rearing of families which a man could not support.

Under these pressures, the administration of Lord Grey appointed a Royal Commission to inquire into the operation of the poor law.

12. Royal Commission 1832; and Poor Law Amendment Act 1834. By its business-like manner, the Commission indicated that the traditional reverence for Elizabethan institutions and legislation such as the 1601 poor law should be discarded in favour of an approach more in keeping with the changing times. Its report of 1834 recommended the following.

(*a*) *The minimum of relief* to the able-bodied and on such terms that the poor would accept it only if genuinely in danger of starvation. This implied the general reimposition of the 1722 "workhouse test", which denied out-relief.

(*b*) *Relief given* should be less than could be earned by the poorest independent worker.

(*c*) *Administrative reforms.* To secure a sounder financial base, parishes should be grouped into poor law unions with boards of guardians employing paid officials (there were 600 unions, which grouped the 15,000 parishes of England and Wales and which survived until 1930). National uniformity was to be achieved through a central Board of Commissioners employing inspectors who would strictly supervise the work of local officials.

(*d*) *Out-relief* should be given only to the sick and to persons over sixty years of age.

These recommendations were given effect in 1834 by the Poor Law Amendment Act.

13. Evaluation of the 1834 Act.

(*a*) *Its obsession was with the abuses* of the poor law to the exclusion of any attempt to relieve genuine distress.

(*b*) *Separate workhouse* for the different categories of pauper had been intended. In practice, for economy's sake, the "general mixed workhouse" was the rule.

(*c*) *Stress was laid upon the responsibility of the individual* for the support of himself and his family, with little appreciation that there might be circumstances in which this was completely impossible, i.e. there was no understanding of the problem of unemployment which resulted from fluctuating industrial activity. In the 1860s, for example, the shortage of raw cotton resulting from the American Civil War caused widespread unemployment in Lancashire.

(*d*) *The desire for economy was given a moral sanction.* Although intended as a means of giving back self-respect and independence to the pauper, it was in practice viewed increasingly as a means of reducing the poor rate.

(*e*) *The administrative reforms* created the pattern in which direction was provided by central government and control by local government. In practice, however, the central Board of Commissioners lacked power to enforce its wishes. A remedy was attempted in 1847, with its replacement by a minor ministry, the Poor Law Board. This was in turn replaced in 1871 by the Local

Government Board. Nevertheless, until the end of the century there remained a lack of national uniformity in the administration of relief.

(*f*) *Hardship*. The allowance system was destroyed but great hardship was experienced by the working population. As a result, it gradually became clearer that as distinct from the problem of pauperism (i.e. destitution) there was also a problem of poverty (i.e. inadequate means).

14. The "collateral aids". The Benthamite framers of the 1834 Act believed that while there should be legislation to deter "voluntary" pauperism the State should provide an environment in which a man was able to cultivate his independence.

In the event, the 1834 Act had made no specific provisions for pauper children, for the aged or for the sick and therefore failed in its broad intention.

The following "collateral aids" were provided piecemeal throughout the remainder of the century.

(*a*) *Education* (*see* Chapter XVIII).

(*b*) *Public health* (*see* Chapter XVII).

(*c*) *Friendly society and trade union benefits*. Since the prevailing feeling was that a man should make his own provision against the eventuality of sickness or the onset of old age, impetus was given to friendly society activity (*see* XIX, **16**).

SOCIAL REFORM, 1905–14

15. Reaction to the principles of 1834. The 1834 poor law saw the beginnings of an intense preoccupation with social conditions. As the century wore on, it became increasingly plain that, although in a climate of *laissez-faire* the problems of production were being solved, the resulting prosperity was ill distributed.

The 1880s finally marked a watershed in Britain's social history with the gradual passing of old doctrines and the acceptance of new.

(*a*) *Government action:* extension of the franchise to the agricultural labourer (1884); extension of public health services (*see* XVII, **9, 10**); the growth of free and compulsory education (*see* XVIII, **12, 16**); the reform of local government (1888).

(*b*) *Private investigation:* a series of accounts, the best known being Salvationist General William Booth's *Darkest England*, gave an alarming picture of poverty and squalor in London. In

1899, Seebohm Rowntree's *Poverty: a study of town life* surveyed living conditions in York. Documentation in each work was so thorough that in a time when little statistical evidence was available much use was made of it in parliamentary debate.

(c) *The "new unionism"* (*see* XIX, **28**). Pressures within the working classes were developing which aimed at social and economic reform. Labour representatives now appeared alongside reforming Liberals in Parliament.

16. The reforming Liberal Government of 1906. The Liberals were by no means united in the strength of their desire for radical reform, but amongst their Ministers were two who subsequently made major contributions to social progress, David Lloyd George and Winston Spencer Churchill.

The "old Liberals", said Lloyd George, had secured the political advancement of the people. It was up to the "new Liberals" to secure their economic advancement. A minimum of welfare below which no one would be allowed to fall should be guaranteed.

Since, however, the Liberals believed implicitly in the freedom of the individual, this could not be provided by socialist schemes of enforced sharing of wealth. With the exception of old age pensions, it would be accomplished by the individual himself through insurance, enforced and extended as necessary by the State to ensure its adequacy.

17. Unemployment. The development of a world economy had underlined the uncertainties of employment in an industrial and trading nation with a high dependence on fluctuating foreign markets.

The problem was aggravated by the lack of organisation of the labour market and the system of casual labour which prevailed in many industries. Men were often without work because they did not know where vacancies existed.

William Beveridge, in his analysis, "Unemployment", in his evidence to the 1905 Poor Law Commission, and in his influence upon Winston Churchill, pressed for labour exchanges as a remedy.

In 1909, as President of the Board of Trade, Churchill secured the agreement of the Cabinet for the establishment of labour exchanges, and Beveridge was given the job of organising them throughout the country (in 1916 they were renamed employment exchanges and passed to the Ministry of Labour, founded in that year).

Having established labour exchanges, Churchill drew up plans for national unemployment insurance which were given effect in Part 11 of Lloyd George's National Insurance Act 1911. The unemployment clauses were cautiously experimental and were at first applied only to a few selected industries. Benefits were kept low to forestall malingering and payment of the compulsory contributions was divided between employer, employee and State. Little opposition was encountered, since there could be no moral objection to a scheme in which the recipient paid in advance for what he might ultimately receive.

18. Old age pensions. In 1889, Bismarck introduced a system of State pensions to Germany as a means of combating socialist agitation. Joseph Chamberlain was influenced by its success and throughout the 1890s pressed Parliament for a similar system.

This pressure was for long resisted, since it was felt that the correct solution to the problems of old age was thrift during one's working life. If savings were eventually exhausted, then the poor law would meet the needs of those who required assistance.

Like Chamberlain, Lloyd George was also influenced by the German example and in 1908 carried the Old Age Pensions Act. A pension was payable to all over the age of seventy, provided that in the previous ten years they had led honest and industrious lives. It was scaled according to income.

Payments were therefore made of right from national funds to a section of the needy and there came into being the first national social service. An important new principle had been established. Previously, relief payments were an act of grace made from local funds and available only after a strict test of destitution.

19. Health. The National Insurance Act 1911 was primarily concerned with making safeguards for the health of the working man. Health insurance, unlike unemployment insurance, applied to all workers but was similarly based upon contributions from employer, employee and State. During sickness, medical attention was provided through a "panel" of doctors and during unemployment through sickness a benefit was paid (*see* XVII, 13).

This Act founded social insurance. Embryonic and fragmentary as it was, it drove wedges into the already disintegrating Victorian poor law.

DEPRESSION BETWEEN THE WARS

20. The setting. There was not yet any real understanding of the nature of industrial unemployment, yet its problems were becoming increasingly acute. Dependent upon a world market which during the war years had been realigned, many of Britain's traditional export industries (e.g. coal, textiles, iron) suffered. At home, moreover, the pattern of consumption was changing. It produced a demand for labour in new consumer goods industries located in the south, while in the north the established heavy goods industries had excess capacity (*see* III, **9**).

The result could be seen in unemployment figures. The national average during the period was above 14 per cent. In certain areas of the north, on occasion the figure reached 75 per cent. The magnitude of the problem was beyond pre-war experience and the poor law and unemployment insurance were not well equipped to meet it.

21. Unemployment insurance. In 1920, the unemployment insurance scheme was extended to the majority of workers but it came too late to build up reserves to tackle the problem with which it was immediately faced.

To relieve the poor law of the strain of growing unemployment there were instituted extended benefits (the "dole") to which, by the strict terms of the insurance scheme, there was no entitlement. This was in fact outdoor relief in a slightly less humiliating form. It was believed at first that the cost would be recovered from continued insurance contributions when the recipient resumed work. By 1930, with depression at its worst, it was apparent that this object would never be realised, whereupon died the hope that the problems of unemployment could be met by the principle of insurance.

By 1931, the "extended benefits" had merged into transitional payments made by the Public Assistance Committees (*see* **23** below) from Treasury grants.

The principle was therefore recognised that unemployment due to fluctuations in industry was not an insurable personal risk. It was a national responsibility and therefore chargeable to taxation.

22. Poor law relief. The pressure upon the poor law increased from men with heavy family responsibilities and from men who were not entitled even to "extended benefits". Throughout the

1920s, the number drawing assistance under the poor law never fell below a million, and there were demands for a review of the law's operation.

In the Poor Law Act of 1930, the 1601 poor law principles were restated in modern form. The Act carefully defined the obligations of the family to support its weaker members. Relief would be granted only subject to a means test embracing the whole family.

The financial burden was not evenly distributed but fell mainly upon about thirty-four poor law unions in areas of heavy unemployment. There consequently arose the paradoxical situation that the poor rate was highest in the areas which could least afford it.

23. Local Government Act 1929. This important Act was largely inspired by the necessity of reorganising the administration of the poor law. The boards of guardians of the poor law unions were abolished and their functions assumed by Public Assistance Committees of county and county borough councils. The cost of relief was thus spread over a much wider area (*see* XVII, **17**).

24. The Unemployment Act 1934.

(*a*) All those who had exhausted their entitlement to insurance benefit, together with those who had never come within the insurance scheme, were to be placed in the care of the Unemployment Assistance Board (U.A.B.).

(*b*) The insurance scheme was placed in the hands of a semi-independent body, the Unemployment Insurance Statutory Committee.

Assimilation of the unemployed from the Public Assistance Committees was completed in 1938, whereupon another nail was driven in the coffin of the poor law, i.e. relief of the able-bodied unemployed was taken out of the hands of local authorities and given to a national agency.

Moreover, a common national level of assistance was laid down, thereby establishing by implication the principle of a "national minimum" of welfare to which all were entitled.

The U.A.B. continued until 1947 (changing its title in 1940 to Assistance Board). In that time, it paid £221 million in relief, but subject to a household means test, i.e. based upon the income of members of the family *household* as distinct from the members of the *family*. It was therefore less exacting than the 1930 poor law.

Nevertheless, there remained the implication of personal failure and the hardship of exacting contributions from members of the same household even though they themselves might have only very small resources.

THE WELFARE STATE

25. Impact of the 1939–45 war on social policies. Under the levelling and unifying influence of war was completed the transition in social thinking which had been taking place since the early nineteenth century. In piecemeal fashion, a complex series of independent social services had been created. The time was now ripe for co-ordination and extension in order to create a Welfare State. Public determination never to return to the old ways was summed up by the Beveridge Report.

26. The Beveridge Report, 1942. In diagnosing and proposing a cure for want, Beveridge outlined a scheme of social insurance against all major eventualities "from the cradle to the grave", which would guarantee minimum subsistence benefits of right and without a means test.

In order that the insurance fund should function without strain, the great assumption of the report was that the Government would play a much more positive part in guaranteeing health and employment, thereby limiting the need for insurance benefits. Hence the absolute necessity for:

(*a*) a comprehensive health service;
(*b*) the avoidance of mass unemployment;
(*c*) family allowances.

In 1944, the Government announced in a number of White Papers its acceptance in principle of much that Beveridge proposed.

27. Legislation of the 1945 Labour Government. Effect was given to the White Papers in the following legislation.

(*a*) *Family Allowance Act 1945.* Allowances were to be paid from taxation and *not* insurance contributions.

(*b*) *National Health Service Act 1946* (*see* XVII, **19**).

(*c*) *National Insurance Act 1946.* This established a comprehensive insurance scheme applicable to the whole nation. Based upon compulsory contributions from employer, employee and State, benefits would be paid for sickness, unemployment, retirement, maternity and death. The Ministry would also administer family allowances.

For any whose basic needs were not met by insurance benefits, there remained the National Assistance system.

28. "National Assistance". The National Assistance Act 1948 set up a National Assistance Board to administer all that was left of the functions of the old poor law. Its duty was to provide for those without resources or whose resources required supplementing.

It was hoped that the scope of the Board's activities would steadily diminish as the social services began to function. What was not anticipated was the pace at which inflation would continuously erode the real value of insurance benefits. This trend became ever more apparent during the 1960s and 1970s with improvements in social security payments always lagging behind rises in the general price level. Not only were insurance beneficiaries adversely affected, but there was also growing hardship amongst low wage earning families.

There was consequently much greater reliance upon "supplementary benefits", (yet another change of nomenclature designed to overcome the stigma of the poor law), and the introduction of a scheme of Family Income Supplements for the lowpaid. However, there still remained the objection that these were means-tested benefits and that because of ignorance or an unwillingness to accept "charity" far too many people were experiencing real hardship.

This was one of the factors which led the Government in 1972 to publish a Green Paper which took a step in the direction of guaranteeing a minimum income for all as of right.

29. Green Paper. "Proposals for a Tax Credit System", October 1972. The Paper set out as a basis for discussion the Government's proposals for radical innovations in the structure of income tax. In essence the system suggested would charge all employees and all national insurance beneficiaries at the basic tax rate, provisionally set at 30 per cent. In the lower ranges, progression would be established by granting tax credits which would replace the existing tax allowances, family allowances and Family Income Supplement. It would also, it was hoped, substantially diminish, if not eliminate entirely, reliance upon supplementary benefits. Where total tax credits exceeded tax liability a cash sum or negative income tax would be paid.   ⌡

With a change of Government in 1974 these proposals were abandoned.

30. Child Benefit Act 1975. This Act implemented the Chancellor's Budget announcement that a new child benefit payment would be made from April 1977. It would be tax free, payable upon all children and wholly to the mother. It would replace the existing dual system of Family Allowances and income tax allowances, the latter having normally been made to the husband.

It was estimated that there were 3 million families with one child only and that in consequence of the new scheme a total of 7 million children would qualify for the first time. Family Allowances had been paid only for the second and subsequent children.

Early impressions were that as a measure to relieve hardship it did not achieve great results since family units as a whole were little better off. "Fiscal drag", the inflationary process through which even the low-paid have been drawn into the tax net, meant that what the mother gained in increased benefits the husband forfeited in increased tax.

31. Full employment. The Beveridge Report emphasised the need for continuing full employment to underpin the system of social security which it envisaged. Keynes had provided an economic analysis which seemed to show that this could be achieved by methods consistent with social democracy (*see* Appendix I). The Government would manage aggregate demand within the economy at a level consistent with full employment without inflation and balance of payments problems.

For two decades the policy appeared to produce acceptable results. It seemed possible to steer a course on which unemployment varied between 1.5 per cent and 2.5 per cent at the expense of a very modest rate of inflation. In the late 1960s and 1970s, however, orthodox Keynesian economists were at a loss to explain the new phenomenon of rising unemployment accompanied by escalating inflation.

Rates of Unemployment (U.K.)
Annual Averages
1961–76 (per cent)

1961	1962	1963	1964	1965	1966	1967	1968
1.6	2.1	2.6	1.7	1.5	1.5	2.3	2.5

1969	1970	1971	1972	1973	1974	1975	1976
2.5	2.6	3.4	3.8	2.7	2.6	4.2	5.8

Source: Annual Abstract of Statistics.

By 1972, unemployment exceeded 1 million for the first time since the 1930s and the Government gave a massive stimulus to aggregate demand. This produced a very short-term relief but the greater part of the additional expenditure was absorbed in higher prices, inflation now trending towards 30 per cent per annum.

By 1977, unemployment had reached 1,341,000 and the figure was still rising. The progressive failure of Keynesian demand management techniques now led to direct Government intervention on an *ad hoc* basis.

32. Employment Protection Act 1975. This Act was in part a response to trade union acquiescence in wages policy and in part an attempt to sustain employment.

(a) *A.C.A.S.* A new Advisory, Conciliation and Arbitrary Service was established. Its functions embraced all disputes including those involving union recognition.

(b) *Payments benefits.* Employees gained guaranteed payments in respect of pregnancy and maternity leave and the right to subsequent continuation of employment.

(c) *Unfair dismissal.* Employees' rights were extended. In practice it then proved extremely difficult to dismiss an employee for whatever reason except at the expense of substantial compensation. Critics have argued that this clause has exacerbated the problem of unemployment since employers, particularly in small businesses where new growth might be expected have been reluctant to engage labour.

(d) *Disclosure of information.* Trade unions were to be kept fully informed of company policies which might produce redundancies.

33. Other measures to alleviate unemployment. In the middle 1970s the Government dispensed large sums under the 1972 and 1975 Industry Acts in an attempt to preserve jobs in many industries but most notably motor vehicles, steel and shipbuilding.

Additionally, relief measures have included the following.

(*a*) *Temporary Employment Subsidies (T.E.S.).* These were introduced in 1975 and were paid to employers willing to retain labour which they would otherwise have shed.

(*b*) *Employment of the disabled.* The Manpower Services Commission (M.S.C.) was empowered to give a £30 per week subsidy for every disabled person given a trial employment period of six weeks.

(*c*) *Small firms.* From 1977, firms in special development areas with fewer than fifty employees qualified for a £20 per week subsidy for each additional worker over a period of six months.

(*d*) *Work experience.* Introduced in 1976 and operated by the M.S.C. this scheme for school-leavers provides that where firms employ young people on temporary projects the Government will pay an allowance to the employee.

(*e*) *Job creation.* Local authorities have been encouraged to employ young people on temporary projects which were considered socially useful.

(*f*) *Employment of school-leavers.* From 1976 the M.S.C. was empowered to subsidise the employment of school-leavers who had been unemployed for more than six months.

(*g*) *Training Opportunities Programme.* From 1976 more funds were allocated to training and retraining schemes.

(*h*) *Job release.* From 1977, employees in assisted areas who were within one year of retirement were to be encouraged to retire early on a special tax-free allowance provided that their firm was prepared to replace them with younger people.

These and other measures were simply palliatives. What was lacking was a long-term strategy which would get to the root of the unemployment problem.

THE EUROPEAN COMMUNITY AND SOCIAL POLICY

34. European Social Fund. As a member of the E.E.C. the U.K. participates in the formulation of social policy aimed at improving Community living standards.

The purpose of the Social Fund is to improve employment opportunities by increasing the mobility of labour. In general it meets up to half the cost of certain Government supported training and resettlement schemes.

35. Social Action Programme. In 1974 the Council of Ministers adopted a programme based upon a number of proposals. The following measures were undertaken.

(*a*) *Financial assistance* was to be provided from the Social Fund for migrant workers and the disabled.

(*b*) *Safety and health.* An advisory committee was set up.

(*c*) *Equal pay.* A directive was issued on equal pay for men and women.

(*d*) *Working hours and holidays.* A recommendation was made for a standard forty hour working week and four weeks' annual holiday.

(*e*) *Dismissals.* A directive was issued on the handling of mass dismissals.

(*f*) *Individual workers' rights.* A directive was issued on the rights of workers in the event of transfers of undertakings.

36. Rights of Community nationals. The general principle is that a Community national is entitled to the social security benefits of the country in which he is working. Similarly he is entitled to medical treatment under the health provisions of that country.

PROGRESS TEST 16

1. In the Middle Ages, who cared for the poor? (**1**)

2. What was the principal cause of the rise in sixteenth-century pauperism? (**2**)

3. Describe the general provisions of the 1601 poor law. Who did it make responsible for the support of the poor? (**3**)

4. How did the growth of *laissez-faire* philosophy affect the general attitude to poor relief? (**4**)

5. How did the Law of Settlement 1662 aggravate the problem of unemployment? (**5**)

6. Why did the eighteenth-century workhouse prove to be an unsatisfactory remedy for poverty? (**6, 7**)

7. How did the Speenhamland system arise and what were its results? (**8–10**)

8. Why in the early nineteenth century was a new approach made to the problem of poverty? (**11**)

9. Outline the provisions of the Poor Law Amendment Act 1834. What administrative improvement resulted? (**12**)

10. How effective was this Act in providing a solution for poverty? (**13**)

11. What was the intention of the "collateral aids"? (**14**)

12. What evidence is there of changing social attitudes in the 1880s? **(15)**

13. In what way did the 1906 Liberal Government's approach to the problems of unemployment differ from that of nineteenth-century Governments? **(13, 16, 17)**

14. In what way did Lloyd George propose to treat the aged differently from other categories of poor people? **(16, 18)**

15. Describe how the "dole" became necessary in the 1920s. **(21)**

16. What major step forward was accomplished by the Local Government Act 1929? **(23)**

17. At what stage did unemployment relief become a national responsibility chargeable to taxation? **(24)**

18. In what way did Beveridge's 1942 proposals for the relief of want differ fundamentally from those of the 1906 Liberal Government? **(16–19, 26)**

19. Through what means has the scope of the old poor law been considerably narrowed since 1945? **(27, 28)**

20. Evaluate the success of full employment policies during the period 1945–78. **(31)**

21. Outline the provisions of the Employment Protection Act. **(32)**

22. What assistance is offered by the E.E.C. in the implementation of social policy? **(34–36)**

CHAPTER XVII

Public Health

CONDITIONS BEFORE THE NINETEENTH CENTURY

1. Population changes and the death rate.

	Population of England
Eleventh century, Domesday survey	2 million
Fourteenth century after Black Death	2½ million *only*
Sixteenth century, Elizabethan era	3 million
Seventeenth century	5 million
1801, first official census	9 million

The estimated figures above illustrate that the population of England expanded slowly until the eighteenth century, at which time there was a fairly rapid increase. The rate of expansion was not closely affected by any variation in the birth rate. This had always been high and remained so. The death rate had been equally high, but in the eighteenth century began to decline, consequent upon improvements in medicine, water supply and social hygiene.

2. Incidence of disease. In the eighteenth century the average expectation of life of working men was no more than forty. This was chiefly attributable to epidemic diseases such as cholera and to endemic fevers, amongst which the greatest killer was typhoid. Both these diseases were water-borne and any hope of control depended upon proper sanitation and water supply.

In an age when illness was often viewed as a judgment of God and when the poor were believed responsible for their own condition, the connection between filth and disease was established only slowly.

3. Impact of urbanisation. The eighteenth-century tendency for the death rate to decline was partially arrested by the growth of factory towns as follows.

(*a*) *Building*. Houses were built with the object of accommodating economically as many workers as possible and with no regard to lighting, ventilation or sanitation. There were no town planning or building regulations.

(b) *Water*. There were no piped water supplies and no means of refuse disposal. There were only open sewers for surface drainage.

By the 1830s, overcrowding in the main industrial towns was so serious and conditions had deteriorated so much that there was a dramatic rise in the death rate.

NINETEENTH-CENTURY REFORM

4. The pressures for reform. A number of circumstances, such as the following, slowly forced public opinion to the view that action must be taken.

(a) The realisation that disease, by incapacitating the worker, increased the burden of the poor rate.

(b) The knowledge that, frequently, disease struck rich and poor alike (e.g. in 1861 the Queen's husband died of typhoid).

(c) The horror caused by the suddenness of epidemics, e.g. cholera outbreaks in 1832, 1848, 1853 and 1866 caused tens of thousands of deaths.

(d) A growing concern for the welfare of the industrial worker. This followed the efforts of reformers such as Chadwick to draw the attention of the public, who were largely ignorant of the facts.

5. Edwin Chadwick (1800–90). As Secretary to the Poor Law Commissioners following the reform of 1834 (*see* XVI, **12**), Chadwick was the initiator of public health controls.

In his *Report on the sanitary condition of the labouring population* (1842) he established the relationship between filth, bad ventilation, disease and the high cost of poor relief.

As a result of this report, a long process began which culminated, in 1948, in the creation of the *National Health Service*.

6. The "collateral aids" (*see* XVI, **14**). The outcome of Chadwick's report was a Royal Commission on the Health of Towns (1844), which made plain the abysmal state of water supplies and drainage and the lack of any co-ordinating bodies to provide them.

The Commission recommended the establishment of a Central Board of Health to supervise the activities of local boards which would be created and made responsible for cleaning, drainage and water supply.

The nineteenth-century dislike of central control delayed legislation until, under the threat of a cholera outbreak, there was passed the Nuisances Removal Act.

7. 1846: the Nuisances Removal Act. Powers were given for the cleaning of towns but no special authorities established. The duty therefore fell upon the Guardians of the Poor, who were slow to act. The position was therefore strengthened by further legislation in 1848.

8. 1848: the Public Health Act. A General Board of Health with limited powers was set up to supervise local boards. The Act was permissive (i.e. there was no compulsion) and full advantage was not taken of it.

The General Board of Health lasted until 1854, by which time it had succeeded in setting up local boards to cover only one-sixth of the population.

Continuing high mortality, reinforced by the cholera outbreak of 1866, again focused public attention on the problem. In 1869, a Royal Commission investigated and its report led to two further Acts.

9. 1872 and 1875: Public Health Acts. The later Act codified and extended previous legislation and formed the base of subsequent advance. Its provisions were as follows.

(*a*) Sanitary authorities were established for the whole country (in the towns, the municipal authorities; in the country, the poor law unions).

(*b*) Medical officers and sanitary inspectors were appointed for each district.

(*c*) The Local Government Board (a government department) was to supervise public health and administer the poor law.

(*d*) Authorities might provide a water supply, baths and wash-houses and were compelled to maintain sewers, street paving, lighting and cleaning and fire services. They were also to deal with infectious diseases and contaminated food.

10. Evaluation of the Act. This Act ranks as one of the great reforming measures of the nineteenth century. It ensured that Britain's cities became fit for human habitation. Its success was reflected in the decline of the death rate from about twenty-three per thousand in mid-century to seventeen per thousand in 1900.

The nineteenth-century approach, however, was to view health as a collateral aid, i.e. a means of providing an environment in which men could take care of themselves.

The shortcomings of this impersonal attitude were to be seen in the infant mortality rate, which persisted at about 150 per thousand throughout the nineteenth century and in the high incidence of tuberculosis, which accounted for about one-sixth of the death rate.

In each case, the remedy was to be found in a more personal approach to the health problems of the individual, but this was not to be achieved until the twentieth century.

TWENTIETH-CENTURY HEALTH SERVICES FOR THE INDIVIDUAL

11. Maternity and infant welfare. Recognition that good health might be dependent upon factors other than sanitary surroundings was first made in provision for mothers and infants:

(*a*) 1902: certification of midwives;

(*b*) 1907: compulsory notification to the Medical Officer of Health of a birth within forty-eight hours of its occurrence. The health visitors which many authorities now employed could therefore call immediately and advise and help as necessary.

The results were to be seen in the drop in the infant mortality rate from 151 in 1901 to 95 in 1912.

12. Sanatoria. The National Insurance Act 1911, provided £1.5 million to build sanatoria open to the whole population and not just to insured persons.

Tuberculosis was a disease arising from the social conditions which nineteenth-century measures had attempted to remedy, not always with success. Its treatment required medical skill and individual care and attention. That the twentieth century was beginning to provide this, establishes the link between nineteenth- and twentieth-century attitudes.

13. National Insurance Act 1911. Weekly contributions of 4*d.* (employees), 3*d.* (employers) and 2*d.* (Treasury) secured a sickness benefit of 10*s.* a week and 30*s.* maternity benefit.

NOTE: 2.4*d.* = 1p; 1*s.* = 5p.

Medical attention could be obtained from a "panel" of doctors, but no provision was made for hospital treatment.

The emphasis of the Act was therefore upon insurance against sickness rather than the creation of a national health service.

An administrative weakness was that the Act did not establish any central supervising body.

14. The Ministry of Health, 1919. Since it was realised that the end of the war would heighten the health problems of the nation, a single Ministry was established which absorbed the public health work of local authorities, housing, the organisation of health insurance and the whole of the poor law administration.

This vast range of duties tended to retard positive action in the field of health but they were not finally disentangled until 1951.

15. Health insurance between the wars. There was no broadening of the principles upon which the 1911 Act had been based, although the number covered by insurance was extended from about 13 million in 1913 to 20 million in 1939. The great weaknesses of the scheme were as follows.

(a) Dependants were not covered and there remained, in consequence, much avoidable illness—especially among young families—because of inability to pay for medical treatment.

(b) With or without justification, there developed the firm belief that there was one class of treatment for the private paying patient and another for the patient "on the panel".

(c) The lack of specialist and hospital facilities left a serious gap in the scheme.

16. Hospitals. The only service was provided by voluntary hospitals of independent foundation and those which had been developed by the boards of guardians. With few exceptions, local authorities had no general hospitals and made provisions only for tuberculosis and infectious diseases. A major step forward was taken in 1929 (*see* **17**).

17. Local Government Act 1929. When, under this Act, local government became responsible for the organisation of poor relief (*see* XVI, **23**) the opportunity occurred to merge the health aspect of this work with the public health services.

The Act encouraged the local authorities to develop local hospital services as a whole, co-ordinating where necessary with the voluntary hospitals.

Progress throughout the country was not uniform, with the result that in 1939 the number of beds was almost evenly divided between voluntary hospitals, those under public health control and those supported by the poor law.

It was estimated that the total number of beds was one-third less than required and that, in general, hospitals were in poor repair and ill-equipped.

18. Government White Paper, 1944. The recommendations for social reconstruction outlined in the Beveridge Report (*see* XVI, **26**) stressed the importance of a much more comprehensive and personal health service than had existed before the war.

The inadequacies of the existing service, particularly in respect of hospitals, had been underlined by the stresses of the war, and in 1944 the Government outlined its plans in a White Paper, *The National Health Service*. With some modification, this was implemented in 1946 (*see* **19**).

19. National Health Service Act 1946. In place of the nineteenth-century guarantee of a healthy environment, the Act marked society's acceptance of its duty positively to ensure the health of each of its members.

To this end, a "free" service financed by contributions from the National Insurance fund, from the rates and from taxation, gave to all the opportunity of having a family doctor and specialist, consultant, hospital, dental, optical and pharmaceutical services.

20. The Health Service in operation. The 1946 Act completed 100 years of development, in which a comprehensive public health service was established. Its beneficial results are to be seen in the continuing decrease in both the adult and infant mortality rates.

The Service has nevertheless operated under certain strains and may be subjected to the following criticisms.

(*a*) The development of the hospital service has lagged, both in the construction of modern buildings and in the recruitment of staff. The result is a continuing shortage of hospital beds.

(*b*) The Service is still strongly orientated to caring for sick people rather than to the prevention of sickness. The exceptions to this criticism are the successful campaigns conducted against poliomyelitis and diphtheria.

PROGRESS TEST 17

1. The eighteenth-century death rate showed some decline. Why? **(1, 2)**

2. What was the effect upon public health of the growth of factory towns? **(3)**

3. To what extent did humanitarian motives inspire early nineteenth-century concern with public health? **(4)**

4. What part was played by Edwin Chadwick in improving the nation's health? **(5)**

5. How was the safeguarding of public health interpreted as a "collateral aid"? **(6)**

6. Assess the effectiveness of the 1848 Public Health Act. **(8)**

7. The date 1875 marks the acceptance of the necessity for stringent public health controls. What evidence is there to support this claim? **(9, 10)**

8. In what major respect have twentieth-century attitudes to public health differed from those of the nineteenth century? Give evidence. **(10, 11, 12)**

9. How adequate to the task of promoting the national health was the National Insurance Act 1911? **(13, 15, 16)**

10. How did the Local Government Act 1929 affect the hospital service? **(16, 17)**

11. In what respects may the 1946 National Health Service Act be regarded as the culmination of 100 years of endeavour? **(19, 20)**

CHAPTER XVIII

Education

EDUCATION IN ENGLAND BEFORE THE NINETEENTH CENTURY

1. Opportunities for education. There existed no national system and the opportunity for a formal education was restricted to the following four types of school.

(*a*) *The grammar schools.* These were of ancient foundation and usually closely connected with the parish church. In the Elizabethan era, their number increased as a result of endowment by the merchant classes, determined to make England a bulwark of Protestantism in a Catholic Europe. By 1600, it was possible for a boy, even in the most remote parts of the country, to secure a free place in preparation for Oxford or Cambridge. However, even had the demand existed, these schools could have catered for only a minute portion of the population.

(*b*) *The public schools.* Difficult to define precisely, they were described (by the Clarendon Commission, 1861) as having grown out of nine great private foundations: Eton, Harrow, Westminster, St. Paul's, the Merchant Taylors', Winchester, Shrewsbury, Rugby and Charterhouse. Bound by certain common ideals and aspirations, they traditionally catered for the ruling classes.

(*c*) *The "dame" schools.* These were frequently run by old ladies or discharged soldiers who, in a rudimentary fashion, taught the "three Rs" and the Bible. They were open to all who could afford the small fees charged.

(*d*) *The charity schools.* From these schools stems the growth of modern primary and secondary education.

2. Society for the Propagation of Christian Knowledge. Formed in 1699, its aim was to provide charity schools for "those whom nature or failure had determined to the plough, the oar and other handicrafts". It was moved by the same zeal which imbued overseas missionaries and was also concerned to safeguard England against the dangers of "Popery".

The Society's great eighteenth-century innovations were as follows.

(*a*) It was the first national body to attempt to organise schools for the poor in the seven to eleven age group.

(*b*) By its attempts to provide some means of teacher training and by approving an embryo teachers' association, it engendered a spirit of professionalism.

3. Weakness of eighteenth-century efforts.

(*a*) *Narrow syllabus.* Education was dominated by religion or, in the case of the public schools, classical studies. An approach which may have satisfied a predominantly agricultural society proved entirely inadequate to the needs of an increasingly industrial society.

(*b*) *Inter-denominational disputes.* The work of the S.P.C.K. was at first inter-denominational but Anglican reaction caused the repression of Non-conformist schools. This schism persisted into the nineteenth century and delayed the creation of a national system.

(*c*) *Insufficient schools.* Two-thirds of the country's children had no instruction.

(*d*) *Insufficient teachers.* There existed no adequate means of teacher training. Added to this, poor salaries meant that the supply of teachers was both insufficient and poor in quality.

NINETEENTH-CENTURY GROWTH
OF ELEMENTARY EDUCATION

4. The schools societies.
An attempt to overcome the shortage of teachers was made by Andrew Bell and Joseph Lancaster, who devised the monitorial system in which senior pupils were placed in charge of younger children.

Lancaster's efforts were supported by the Quakers, who in 1808 founded the British and Foreign Schools Society, the aims of which were outlined in its original title: "The Institution for promoting the British system of education of the labouring and manufacturing classes of society of every religious persuasion."

Moved by the increasing need for educating the children of the growing industrial towns and by the desire to ensure that they were educated in the Anglican faith, members of the S.P.C.K. in 1811 formed "The National Society for the education of the poor in the principles of the established Church throughout England and Wales."

The two societies vied with each other in the establishment of schools in industrial areas. The National Society had the advantage of the diocesan and parish organisation of the S.P.C.K. and a considerable number of schools with which to begin (in 1814, 230).

The practice developed that Non-conformist parents would, when possible, send their children to the schools of the British and Foreign Schools Society while Anglican children attended the National schools.

5. Teacher training. The monitorial system demanded some training, and Lancaster began a system of selecting certain monitors as apprentices. This idea was quickly extended, especially by the National Society, which in its year of foundation, 1811, established a central training school. Other central schools followed which formed the embryos of the subsequent training colleges.

6. Collateral aids (*see* XVI, **14**). The 1834 poor law report stressed that if the poor rate was to be diminished and the working man's lot improved, not only must the Government supervise the health of towns but it must also "promote the religious and moral education of the labouring classes". The intention was that literacy should be encouraged to the extent that the working man understood and accepted his duties and responsibilities.

7. Government subsidies. As in matters of health, the Government was slow to interfere with voluntary activity. When it did so, it was not in order to provide State schools but to subsidise the work of the National and the British and Foreign Schools societies.

In 1833 they received a mere £10,000 each but subsequent annual grants were increased, and in 1838 a committee of the Privy Council under Dr. Kay-Shuttleworth was set up to administer them.

8. Inspectors and teachers. The committee appointed inspectors and attempted to remedy the teacher shortage by setting up training colleges. It failed to do so, through the desire of the Church to have sole control. After some delay, Anglicans and Non-conformists set up their own training colleges, of which, in 1846, there were twenty-five.

In the face of continuing shortage, a new system of training pupil-teachers in selected schools was adopted.

9. 1857: Department of Education. By 1857, annual grants had risen to well over £500,000 annually and, to administer this sum, a Department of Education was established.

10. 1858: Parliamentary commission. An inquiry into the state of education had its main recommendations put into effect as follows:

(*a*) state grant increased;

(*b*) work of inspectors to be accompanied by examinations;

(*c*) amount of grant to be based upon examination results— "payment by results". The defects of this system became more and more apparent and, with half the country's children receiving no instruction at all, the voluntary schools were clearly unequal to the task.

11. The 1860s: final incentives for a national system.

(*a*) *Prussian example.* In Prussia, State education existed and its value in military matters was being demonstrated to all Europe.

(*b*) *Trade union pressure.* The trade unions and other working-class organisations had long been pressing for compulsory education.

(*c*) *Employers' consent.* Fearful of growing German and American competition, manufacturers finally saw that education meant increased efficiency.

(*d*) *Extended franchise, 1867.* The artisan now had the vote and it was seen to be imperative that he should exercise it intelligently.

In 1869, the National Education League was founded in Birmingham to press for free, compulsory and secular education. The time was ripe for the most important measures which marked the State's acceptance of its duty to guarantee an education for all.

12. Education Act 1870. The aim was "to cover the country with good schools".

(*a*) School boards were established for each district, with the power to raise rates and build schools where voluntary provision was inadequate.

(*b*) The church schools were fitted into the national system through a continuance of grants.

(*c*) Small fees were charged which could be remitted if the board thought fit.

(*d*) Children were permitted (not compelled) to attend between the ages of five and thirteen.

13. Results of the Act.

(*a*) Some 2,500,000 new places in new buildings were provided in the thirty years' existence of the boards.

(*b*) Education was now a right and not a charity.

(*c*) The dual system of church schools and board schools proved a handicap to further development. The first based its teaching in religion but had insufficient income to ensure efficiency. The second separated religion from secular education and, with a higher income, reached higher technical standards.

NINETEENTH-CENTURY GROWTH OF SECONDARY, TECHNICAL AND UNIVERSITY EDUCATION

14. Reform of the public schools. Since primary education was taking so long to establish, there was no question of secondary education for other than the upper and middle classes.

Public schools were criticised because of their narrow curriculum, hard and brutal life and poor masters. They were recreated by a handful of remarkable men, notably Thomas Arnold (1828–42) at Rugby and Edward Thring (1853–87) at Uppingham. Aiming to produce scholars and Christian gentlemen, they widened the teaching syllabus and employed better masters at higher salaries.

The Clarendon Commission, 1861, reported on the nine great public schools (*see* 1). The subsequent Public Schools Act 1868 revised the constitution and curriculum of seven of them on the lines of Rugby.

15. Grammar and private schools. In 1865, the Taunton Commission showed that the number of grammar schools had shrunk to seventy-two. In addition, there existed some 10,000 private schools of no particular repute which, for many years, catered for the bulk of the middle and upper classes.

The Endowed Schools Act 1869 attempted to rejuvenate the grammar schools by reorganising the use of their endowments. No effort was made, however, to make them conform to a national pattern.

16. Secondary schools. The primary education offered by the 1870 Act was rudimentary and often ended early. This was not surprising in times when parents depended partly upon their children's earnings.

Attendance was only made compulsory to the age of ten in 1880, to the age of eleven in 1893 and to the age of twelve in 1899. There was no attempt to provide secondary schooling until the second great education Act in 1902.

17. Education Act 1902. Administrative reforms were effected and schooling extended as follows.

(*a*) A broader administrative base was achieved by the substitution of 328 local education authorities (i.e. local councils) for the 2,568 school boards.

(*b*) The local education authorities were empowered to create their own "grammar type" secondary schools, charging small fees but providing free scholarships to elementary school candidates.

(*c*) The local education authorities were encouraged to integrate the existing endowed grammar schools into the system.

Criticism: for many years, both types of secondary school catered mainly for the middle classes. Barely 5 per cent of elementary school children were able to secure places. This confirmed the fundamental class character which the English education system was acquiring by the end of the century and which today continues to cause concern.

18. Technical education. Malthus taught that population must inevitably outstrip the means of subsistence. Others argued that science would keep pace with man's needs provided that there was sufficient professional training.

The London Mechanics' Institute opened in 1824 and was quickly followed by others, particularly in the industrial areas of the north. In the 1830s and 1840s many institutes formed associations, and in 1852 a National Union was founded by the Royal Society of Arts. Through this body a system of examinations, administered by the regional unions, was inaugurated (the Union of the Lancashire and Cheshire Institutes survives as an examining and consultative body).

19. University education. Until the nineteenth century, the only universities in England were the ancient foundations of Oxford and Cambridge. They catered almost exclusively for the ruling classes and admitted only Anglicans.

The desire for a secular education of high technical standard which inspired the Mechanics' Institutes led also to the foundation of the first English university which imposed no religious test (*see* (*a*)).

(*a*) *1826: University of London.* Emphasis was upon medical training but gradually its structure was changed, so that by 1851 it embraced twenty-nine general colleges and nearly sixty medical colleges, not only in London but throughout the country.

(*b*) *1832: Durham University.* Organised on the pattern of Oxford and Cambridge, its work was primarily scientific.

(*c*) *1851: Manchester University.* Formed to meet regional needs.

(*d*) *In the second half of the century*, increasing interest in scientific discovery, spurred on by German and American competition, led to the foundation of many university colleges which subsequently acquired full university status:

    (*i*) Newcastle Royal College of Science (1871);

    (*ii*) Yorkshire College, Leeds (1874);

    (*iii*) Firth College, Sheffield (1879);

    (*iv*) university colleges at Liverpool (1881), Nottingham (1881), Reading (1892), Exeter (1893);

    (*v*) a provincial college at Bristol (1876);

    (*vi*) Birmingham University (1900).

The work of each college reflected the technical activities of its region.

EXTENSION OF THE EDUCATION SYSTEM, 1918–39

20. Increased desire for education. From the years of the First World War, demand for the extension of elementary education grew within the working class itself.

(*a*) Parents did not have quite the same dependence upon their children's wages.

(*b*) There was a growing realisation of the importance of education to economic security.

(*c*) It was felt that equal sacrifice in war demanded equal opportunity in peace. This was reflected in the increase in the numbers receiving secondary education from 56 per 1,000 in 1914 to 97 per 1,000 in 1921.

21. 1918: the "Fisher Act". Lloyd George realised the importance of education to post-war reconstruction and appointed H. A. L. Fisher as President of the Board of Education. The latter was responsible for the third great education Act, which provided that:

(*a*) the school-leaving age be raised to fourteen, with the option of an extra year to the age of fifteen;

(*b*) part-time "day continuation" classes be offered to the age of eighteen.

The great step forward was the acceptance of the principle that continued education was of importance not only to the individual but also to society.

22. 1926, Hadow report. Handicapped by the economics of the 1920s, progress was slow. The Hadow recommendations sought to accelerate it.

(*a*) Secondary education for all accepted as a principle, with the division from primary established at the age of eleven.

(*b*) The 1902 secondary schools to be rated grammar schools. The top forms of the elementary schools to become the new "moderns".

(*c*) The leaving age to be raised to fifteen.

With the exception of the last, the implementation of which was delayed, these proposals were accepted.

23. Grammar school admission. In the 1930s the practice was adopted of opening the grammar schools to all, subject to an examination at the age of eleven. Contributions to fees were made according to parents' means.

24. Evaluation of the period. Whereas nineteenth-century education had been concerned to fit working men to their role in the complex techniques of industry, twentieth-century education unconsciously adapted itself to changing needs, blurring the distinction between the working class and middle class in order to create a new administrative and managerial class.

However, in the system which had evolved by 1939 there remained serious gaps in technical and higher education.

DEVELOPMENT SINCE 1944

25. Education Act 1944. The Second World War drove home the half-digested lesson that the eminence of a modern industrial nation rests upon the education of its people. Post-war development was to be based upon the major extension and reorganisation of education set forth in the Act of 1944.

(a) A Ministry was established with far wider powers than its predecessor, the Board of Education (*see* **21**).

(b) It would ensure that local education authorities provided "a varied and comprehensive educational service".

(c) Children would receive an education suited to "their age, ability and aptitude".

(d) Progressive education would be in three stages, primary, secondary and further (the tripartite division at the secondary level into grammar, modern and technical was generally adopted although *not* specifically directed by the Act).

(e) The principle of "day continuation" was reaffirmed and was to be implemented when practicable.

(f) The school-leaving age would be raised to fifteen (implemented in 1947) and to sixteen when practicable.

(g) School meals, milk and medical services were regulated.

(h) Provision was to be made for adults in full-time and part-time education and in cultural pursuits.

26. Evaluation of the 1944 Act. It was undoubtedly the greatest legislative measure in education to date. Post-war criticism has been aimed not at the Act itself but at the failure to achieve some of its objectives and at its application in particular fields.

(a) The merits and weaknesses of the tripartite secondary system have been hotly disputed. As a remedy, in many areas comprehensive schools have been established which absorb the functions of modern, grammar and technical schools.

(b) There was a marked lack of success in extending "day continuation classes" in the county colleges proposed by the Act and the concept was subsequently dropped in favour of raising the school-leaving age to sixteen.

(c) Despite extensive building programmes, a vast number of school buildings throughout the country remain inadequate and wholly unsuited to their purpose.

(d) Dissatisfaction with remuneration has periodically affected teacher recruitment both in numbers and quality.

(e) Recurrent shortages of teachers and accommodation and, in the 1970s, public expenditure constraints which left many newly trained teachers unemployed, have kept the average numbers in classes well above what is desirable.

27. The Robbins Report, 1963. The immediate post-war years saw substantial growth in the higher education sector. Even so, competition for the places available became intense and it was felt that too many gifted young people were not receiving the opportunity which they merited.

In 1960, a committee under Lord Robbins was appointed to inquire into the higher education system. It was the first comprehensive survey ever conducted and the report which was published in 1963 was described by the Minister as "the most important social document since the Beveridge Report". Its principal proposals were:

(a) the immediate creation of six new universities and the expansion of the existing ones;

(b) the creation of a Ministry of Arts and Science with over-all responsibility for higher education.

(c) the creation of five new "special institutions for scientific and technological education and research" operating along similar lines to the Massachusetts Institute of Technology;

(d) there should be continuous planning for the period ten years ahead;

(e) the creation of a Council for National Academic Awards (C.N.A.A.) which would afford the opportunity of degree courses to students in Regional and Area colleges;

(f) the foundation of two new management education centres.

These proposals, which were estimated to involve capital expenditure of £1,140 million by 1980–1, were immediately accepted by the Government. However, by 1965 there had been second thoughts on how the Robbins proposals were to be achieved. The Minister then told the House of Commons that while the Government accepted the Robbins target of 390,000 full-time places of higher education by 1973–4, no new universities would be built in the following ten years nor would the five "special institutions for science and technology".

Attention was subsequently focused upon the development of regional polytechnics.

28. Polytechnics. In April 1967 the Secretary of State for Education and Science announced that thirty polytechnics would be established in England and Wales in line with proposals contained in a White Paper of May 1966.

In selected areas, local colleges of art, commerce, building and science and technology would be brought together into a single institution concentrating primarily upon courses leading to higher national certificates and diplomas and to degrees approved by the C.N.A.A.

29. Newsom Report, 1963. Concurrently with the Robbins Report, a second report was published by a committee which had sat under Sir John Newsom to consider "the education of pupils aged thirteen to sixteen of average and less than average ability".

The report concluded that there was "very little doubt that among our children there are reserves of ability which can be tapped if the country wills the means. One of the means is a longer school life." It accordingly recommended that the school-leaving age should be raised to sixteen for those reaching the age of fifteen in the school year 1969–70.

While agreeing to the principle, the Government said that the proposal could not be implemented until the 1970–1 school year because of the shortage of teachers. In the event, it was delayed still longer and finally put into effect in 1973.

30. Plowden Report, 1967. The first comprehensive inquiry into primary education for more than thirty years was instituted under the chairmanship of Lady Plowden in June 1963. Its terms of reference were "to consider primary education in all its aspects and the transition from primary to secondary education". Its main proposals were as follows.

(*a*) *Special assistance for schools in slum areas*, to be designated "educational priority areas", in the form of more teachers and additional finance for buildings and equipment.

Educational priority areas were defined as those where poor homes and a bad neighbourhood put children at a disadvantage for life, the report commenting "the loss of them, the loss to the community that arises because of the inequality of educational opportunity is avoidable and in consequence intolerable".

(*b*) *Recruitment of more than 50,000 "teacher aides" by* 1973–4.

(*c*) *Expansion of nursery schools.*

(*d*) *Smaller classes*, not to exceed thirty in educational priority areas.

(*e*) *The abolition of corporal punishment.*

Real progress on these proposals remains to be achieved. To the detriment of the whole educational system, the primary sector appears in the post-war period not to have enjoyed the enthusiastic support which it merited.

31. Comprehensive education. In 1965, a Labour Government circular requested local education authorities to submit within one year plans for reorganising secondary education on comprehensive lines and set out patterns which the Ministry would accept.

The following year, pressure was applied in a further circular which stated that approval would not be given to any new secondary school building projects which would be incompatible with a non-selective system of secondary education.

The Education Bill which would have imposed a system of comprehensive secondary education throughout the country was overtaken in 1970 by the dissolution of Parliament and a change of Government.

The new Conservative Government took a different view of secondary school reorganisation. In 1970, a Ministry circular stated that the Government's aim was to ensure that children should have secondary education opportunities suitable for their needs and abilities. The Government, however, believed it was wrong to impose a uniform pattern of secondary organisation on local education authorities by legislation or other means. The Labour Government circulars of 1965 and 1966 were therefore withdrawn.

The Labour Government of 1974 reverted to the earlier policy. During the following four years the comprehensive system was gradually imposed upon the whole of secondary schooling with only a few local authorities fighting a rearguard action.

Direct grant schools were given the choice of joining the system or becoming fully independent. Many chose the latter course.

During 1978, Labour Party discussion indicated an intention to continue the pressure on the independent sector in order that in due course this too would be absorbed into the system.

32. The Open University. In 1966, a White Paper had proposed the foundation of a "University of the Air". The proposal finally bore fruit in 1969 when the Open University became an autonomous institution.

The aim was to provide opportunities for university education to those "precluded from achieving their aims through existing institutions of higher education". It was therefore intended to cater primarily for adult students of whom surveys suggested there might be 100,000 potential candidates.

It was also anticipated that the opportunity of a higher education would now be afforded to those with few formal qualifications. This expectation has not been realised. While enrolments have been encouraging, the university has in the main catered for students already holding substantial qualifications such as teachers and other professional people who might well have followed part-time degree courses now offered in the polytechnics.

PROGRESS TEST 18

1. What educational opportunities existed for the working classes before 1800? (1)

2. "Until 1760, facilities for a formal education were quite equal to the needs of society." Examine this view critically. (2, 3)

3. For what reason may it be said that an obsession with doctrinal religion delayed educational advance in the eighteenth and nineteenth centuries? (3, 4, 8)

4. In the 1830s, the State began in a small way to subsidise education. How far were its motives altruistic? (6)

5. Why in the 1860s was education for all seen to be imperative? (11)

6. Assess the importance of the 1870 Education Act. (12, 13)

7. Describe the structure of secondary and further education prior to the Act of 1902. (14–16, 18, 19)

8. How far did the 1902 Act broaden educational opportunities? (17)

9. In what ways had public attitudes to education changed by 1939 and how were they made manifest in the period between the wars? (20–24)

10. Assess the strengths and the weaknesses of the 1944 Education Act (25–26)

11. Why was the Robbins Report described as "the most important social document since the Beveridge Report"? (27)

12. What was the outcome of the Newsom Report? (29)

13. What were the main recommendations of the Plowden Report? (30)

14. Outline the development of the dispute over comprehensive education. (31)

CHAPTER XIX

Trade Unionism

EIGHTEENTH-CENTURY LABOUR COMBINATIONS

1. Functions of trade unions. The proper role of trade unions in the changing economic order of modern times is frequently disputed. It is argued that they now have a positive part to play, in co-operation with the employer, in order to secure a better standard of life for the whole nation.

The history of trade unionism, however, is one of antagonism to the employer, since the movement had its birth in times when labour was oppressed and powerless to protect its interests in a society which had accepted the ideal of *laissez-faire*.

Combinations sprang from the need to provide this protection by negotiating collectively (*a*) wages, (*b*) hours, (*c*) conditions of work.

2. Labour relations under the domestic system. While industry was carried on in the home, workers seldom came together in large numbers and there was therefore little opportunity for collective action. There was, moreover, little need as long as medieval custom prevailed or the State regulated labour relations by the Statute of Artificers 1563 (*see* I, **31**). This Act:

(*a*) controlled conditions of entry and periods of apprenticeship to be served in different trades;

(*b*) gave to local J.P.s the task of drawing up schedules of wages which were revised annually.

The indications are that the system worked tolerably well while it was observed, although the latent antagonism of employer and employee was becoming increasingly manifest from an early date (*see* I, **24**).

3. The growth of industry. The growth of industry in the eighteenth and nineteenth centuries had two implications.

(*a*) It was a product of *laissez-faire*, and the acceptance of this doctrine enshrined the idea that wages should be negotiated freely between master and man.

The Statute of Artificers was therefore increasingly disregarded. Unprotected, the working man found himself in a hopelessly weak bargaining position and his condition deteriorated accordingly.

(*b*) For the first time, workers not only assembled in large numbers at their workplace, but also lived in close proximity in the new towns. There was therefore an increasing awareness of their common misfortunes and an opportunity to take some collective action.

4. Trade clubs. In certain crafts, social clubs for journeymen existed at a very early date. By the eighteenth century, they were well established in all crafts in the urban areas. Their purposes were:

(*a*) social evenings;

(*b*) the ceremonial initiation of apprentices after they had served their time;

(*c*) providing a form of labour exchange where masters could engage workers;

(*d*) the preservation of traditional practices within the trade.

From time to time, as the need arose, these trade clubs would federate temporarily to form a trade union in order to defend wage rates by strike action or by pressing for the observance of the Statute of Artificers. The eighteenth century provides a great deal of evidence of fairly powerful societies which were able, in this way, to take effective action.

EXAMPLE: (1) 1752: the Norwich woolcombers, through strike action, secured the dismissal of an unapprenticed man. (2) 1773: the Spitalfields silkweavers secured a specific Act of Parliament to regulate their wages and conditions. (3) 1777: the London goldbeaters, by this date, had built up a fairly substantial strike fund.

5. The repression of unions. The trade clubs were viewed by the employers with a certain amount of indifference, but when they united they caused much more concern. The law was vague, but it was generally agreed that labour combinations were of doubtful legality and almost any judge would decide against them when they were formed with the specific object of raising wages.

However, a combination formed to secure the observance of the Statute of Artificers was a different matter, and Parliament willingly received many petitions which had this object.

It was therefore a simpler matter for the employers to move against unions which actively pressed for increased wages. During the eighteenth century some forty Acts were passed, outlawing such combinations in specific trades. These measures culminated in the Combination Acts.

6. The Combination Acts 1799 and 1800. These were general laws which provided summary remedies against combination, thereby easing the employer's task of strike-breaking. The Acts prohibited:

(*a*) any combination between two or more workmen to gain either an increase in wages or a decrease in hours;

(*b*) incitement of another to leave work;

(*c*) refusal to work with any other workman.

7. Effect of the Combination Acts. Previously, the employer's remedy against combination had been to resort to the High Court, where he had almost always been successful. But this procedure was time-consuming, and workmen, by strike action, had been able to maintain their position on many occasions despite the fact that, later, their leaders may have been penalised.

The new laws provided that magistrates could deal summarily with offenders and therefore strikes could be quickly broken.

Moreover, in practice, the simple act of combination, without proof of further intent, was sufficient to secure conviction. Almost all forms of workers' association were therefore made impracticable.

OPPRESSION, UNREST, REFORM, 1800–24

8. Attempts to enforce statutory regulation of wages. Despite the difficulties of any form of collective action, workmen were able on a number of occasions to bring prosecutions against employers for failure to observe the Elizabethan statutes which governed their wages and the conditions of their trades. The Courts and Parliament proved hostile, and they had little success, e.g. in 1802 the West of England and the Yorkshire weavers prosecuted their employers for failure to adhere to apprenticeship and wage-fixing statues governing their trade. Parliament immediately suspended these statutes and renewed the suspension annually.

Continued pressure by different groups of workmen brought the repeal of all Acts empowering magistrates to fix wages (1813) and the repeal of the apprenticeship Acts in 1814.

9. Clandestine trade unions. Trade unions were illegal between 1800 and 1824, yet they did not cease to exist.

(*a*) *Friendly societies* enjoyed legal recognition under an Act of 1793. Their function was to assist distressed members from contributions made by other members of the society. Some trade unions were able to survive by adopting this disguise.

(*b*) *Other unions* were formed in defiance of the law and met in secret, e.g. the Society of Ironfounders, established in 1810, met by night on the moors in the Midlands and kept its records buried in the ground.

10. Deteriorating working conditions. The period was one in which any attempt to ameliorate the condition of the workman was savagely suppressed. His life became correspondingly more wretched.

(*a*) Penalties for combination included severe prison sentences and public whipping.

(*b*) The growing substitution of machinery for labour made the workman's position precarious.

(*c*) Fluctuating demand led to the use of much unapprenticed labour in periods of boom, with correspondingly greater unemployment difficulties in periods of depression.

11. The Luddites. Deprived of any legitimate means of resistance, workmen turned to violence. In 1811 and 1812 occurred a number of disturbances known as the Luddite riots (after the reputed leader, Ned Ludd, who supposedly had his headquarters in Sherwood Forest).

Possibly with the support of the trade clubs and the clandestine unions, bands of workmen up and down the country systematically attacked factories, particularly of despotic employers, and destroyed the machinery which they believed was undermining their livelihood. These disturbances were renewed in 1816 and were supported by hunger marches and popular demonstrations.

Government reaction was predictable. Sentences of death and transportation were imposed upon convicted "Luddites" and political agitation was curbed by the "Six Acts" of 1819 which in effect denied freedom of public meeting, freedom of speech and freedom of Press.

12. The reformers. Perhaps strangely, little working-class agitation was directed towards securing the repeal of the combination laws. Direct action to remedy immediate ills was preferred to the long-term benefits which legalised combination might bring.

However, men of great foresight were at work to educate public opinion. At the centre of these was Francis Place, formerly a master tailor. In 1818 he devoted himself wholly to the task of legalising the trade union movement. He gained the support of a group of radical M.P.s led by Joseph Hume and of a number of economists led by J. R. McCulloch.

Their skilful parliamentary manoeuvring led in 1824 to the repeal of the Combination Acts. With this repressive measure removed, they believed that the way was now open to a greater harmony between workman and employer in which all would share in the resulting prosperity. This belief was shattered by an immediate rash of strikes, and an alarmed Parliament sought to reimpose prohibition.

Hume and Place managed to forestall this reaction but an amending Act of 1825 reduced the area of freedom.

Nevertheless, a victory had been won, since the right to combine was now recognised in law, provided that:

(a) unions confined themselves to bargaining about wages and hours;

(b) there was no attempt made to picket, i.e. dissuade other employees from working.

Extension of this basic liberty took many years, but never again was the movement driven underground.

ABORTIVE ATTEMPTS AT COMBINATION, 1825–40

13. 1825–30: local unions. Once legalised, underground associations came out into the open and many new unions were formed, e.g. the London Shipwrights declared themselves and the Northumberland and Durham Colliers' Union was reformed.

Since they were purely local organisations, their financial base was narrow. In the years of expanding trade until 1829, when labour was in demand, they managed to survive, but depression in that year caused many to dissipate their funds in abortive strikes aimed at maintaining wages. The men were forced back to work on the employers' terms and the unions collapsed.

Among the unions defeated in this way were the Lancashire Cotton Spinners led by John Doherty. The moral which Doherty drew was that for a union to be effective it had to be national in its membership in order to prevent one district "blacklegging" on another and in order to build up a sufficiently sound financial base.

14. Doherty's National Association, 1830. In 1829, Doherty persuaded a conference of English, Irish and Scottish spinners to found the "Grand Central Union of all the Spinners in the United Kingdom".

He saw this as a first but necessary step towards the ultimate creation of a national union of all workmen. In 1830, at a representative conference of many trades, he succeeded in launching the National Association for the Protection of Labour, which every trade union in the country was urged to join. The Association prospered; by 1831 it had a membership of 100,000 and substantial dues were being paid to its central office in Manchester.

The employers fought back and, shortly, individual unions were too preoccupied with their own regional conflicts to spare a thought for building up the wider organisation.

By 1832, the National Association had disintegrated but many of the member unions which Doherty had helped into being survived despite the adverse state of trade and employment.

15. Owen's National Union. The Parliamentary Reform Bill had been much discussed and had led the working man to believe that his lot would be improved by constitutional action. In the event, the Reform Act of 1832 extended the franchise to the middle but not the working classes and the consequent disappointment gave a new impetus to union activity. In 1833 and 1834 the trade union movement, which since 1825 had advanced at only a very sedate pace, suddenly sprang to life and total membership expanded to an estimated 800,000.

Out of this upsurge was born in 1833 the Grand National Consolidated Trades Unions. Promoted by the socialist philanthropist, Robert Owen, this organisation had a membership in excess of half a million and embraced every sort of trade and every part of the country.

The enthusiasm which it generated was quickly dissipated by internal dissension, financial disorder and unsuccessful strikes; by the end of 1834 it had begun to crumble. Disillusioned, the working man began to turn once more to political action and union membership declined.

STRUGGLE FOR A SECURE FOUNDATION, 1840–75

16. "New model unionism". In the 1840s began a revival whose principles characterised "new model unions" (in contrast to principles which were developed at a later date).

Reacting to the disastrous experience of the 1820s and 1830s, the new movement favoured prudence, respectability and financial stability. Many unions rejected strike action, preferring to conserve their funds (which were derived from very substantial membership subscriptions) for the payment of friendly society benefits.

This aspect of their work was considered of equal importance with their trade activities. The latter were furthered by attempting to secure a control over admittance to the trade, thereby assuring a scarcity value to their labour.

Caution, sound organisation and the improving financial condition of skilled labour brought success and the formation of large amalgamated unions covering specific crafts, e.g. the Amalgamated Society of Engineers, formed in January 1851 and by the end of that year having a membership of 11,000 who paid a shilling (5p) a week, hitherto an unbelievable subscription.

17. Trades councils and the T.U.C. Trades councils are made up of the representatives of all the different unions in a given town. They were active in the 1820 and 1830s but only took firm root in the 1860s when unionism was more securely established.

The London Trades Council, founded in 1860, exercised considerable influence for about eleven years. (Many of the powerful new amalgamated unions had their offices in London and their General Secretaries sat on the Council.)

The "Junta", as it was described, was at pains to propagate the new principles of unionism. In this, it was not always successful and in the north, particularly, some unions preferred the decentralised, loosely organised but often bellicose organisations which had previously foundered. That they, too, did not meet the same fate was due to the general expansion of trade which ensured a high demand for labour.

Dissension within the movement delayed the convening of a fully representative Trades Union Congress, and the first "official" conference did not meet until 1868. The next, in 1869, formed the first "Parliamentary Committee", which was for many years the only central organisation of the trade union movement.

By 1871, the ideas of the Junta had prevailed and the ranks of the trade unions had closed. Unity came just in time to meet a challenge to the very existence of unionism.

18. A double threat to trade unionism.

(a) *The parliamentary threat.* A number of minor incidents and a crop of strikes led to the appointment of a Royal Commission to inquire into trade unions as a whole.

Antagonistic witnesses claimed that the unions had destroyed the "friendly relations" which existed between master and man; that they promoted strikes which harmed the workman financially; that they operated in restraint of trade.

Hopes were expressed in Parliament that the combination laws would be restored.

(b) *The threat from the judiciary.* In 1867 (the case of *Hornby* v. *Close*) a court decision prevented the Boilermakers' Society from suing an offical who had misappropriated union funds. In effect the court said that, while combination was not illegal, the law did not recognise the existence of trade unions and therefore they could not claim the law's protection of their funds.

19. Conclusions of the Royal Commission.
Having examined a great many trade union witnesses, who were able to put forward a very substantial case, the Commission's findings were far from what had been expected by those who had inspired the inquiry.

(a) *The majority report* was not too well disposed to the unions, but conceded that the inclination to strike did not increase with the strength of the union. It recommended some amelioration of the union's position.

(b) *The minority report* was much more favourably inclined and found that the disposition to strike grew less as the size and power of the union increased. It recommended:

    (i) full protection of funds;

    (ii) total repeal of the combination laws;

    (iii) registration and recognition of trade unions.

The report led to two Acts of Parliament.

20. Two conflicting Acts of Parliament, 1871.
In 1871, the Gladstone Government decided to regularise the whole postion of the trade unions with two simultaneous Acts of Parliament.

(a) *The Trade Union Act.* This favoured the unions by substantially adopting the recommendations of the 1867 Commission's minority report.

(*i*) A trade union was not illegal simply because it was "in restraint of trade".

(*ii*) A union could, if it desired, register with the Registrar of Friendly Societies.

(*iii*) A registered union could hold property and bring court actions.

(*b*) *The Criminal Law Amendment Act.* This Act almost completely nullified the advantages gained. It codified a vast number of recent magisterial decisions hostile to the unions.

Picketing and intimidation were made illegal and the magistrates' interpretation of intimidation was often ludicrous, e.g. "unfriendly looks"; persistently following; "watching premises"; presence of strikers in large numbers; urging others to strike.

All these actions now became crimes subject to heavy penalties. The campaign of protest which followed was conducted by union leaders of the Trades Union Congress.

21. Conspiracy and Protection of Property Act 1875. The Liberals having failed them, the trade unions took the reluctant decision to oppose them in the 1874 general election. The Gladstone Government toppled and the new Conservative Government fulfilled its part of a tacit bargain by repealing the Criminal Law Amendment Act.

In its place was passed the Conspiracy and Protection of Property Act.

(*a*) Peaceful picketing (but not peaceful persuasion) was expressly legalised.

(*b*) No action in furtherance of a trade dispute should be regarded as criminal when performed by a combination of workmen if it were not criminal when performed by individuals.

The Act effectively recognised the right of workmen to bargain collectively with their employers and to press their case by strike action and by peaceful picketing.

22. New unions and militancy, 1871–5. This was a period of national prosperity in which the big, long-established "amalgamateds" pursued their conciliatory policies to the point of becoming little more than rich friendly societies with dormant trade union purposes.

The union membership, dissatisfied with its leaders and wishing to take advantage of the high demand for labour, in a number of instances (e.g. the engineers) formed "splinter" groups and, before long, a wave of strikes swept the country. These were aimed chiefly at securing a nine hour day and they were frequently successful.

By 1875 trade unionism had reached a height of prosperity and security never previously experienced and had penetrated trades, such as agriculture and railways, which had hitherto seemed closed to it.

THE ORGANISATION OF UNSKILLED LABOUR, 1880–1900

23. The recruits. While skilled craftsmen had steadily improved their position, trade unionism had forgotten an army of unskilled workers who, as late as the 1880s, lived in the most deplorable conditions. Moreover, no move had yet been made to organise women's trades. The difficulties of organisation were as follows.

(*a*) In the event of a strike, unskilled labour could be easily replaced.

(*b*) Unskilled wages were low but current union subscriptions high.

(*c*) Of generally lower intelligence, the unskilled man was slower to appreciate the advantages of combination.

24. The "match strike". The spark which gave rise to the rapid spread of unionism amongst the unskilled was provided by a strike of 700 match girls. To everyone's surprise, the strike was well organised and the girls' claims were met.

25. The gasworkers' eight hour day, 1889. Labourers in gasworks, hastily organised by Tom Mann, John Burns and Will Thorne, pressed a claim for an eight hour day and, again to everyone's surprise, were successful. These incidents were the prelude to a major action.

26. The London dock strike, 1889. Tom Mann, John Burns and Ben Tillet (professional trade union organisers) led the London dock labourers in a strike which paralysed the port from the 20th August until the 16th September.

Sustained by help from well-wishers in various parts of the world, their claim for "the docker's tanner" (2½p) an hour was fully met.

The dock labourers had proved that unskilled workers could be effectively organised and during the 1890s the trade union movement was extended to embrace many more workers, on the railways, at sea, in the mines and in manufacturing.

27. Women's Trade Union League, 1889. Previously there had been suspicion of women in industry who might take men's jobs but 1889 saw the beginnings of a change of heart when the Women's Trade Union League was established and taken under the wing of the T.U.C.

In general, women workers proved more reluctant to adopt unions, but there was a steady extension of the movement, and from this time forward their interests were always considered in industrial negotiations.

28. The "new unionism". Towards the end of the century, the trade union movement began to adopt new principles.

(*a*) The importance of friendly society benefits began to recede as it was argued that the State should provide such benefits.

(*b*) The importance of political action, to secure such a state by constitutional means, grew accordingly.

The vote had been extended to town artisans in 1867 and to agricultural labourers in 1884. At first, union support went to Liberal candidates who were sympathetic to their cause, but the influence of Keir Hardie, the dominant socialist figure of the 1890s, led to the formation of the Independent Labour Party in 1893.

The object of the party was to persuade workers who already identified themselves as "Labour" (in particular, trade unionists) to return them to Parliament where, in time, a constitutional socialist state could be built.

VARYING FORTUNES OF UNIONISM, 1900–14

29. Loss of vigour. The early years of the twentieth century saw some deterioration in the workers' position. There was gradual inflation and a consequent decline in the value of real wages, which the unions seemed unable to oppose, since by now:

(*a*) they had become inefficiently organised;

(*b*) they were too apathetically led;

(*c*) they were too inclined to quarrel amongst themselves.

This impotence was exploited by two blows from the employers (*see* **30** and **32**).

30. The Taff Vale judgment. In 1900, a strike on the Taff Vale Railway was followed by a court action in which the Company secured substantial compensation from the men's union (the Amalgamated Society of Railway Servants) for the loss they had sustained.

This decision put the unions in an intolerable position. By assuring compensation to the employers, the right to strike was virtually removed.

It was seen that parliamentary action would provide the only remedy, but the Conservative Government was unwilling to move. The 1906 general election saw the Liberals returned with a large majority but accompanied by a substantial number of Labour members, who immediately pressed for a new Act.

31. The Trade Disputes Act 1906. This Act:

(*a*) protected the unions from civil law-suits when none could have resulted had the action been performed by an individual;

(*b*) legalised peaceful picketing in very positive terms;

(*c*) positively legalised actions in restraint of trade provided that they were not violent.

32. The Osborne judgment, 1909. W. V. Osborne, a branch secretary of the Amalgamated Society of Railway Servants, contested the right of his union to devote funds to political purposes.

Taken to appeal, the House of Lords found in his favour on the ground that the 1871 statute and subsequent Acts had never expressly included political activity within the purposes of the trade unions.

Unions had, in fact, devoted funds to political objectives—certainly since the Labour Representatives League of 1869 and probably long before that. The new-born Labour Party depended for its very existence upon such subscriptions, which paid its M.P.s' salaries and election expenses.

Labour M.P.s managed to scrape sufficient funds to struggle back to Parliament through the two general elections of 1910 and immediately pressed for a reversal of the Osborne judgment.

The Liberal Government was in no hurry to oblige but saved the Labour members from starvation or resignation by giving all M.P.s an immediate salary of £400 per annum.

Relief from the Osborne judgment was not granted until 1913.

33. Trade Union (Amendment) Act 1913. This Act provided that:

(*a*) political activity was legal if it was approved by a majority of members;

(*b*) political funds should be kept separate;

(*c*) members wishing to refrain from political contributions should be permitted to do so without victimisation.

Neither trade unionists nor their opponents were satisfied by this measure. The former saw it as only a partial restoration of their freedom of political action and the latter feared the indirect coercion of the union members who were not Labour Party supporters.

UNIONISM BETWEEN THE WARS

34. Unfavourable conditions. Trade unionism has always found its greatest strength in periods of expansion and prosperity, when it has been able to take advantage of labour's scarcity value. Conversely, in periods of depression and unemployment its bargaining position has been weakened and workers have doubted its effectiveness in protecting their interests. A corresponding tendency may be noted in the alternation of industrial and political action.

The period between the wars was, in general, one of depression and high unemployment in which unionism lost ground which it only regained in the late 1930s.

35. Loss of membership, 1921–4. The brief post-war boom was followed by a steep decline in trade. In 1921, organised labour fought and lost a crucial battle.

The coal mine owners announced a cut in wages which the miners resisted with a strike, calling upon the other two great members of the 1914 Triple Alliance for support. The railwaymen (N.U.R.) and the transport workers (T.W.F.) hesitated, issued a strike order and then withdrew it. The miners fought alone and, in the summer, were defeated.

Whether this defeat was in fact attributable to lack of solidarity may be questioned, but certainly the rank and file membership believed so, and by 1924, 3 million members had been lost.

However, an increasing number of Labour Members were now being returned to Parliament, and in 1924, with Liberal support, Ramsay MacDonald was able for a few months to form a government.

Inspired by a revival in trade and the presence of a Labour Government, there was, in 1924, a renewed burst of union activity in which dockers, miners and transport workers secured gains.

This success was, however, short-lived.

36. General Strike, 1926. In 1925, trade took a further plunge and the mine owners were the first to announce cuts in wages. The miners appealed successfully to the General Council of the T.U.C. (a standing body formed in 1920) for support and a general strike was decided upon.

The Government having refused assistance, in May there was an almost complete stoppage of work throughout the country.

Inadequacy of strike funds, but more particularly the vacillating leadership of the General Council, led to the breaking of the strike after nine days and, with the exception of the miners, who fought on alone, there was a gradual return to work.

37. The results of defeat. The resounding defeat of the whole labour movement led to the following.

(*a*) A steep decline in union membership.

(*b*) A general attack on wages, which was resisted with partial success.

(*c*) The Trade Disputes and Trade Unions Act 1927. Union political activity was weakened by making it necessary for members expressly to contribute to the political levy. By the 1913 Act, they had to choose not to contribute. The new Act meant a potential loss of subscriptions from politically apathetic members. It also placed fresh restrictions upon picketing; forbade Civil Service unions to affiliate to any other organisation; and forbade general strikes and most sympathetic strikes.

38. The 1930s. The crash on the New York stock exchange in 1929 heralded a depression which sapped the strength of the trade union movement, as the following membership figures illustrate: 1929, 5.5 million; 1927, 5 million; 1932, 4.5 million. During the worst of the depressions, the unions could only try to hold on, avoiding disputes and making no attempt to extend unionism into new industries.

The employers for their part refrained from any further attacks, secure in the knowledge that if the unions should become troublesome, they could be tamed with the 1927 Act.

Only after 1933, with the slow upswing of trade and the gradual decrease in unemployment, did the fortunes of the unions begin to recover.

THE TRADE UNIONS SINCE 1945

39. The Trade Disputes and Trade Union Act 1946. The 1927 Act had been much resented, but all attempts to have it modified were unsuccessful. The 1945 Labour Government remedied this with a repealing Act which said that the law should be as if the previous measure had never been enacted.

40. Rookes v. Barnard (1964). A judicial decision having far-reaching effects on trade union law was delivered on the 21st January 1964, when the House of Lords found that under certain circumstances trade union officials were not protected by the 1906 Trade Disputes Act and were liable to be sued for intimidation.

In 1961, an action had been won by a Mr Rookes against his union, the Association of Engineering and Shipbuilding Draughtsmen. This union had an agreement with B.O.A.C. whereby its members contracted not to strike without first making use of all the negotiating machinery. It also insisted upon a closed shop and when Rookes resigned from the union threatened strike action if he were not dismissed. Under duress, B.O.A.C. complied.

The court found that this dismissal had been secured by an incitement to illegal action by the union, namely breach of contract and therefore the dismissal itself was illegal. The High Court decision was reversed by the Appeal Court in 1962 but reversed yet again when the case was taken to the House of Lords.

The decision caused grave concern in the trade union movement since it removed an immunity which it believed it enjoyed. The case prompted immediate action by the incoming Labour Government in 1964 in two directions:

(a) *a Royal Commission* (*see* **42**);
(b) *amending legislation* (*see* **41**).

41. Trade Disputes Act, August 1965. The substance of this Act was as follows.

An act done in furtherance of a trade dispute shall not be actionable in tort on the ground only that it consists in threatening that:

(*a*) a contract of employment will be broken;

(*b*) a third party will be induced to break a contract of employment. (It was this clause which would have been applicable in the *Rookes* v. *Barnard* case.)

42. Donovan Report, 1969. A Royal Commission under Lord Donovan was appointed in February 1965 "to consider relations between management and employees and the role of trade unions and employers' associations in promoting the interests of their members and in accelerating the social and economic advance of the nation with particular reference to the law affecting the activities of these bodies".

The Commission reported in 1969. While largely rejecting curbs on unofficial strikes the Report urged improvements in industrial relations by voluntary collective bargaining at local level and recommended the following.

(*a*) *An Industrial Relations Commission* to investigate labour difficulties.

(*b*) *Labour Tribunals* to hear individual complaints of breach of contract.

(*c*) *An independent review body* to hear complaints against individual trade unions.

The joint C.B.I. and T.U.C. reaction was to agree to the formation of an Industrial Relations Commission with powers to investigate a firm or an industry provided that it restricted itself to procedural arrangements and did not attempt to influence the content of collective bargaining.

43. "In Place of Strife" White Paper, 1969. The Government reacted to the Report with a White Paper which in the main accepted the Donovan proposals. Additionally, it proposed to confer upon the Secretary of State for Employment and Productivity the power to order a twenty-eight day conciliation pause and to order a ballot of a trade union's members before it could call an official strike.

These proposals were to be introduced in a comprehensive Industrial Relations Bill. Organised labour was not very sympathetic to the Government's intentions, particularly where it seemed that the power of strike action might be restricted.

In 1970, with a change of Government, the Bill was dropped. However, one proposal had already been implemented, namely a Commission on Industrial Relations.

44. Commission on Industrial Relations, 1969. The C.I.R. was set up by Royal Warrant in 1969. General or particular problems in industrial relations could be referred to it, e.g. collective bargaining, procedural agreements, recognition and negotiating rights.

It was to publish reports on its inquiries together with an annual general report.

45. Industrial Relations Act, August 1971. Upon assuming office the Conservative Government introduced its own industrial relations legislation. The purpose of the Bill was stated to be the promotion of good industrial relations in accordance with the following four general principles.

(*a*) Collective bargaining freely and responsibly conducted.

(*b*) Developing and maintaining orderly procedures in industry for the peaceful settlement of disputes by negotiation and with regard to the interest of the whole community.

(*c*) Free associations of workers in independent trade unions and employers in employers associations, so organised as to be responsible and representatvie.

(*d*) Freedom and security for workers, protected by adequate safeguards against unfair industrial practices whether on the part of employers or others.

Despite massive opposition in Parliament from the trade union movement the Bill was enacted on the 5th August 1971.

Its main provisions were as follows.

(*e*) The formulation of a code of industrial relations practice. The final draft of this code was published in January 1972. It set out the responsibilities of management, trade unions, employers associations and workers. It also set standards for effective communication and consultation status, security and working conditions.

(*f*) The protection of the rights of the individual in respect of trade union membership and unfair dismissal.

(*g*) The enforceability of written collective agreements.

(*h*) New regulations for the registration and conduct of trade unions and employers associations.

(*i*) The extension of the jurisdiction of the Industrial Tribunals set up in 1964.

(*j*) A National Industrial Relations Court to be set up with the power to fine and award damages against employers and trade unions who acted illegally. There would also be power to take civil proceedings against unofficial strike leaders.

(*k*) A statutory basis was now given to the Commission on Industrial Relations.

46. Resistance to the 1971 Act. The attempt to bring the conduct of industrial relations within the framework of law was bitterly resisted by the trade unions who viewed it as an attack upon the privileges which they enjoyed under the Acts of 1906 and 1965. Particularly resented were the attempt to give the force of law to collective agreements, the threat to the principle of the closed shop and the requirement to register in order to enjoy certain tax advantages.

Registration was viewed as an acceptance of the legislation and the T.U.C. indicated that its members should not comply. Meanwhile the Labour Party declared that on being returned to office the whole Act would be immediately repealed.

47. Trade Union and Labour Relations Act 1974. Upon election in 1974 the new Labour Government immediately enacted legislation with the following provisions.

(*a*) *Repeal of the 1971 Act.*

(*b*) *Institutions abolished.* The Commission on Industrial Relations, the National Industrial Relations Court and the Registrar of Trade Unions and Employers' Associations were abolished.

(*c*) *Legal immunities.* The pre-1971 position was restored and extended.

    (*i*) Disputes over union recognition by employers would be included within the definition of a trade dispute.

    (*ii*) Union officials would be protected against action for civil conspiracy.

    (*iii*) There would be immunity for breach of contract with an extension to all types of contract including commercial contracts. Equally, the immunity provided by the 1965 Act for threats to induce a breach of contract was restored.

(*d*) *Torts.* Protection for action against torts was restored and extended to threatened torts.

(*e*) *Picketing.* The right of picketing was restored to the 1906 position and extended to the right to communicate with the occupants of vehicles.

In return for these legal privileges the trade unions largely surrendered their function in respect of free collective bargaining, agreeing to support the Government in the operation of a voluntary wages policy (*see* XII, 24(*f*)).

PROGRESS TEST 19

1. What was the original function of labour combinations? **(1)**

2. What institutions favoured harmonious labour relations under the domestic system? **(2)**

3. What new circumstances created an environment which was favourably disposed to labour combinations? **(3)**

4. Would it be true to say that the functions of the eighteenth-century trade clubs were identical with those of the later trade unions? **(4)**

5. By what strategy were the employers able to gain the support of Parliament and the enactment of the combination laws? **(5, 6)**

6. Who were the Luddites? Describe the conditions which gave rise to their activities. **(8–11)**

7. Who were Frances Place and Joseph Hume? Would you say that they favoured militant trade union action? **(12)**

8. Assess the importance of John Doherty in the history of the trade union movement. **(14)**

9. Would you say that the trade union movement was assisted or retarded by the activities of Robert Owen? **(15)**

10. What were the outstanding characteristics of the new trade unions of the 1840s? **(16)**

11. Who were the "Junta" and what part did they play in promoting the new ideals of trade unionism? **(17)**

12. What difficulties did the unions encounter in the 1870s? **(18)**

13. Explain the paradox of Gladstone's trade union legislation of 1871. **(20)**

14. How was this legislation amended by the Conservative Government of 1874? **(21)**

15. Comment on the general position of the trade union movement in 1875. **(22)**

16. Outline the course of events in 1889 which led to the extension of unionism into the unskilled trades. **(23–26)**

17. Describe the principal characteristics of "new unionism". (28)

18. What was at stake in the Taff Vale case and how was the trade union position subsequently strengthened? (30, 31)

19. How was organised labour adversely affected by the Osborne judgment and how was the position remedied? (32, 33)

20. What circumstances weakened the trade union movement during the 1920s and resulted in the Act of 1927? (34–37)

21. In what respect did the *Rookes* v. *Barnard* case expose a flaw in the 1906 Trade Disputes Act? (31, 40)

22. Outline the provisions of the Industrial Relations Act 1971. (45)

23. Why was the 1971 Act bitterly resented? (46)

24. What was the response of the 1974 Government? (47)

CHAPTER XX

Factory Legislation

REGULATION OF THE TEXTILE INDUSTRY

1. The factory system. In the eighteenth century, the harnessing of power to machinery had results of the most profound importance.

(*a*) *Destruction of the domestic system.* It was now no longer possible for the worker to practise his craft in his cottage. Power could only be made available if a number of machines and their operators were assembled together in the same building. The surviving domestic workers were subjected to the increasingly severe competition of machines, and by 1850 the domestic system had been entirely displaced.

(*b*) *Poor working conditions.* When the employer lacked capital, the factories were makeshift and often completely unsuited to their purpose. When they were specially designed, it was with a view to maximising profit, without any regard to the interest of the workman. In an age which had rejected Government control, the buildings were therefore insanitary, badly lit and unventilated, while machinery was often dangerous and fatal accidents frequent.

(*c*) *Child labour.* Power-driven machinery could often be supervised well enough by a child. Since their wages were much lower than those of an adult, an increasing number of children were employed.

This was made easy by the 1601 poor law, which provided for pauper children to be apprenticed to a trade. They worked seven days a week for hours which scarcely gave them time for eating or sleeping.

NOTE: The conditions of child labour under the factory system were probably no worse than they had been under the domestic system. The difference lay in the fact that they could now be more readily observed.

(*d*) *Final destruction of workman's independence.* Even the semblance of independence enjoyed by the workman was shattered. Previously he had used his own tools in his own premises and for a number of employers. Now he was brought together with many others to work for a single employer in a factory in which he owned no share. The divorce of labour and capital was complete.

(e) *Urbanisation.* Concentration of industry in factories called for an equivalent concentration of workers in the towns. Terraces of houses were run up back-to-back by the factory owners with the object of accommodating as many people as possible in the smallest space at the lowest cost. There resulted slum conditions of the worst kind.

2. Decay of Elizabethan labour statutes (*see* XIX, 3). The rising spirit of *laissez-faire* brought all forms of State regulation into disrepute and the Elizabethan statutes which governed wages and conditions of work were increasingly disregarded (*see* X1X, 8). By 1814, they had all been formally repealed.

It was argued that the fairest possible contract of employment would always be reached by free bargaining between master and man. Since the bargain was always struck from positions of unequal strength, the workman was now at the mercy of his employer.

The argument was particularly absurd when applied to children, who plainly were in no position to protect their own interests. It was on their behalf that action was first taken by humanitarians who were outraged by the excesses of the early stages of the Industrial Revolution.

3. Decision of Manchester magistrates, 1784. The Manchester magistrates refused to indenture apprentices who might be compelled to work at night or more than ten hours a day.

NOTE: The magistrates were only extending their duties in administration of the 1601 poor law. They did not show any desire to exercise control over industry.

4. Manchester Board of Health, 1795. In 1784, fever was rife in many Lancashire cotton mills. Investigation showed it to be the result of the insanitary conditions of work of pauper children and there were recommendations that more control should be exercised.

In 1795, the Manchester Board of Health was set up to carry out further investigations into the conditions in which children were employed. They found them deplorable (although recognising that all factories were not equally bad) and made recommendations which passed into law (*see* 5).

5. The Health and Morals of Apprentices Act 1802. Sir Robert Peel (senior) passed this first Factory Act, which, like the Manchester magistrates' decision, is to be seen as an aid to J.P.s in discharging their duties under the 1601 poor law rather than an attempt at direct control of industry. The Act provided that:

(a) no apprentice in the cotton or woollen industries should work more than twelve hours a day and should not in any case work later than 9 p.m.;

(b) apprentices were to be adequately clothed and accommodated;

(c) provision was to be made for their religious instruction;

(d) two "visitors" were to be appointed, a Minister and a J.P., to enforce the Act.

Evaluation of the Act. There was much evasion and the system of inspection proved ineffective, probably because the "visitors" were often friends of the employers.

Its true importance therefore lay not in its intrinsic merits but in the fact that it paved the way for later Acts.

6. Employment of unapprenticed children. The Act protected only those bound by articles of apprenticeship. There was, therefore, a strong incentive to avoid the obligations of the Act by employing wage-earning children, of whom there was no shortage. It was still cheaper than employing adults, who themselves were not loth to put their children into the factories to supplement their own meagre earnings.

In 1815, Sir Robert Peel introduced a Bill to regulate all child labour. It was not carried out, but an inquiry resulted which, together with the agitation of the wealthy philanthropist and industrialist Robert Owen, led to the 1819 Act.

7. Factory Act 1819. It applied only to cotton mills but was more comprehensive than its predecessor.

(a) No child under the age of nine was to be employed.

(b) A maximum twelve hour day was set for those under sixteen.

(c) One and a half hours were to be allowed for meals, to give a maximum daily attendance of thirteen and a half hours.

Evaluation of the Act. Inspection was difficult and the Act was never properly enforced. It did, however, set a precedent in acknowledging that where children were employed protection was necessary.

In the following decade, agitation continued and there were amending Acts, in 1820, 1825 and 1830, all of which were repealed by the Factory Act of 1831.

8. Factory Act 1831. Cotton mills only were affected.

(*a*) A maximum twelve hour day was extended to all under the age of eighteen.

(*b*) Night work was prohibited to all under the age of twenty-one.

Like the previous Acts, enforcement proved difficult and evasion was extensive. By now, however, there was growing concern that Parliament's wishes should be so disregarded. Champions of factory reform such as Richard Oastler, Michael Sadler and Anthony Ashley Cooper (who became Earl of Shaftesbury in 1851) were attracting public attention and, in 1833, Ashley's efforts in the Commons produced a new Factory Act.

9. Factory Act 1833. It applied to the whole textile industry with the exception of silk. Its provisions were:

(*a*) prohibition of the employment of all children under nine;

(*b*) a maximum working week of forty-eight hours for children of eight to thirteen, with no more than nine hours in any one day;

(*c*) two hours' compulsory schooling each day;

(*d*) a maximum twelve hour day for young persons under eighteen;

(*e*) four full-time factory inspectors were appointed to enforce the law and were given power to impose penalties for infringements.

Evaluation of the Act. The Act's broader scope had been made necessary by the extension of capitalist methods of production from the cotton industry into the more conservative woollen industry. Since conditions in the former had been regulated without economic ill-effects, there was plainly every reason to extend controls when the same conditions arose in other industries.

In its operation, the importance of this Act cannot be overstated:

(*i*) It established an impartial professional Factory Inspectorate, which was shortly expanded. Beyond their enforcement of the law, the inspectors in their quarterly reports provided the Government with information on factory conditions which was the basis of most subsequent legislation.

(*ii*) It provided the beginnings of compulsory education (but only for children who worked in the factories).

10. Obstacles to the efficient operation of the Act. Many employers remained unconvinced that the Act would not damage trade by inflating costs. They therefore obstructed the inspectors, often with the connivance of their employees.

(*a*) *Baptismal certificates* were often unreliable evidence of a child's age, since they gave rise to fraudulent practices, e.g. they were frequently bought and sold.

(*b*) *The relay system* was operated and this made it difficult for the inspector to ascertain how long a child had worked in a day. Teams of children began and finished work at different times.

(*c*) *Fear of employees* hindered the inspectors, as the employees knew that in making a complaint they were jeopardising their livelihood.

(*d*) *Bribery* might accomplish the same objects as fear.

11. Peel's Factory Act 1844. The Act embraced all textile factories, with the exception of silk.

(*a*) The age limit for child labour was reduced from nine to eight (as some compensation, compulsory registration of births (introduced in 1836) now made evasion of the age limit more difficult).

(*b*) A maximum six and a half hour day with three hours' schooling for children of eight to thirteen.

(*c*) A maximum twelve hour day for young people under eighteen and all women.

(*d*) Fencing was to be provided for dangerous machinery.

12. Fielden's Factory Act 1847. Agitation for a ten hour day had begun in the 1830s and now reaped its reward in the second major Factory Act.

(*a*) *Its supporters argued in its favour as follows.*

(*i*) Excessive hours of work were sapping the nation's vitality and stunting its physical, intellectual and moral growth. Unless the position were remedied, Britain would yield her foremost place amongst the nations to others who were more enlightened.

(*ii*) In the long run, the nation would benefit, even commercially, from shorter hours, since a tired worker was an inefficient one.

(b) *The Act's opponents argued as follows.*

(i) The employer's profit was made in the last hour of the day. The value of the product of the preceding hours simply covered costs. To remove profit would be to remove all incentive to enterprise.

(ii) The social consequences of more leisure would be undesirable. The assumption of the mid-nineteenth century was that the working man was instinctively degenerate and that leisure time would always be spent in immoral pursuits. In any case, the manufacturers were for the most part Non-conformists with a strong Puritan streak. They saw virtue in work for its own sake.

The Act applied only to the textile mills and conceded a ten hour day to young persons and women. Because of the correlation of their work, however, it was anticipated that men would benefit indirectly.

13. Amending legislation. The employer reacted to the 1847 law by reviving the "relay stystem". The factory was open from 5.30 a.m. until 8.30 p.m. It was therefore difficult to ensure the observance of the Act. The position was remedied by the following.

(a) *Factory Act 1850.* The hours of work of women and young persons were specified (6 a.m. to 6 p.m. with a one hour break for meals and a 2 p.m. finish on Saturdays). There was thus an extension of the working day to ten a half hours.

(b) *Factory Act 1853.* The 1850 Act did not cover children, who might still be employed as early as 5.30 a.m. and as late as 8.30 p.m. The 1853 Act blocked this loophole.

14. The importance of Fielden's Act. The 1847 Act marked a turning-point. The principle of *laissez-faire* was virtually abandoned in the textile mills and when experience proved that Britain's competitive position was not weakened and that costs did not rise, the hostility of the employers to factory legislation diminished.

At this time, in the textile factories, the law directly regulated the employment of women, children and young persons and indirectly the employment of men in so far as their work was dependent on that of the former.

THE EXTENSION OF LEGISLATION IN FACTORIES AND WORKSHOPS

15. The inclusion of subsidiary textile trades. The improved conditions of the textile workers contrasted sharply with those obtaining in associated trades.

In Parliament, Shaftesbury continued to press for reform and in 1862, secured the extension of the Acts to lace-making factories and subsequently to calico printing and bleaching and dyeing.

16. The inclusion of non-textile trades. A Royal Commission inquired into conditions in the non-textile trades between 1862 and 1866. Its reports led to the following legislation.

(a) *Factory Act 1864.* Working conditions having been proved deleterious to health, regulation was extended to the manufacture of earthenware, matches, cartridges, percussion caps, paper staining and fustian cutting.

(b) *Factory Acts (Extension) Act 1867.* Existing legislation was extended to all factories where more than fifty people were employed and to certain specified industries, irrespective of the numbers employed, e.g. blast furnaces, iron and steel mills, glass, paper making, tobacco, printing and bookbinding.

(c) *Workshop Regulation Act 1867.* This was a comprehensive measure which applied to all establishments where less than fifty were employed. A distinction between factories and workshops was thereby made. This Act provided that:

(i) children could not be employed below the age of eight and only half-time between eight and thirteen;

(ii) the maximum working hours for women and young persons were set at ten and a half, but these might be at any time between 5 a.m. and 9 p.m.;

(iii) the local sanitary authorities would enforce the law.

Criticism. The Act was defective in being permissive, i.e. the local authorities might or might not take action. Moreover, like earlier legislation, it failed to define the working day, thereby exposing the workshops to the dangers of the "relay system".

17. Amending legislation.

(a) *Factory and Workshop Act 1871.* Enforcement was made the responsibility of the Factory Inspectorate, and junior inspectors were appointed for the additional work. In view of the amount of this, for many years enforcement proved difficult.

(b) *Factory Act 1874.* The working day in the textile industry was reduced from ten and a half hours to ten for women and young persons and the minimum age for the employment of children was raised to ten.

(c) *A demand now arose* for the codification of the various Acts and, in 1875, a Royal Commission was appointed. This led to a further Act in 1878 (*see* (*d*)).

(d) *Factory and Workshops Act 1878.* The distinction between factory and workshop was redefined. Irrespective of the number of people employed, an establishment using power-driven machinery was described as a factory.

Workshops were described as establishments which did not employ mechanical power and they in turn were sub-divided into various categories to which different regulations would apply.

Criticism. Some weakness resulted from the division of responsibility for the enforcement of sanitary regulations. In some cases, it lay within the province of the Factory Inspectorate and in other cases was the responsibility of the local sanitary inspectors.

18. Factory and Workshop (Consolidating) Act 1891. The whole subject was reviewed, with greater emphasis laid upon sanitary and accident regulations. The minimum age for the employment of children in factories was raised to eleven, and the Factory Inspectorate was given greater powers of access.

19. Labour of children.

(a) *The Factory Act 1895* limited the working week of children to thirty hours.

(b) *The Factory and Workshops Act 1901* codified existing legislation. It also raised the age at which a child might enter a factory to twelve.

(c) *The Education Act 1918* (*see* XVIII, **21**) provided that all children should attend school full time until the age of fourteen. Only then could they enter a factory.

(d) *The Education Act 1944* (*see* XVIII, **25**) raised the school-leaving age to fifteen, with provision for it to be raised again to sixteen.

20. The Factories Act 1937. The 1901 Act provided the basis of factory law until 1937, when a review was made. There were no innovations but modifications included the following.

(a) *The maximum working week* for women and young persons was reduced from fifty-five and a half hours in textile and sixty hours in non-textile factories to forty-eight hours, and for young people aged under sixteen to forty-four hours. Limits were also set to the amount of overtime permissible.

(b) *Factory law was extended* to a variety of other industries, e.g. building and engineering.

(c) *A great many detailed health regulations* were laid down, e.g. lighting, ventilation, sanitation. The Act was supported by:

(i) the Young Persons Employment Act 1938, which extended the protection of the 1937 Act to occupations not previously covered, e.g. delivery boys;

(ii) the Shops Act 1938, which regulated the hours of young shop employees.

21. Factories Act 1961. The mainstream of factory legislation was continued with this Act which, while making no major innovations, updated the detailed Regulations of the 1937 Act. It remains the principal legislation governing the conditions in which some 8–9 million workers are employed.

22. Offices Act 1960. Hitherto, white-collar workers had received no protection from factory legislation. A private member's Bill was enacted in 1960 giving the Home Secretary permissive powers to issue Regulations. In the event, no Regulations were made since the Government was about to introduce more comprehensive legislation of its own.

23. Offices, Shops and Railway Premises Act 1963. The Act applied to all shops and offices and to most railway buildings adjacent to the permanent way. The main provisions were as follows.

(a) *Cleanliness.* Appropriate standards of cleanliness of all fittings.

(b) *Space.* A minimum 40 square feet (about 3.7m²) of floor space for each permanent employee.

(c) *Temperatures.* Reasonable temperatures of not less than 60.8° F (16° C) to be maintained.

(d) *Ventilation and lighting* of adequate standards to be maintained.

(e) *Fire escapes and fire-fighting equipment* to be provided.

(f) *Sanitation and washing facilities* to be provided.

Enforcement was placed in the hands of local authority inspectors in the case of shops and offices. The Factory Inspectorate was made responsible for offices in factories and railway buildings.

24. Health and Safety at Work etc. Act 1974. The intention of this Act was to rationalise and extend preceding legislation into a comprehensive system of law dealing with the health and safety of people at work and with the protection of the public where they might be affected by work activities.

It also established a Health and Safety Commission and an Executive responsible for the administration of the legislation. The members of the Commission are drawn from employers' organisations, trade unions, local authorities and professional bodies. The Factory Inspectorate was transferred to the Executive from the Department of Employment and was given powers to issue improvement and prohibition notices.

Upon the recommendations of the Executive and the Commission, the appropriate Minister, usually the Secretary of State for Employment, makes detailed Regulations to supplement the general requirements of the Act. The Commission can also issue codes of practice giving practical guidance on how to comply with the legislation.

The aims of the Act can be summarised as:

(*a*) the protection of all people at work;

(*b*) the protection of the public against hazards arising from work activities;

(*c*) the control of dangerous substances;

(*d*) the control of emissions into the atmosphere;

(*e*) the placing of responsibilities on employers, the self-employed, employees, designers, manufacturers and suppliers to ensure that their activities do not endanger health and safety.

PROGRESS TEST 20

1. State briefly the principal social consequences of the mechanisation of industry. **(1)**

2. Outline the circumstances which led up to the first Factory Act in 1802. **(2–5)**

3. What was the weakness of the 1802 Act and how was it remedied? **(6, 7)**

4. Assess the importance of the 1833 Factory Act and explain why its scope was broader than its predecessors'. **(9)**

5. How was the full operation of the Act impeded? **(10)**

6. What arguments centred on the ten hour day introduced by the Act of 1847? Why was the passage of the Act of such importance? **(12–14)**

7. Describe how in the 1860s the scope of factory legislation was broadened to cover non-textile trades. **(16)**

8. What was the administrative weakness of early legislation governing workshops? **(16, 17)**

9. By what measures was the employment of children progressively restricted after 1891? **(18–20)**

10. To what extent are employees in 1978 better protected than they were in 1937? **(20–24)**

CHAPTER XXI

Central Government Finance

SCOPE, ORIGIN AND DEVELOPMENT TO 1697

1. Scope of national finance. There are the following three aspects.

(*a*) *Expenditure*. While the doctrine of *laissez-faire* was prevalent, the function of Government was seen to lie only in the maintenance of national security, i.e. the provision of defence and the presentation of law and order. Government spending increased therefore only during periods of war.

The slow growth of health, welfare and education services during the nineteenth century was financed almost entirely by local government. Only during the twentieth century has there been a great enlargement of the public sector of the national economy, with central Government assuming responsibility for a wide variety of services. Moreover, since 1945, public expenditure has been used as an instrument of economic policy to regulate the level of business activity (*see* Appendix I).

(*b*) *Taxation*. The level of taxation has risen in step with the growth of public expenditure. However, whereas in the nineteenth century taxation existed simply to provide Government with a revenue, today it is seen also as a major instrument of economic planning.

(*c*) *Borrowing*. When revenue has been insufficient to cover expenditure, Government has of necessity borrowed from the public. The National Debt would therefore be more understandably described as the Government debt. It comprises the following.

(*i*) The funded debt: no date is set for repayment. It is composed almost entirely of securities publicly quoted on the stock exchange, e.g. 3½ per cent War Loan (*see* X, **12**).

(*ii*) The floating debt: short-term borrowing. Expenditure is fairly uniform throughout the year, while revenue tends to be concentrated at the end of the year.

(*iii*) The unfunded debt: various dates are set for repayment.

Non-existent at the beginning of the twentieth century, it now accounts for the bulk of the National Debt. Also in this category fall National Savings certificates.

(*iv*) Foreign debt: the smallest category, it comprises chiefly dollars borrowed from the U.S.A. and Canada for reconstruction since 1945.

2. Origin. Central Government finance in the modern sense dates from the Revolution of 1688, after which time the supreme authority of Parliament was undisputed.

Previously, Parliament wielded power only through its ability to deny funds to the Crown. Public finance had therefore been a political weapon, but now it could be managed on sounder principles.

National expenditure was separated from the monarch's personal expenditure and money was now raised for designated purposes.

3. Financial methods in the late seventeenth century.

(*a*) *Expenditure*. War with France caused a steady growth in expenditure during the last decade of the century.

(*b*) *Taxation*. Customs and excise duties (indirect taxes) were the traditional source of revenue, but in 1692 a direct tax on the annual rentable value of land was set at 4*s*. (20p) in the £.

(*c*) *Borrowing*. Parliament offered greater security against loans than had been afforded by the Crown. Certain taxes were specified for the payment of interest and the repayment of capital.

In 1693, however, public borrowing followed a new trend. A loan of £1,200,000 was made to the Government by a group of businessmen who, the following year, received a charter to found the Bank of England (*see* IX, 6). No date was set for repayment and this was the beginning of the funded debt. By the end of the war with France, in 1697, the debt had grown to £21 million.

GROWTH OF THE NATIONAL DEBT TO 1816

4. The financial burden of wars. The magnitude of the Debt was believed to be a serious drain on national prosperity but, despite the efforts of statesmen such as Walpole and Pitt, it continued to grow, in consequence of increasingly costly wars:

Period	Size of the Debt
War of the Spanish Succession, 1702–13:	£54 million
A period of peace under Walpole, 1721–39:	£44 million
War of the Austrian Succession, 1740–8:	£71 million
Seven Years' War, 1756–63:	£128 million
War of American Independence, 1776–81:	£238 million
Reduction effected by Pitt's sinking fund, 1783–93:	£228 million
French Revolutionary wars, 1793–1802:	£488 million
Napoleonic wars, 1803–15:	£819 million

5. Sir Robert Walpole in office, 1720–42. His reforms reduced the Debt and pointed toward the free trade age of the nineteenth century.

(*a*) *Taxation.* He appreciated the stifling effect upon trade of innumerable customs duties. If the volume of trade could be stimulated by reducing them, the revenue would also benefit. This he accomplished, simultaneously giving further assistance to importers by setting up bonded warehouses for certain commodities. Importers were thereby enabled to pay duty when they withdrew goods from bond instead of having to find large sums for payment immediately after ships were discharged.

These reforms increased revenue so that it became possible to reduce the land tax from 4*s.* (20p) to 1*s.* (5p).

(*b*) *The National Debt.* A sinking fund of £1 million per annum was set aside from revenue for repayment of the Debt. But for its periodic diversion to other purposes, the Debt would have been reduced further than the £44 million achieved by 1739.

6. Pelham's conversion, 1749. The burden of the Debt was increased by the War of the Austrian Succession, both in respect of size and in the rise in interest rates to 4 per cent.

However, the post-war period was a time of prosperity and cheap money in which Henry Pelham succeeded in reducing the weight of interest payments by making a conversion.

Holders of 4 per cent stocks were offered a security yielding $3\frac{1}{2}$ per cent to 1757 and 3 per cent thereafter. One of the major Government stocks for over a century, the $3\frac{1}{2}$ per cent Reduced Annuities were thus created.

In 1751, Pelham also introduced another famous stock, the 3 per cent Consolidated Bank Annuities (Consols) by merging a number of earlier 3 per cent annuities (*see* **X, 12**).

7. Subscribers to the National Debt. The costly wars of the mid-eighteenth century ended the policy of relying upon the banks and the great trading companies. Although the Bank of England lent £2.5 million and the East India Company £1 million during the War of the Austrian Succession, these sums were a small fraction of the amount advanced by the general public.

8. Lotteries. When the general level of interest rates was high, the public were induced to invest in Government stocks by means of lotteries. Lottery tickets were given free or sold on favourable terms to purchasers of a stock. The prizes were in the same stock.

Between 1755 and 1826, lotteries of a different kind became a regular feature of national finance. The cash subscribed exceeded the amount distributed as prizes, the profit going to revenue.

9. Eighteenth-century taxation principles.

(*a*) *Direct taxes.* In the absence of adequate administrative machinery, a direct tax on income was not favoured. Moreover, a compulsory income return was thought to be an infringement of an Englishman's liberty.

(*b*) *Indirect taxes.* Practically every article in general use was taxed. This was considered the most equitable method of spreading the burden. It also gave the alternative of avoiding the tax by rejecting a purchase.

In fact, the system was unjust and inefficient. Taxation of necessities struck at the poor rather than the rich, while the great diversity of taxes hampered trade and made collection difficult.

10. Financial reforms of the younger Pitt. Pitt came to office in 1783 at a time when the financial affairs of the nation were in disorder following the costly War of American Independence. The Debt had grown and the weight of taxation, already irksome, nevertheless failed to balance the budget.

Even more than Walpole, Pitt could see the benefits which might result from a liberalisation of trade, and he introduced reforms accordingly.

(*a*) *Taxation.* Despite opposition, he was able to cut customs duties. He also simplified the basis for duty and extended Walpole's system of bonded warehouses.

To compensate for the short-term loss of revenue, he resorted to loans and to a variety of direct taxes on windows, hats, candles, servants, wagons, etc., the main burden of which fell upon the rich.

Moreover, in 1785 he set up a body of commissioners to audit public expenditure ˎand, to facilitate this, established the Consolidated Fund into which all revenue was paid.

(b) *The National Debt.* A new sinking fund of £1 million per annum was established. The National Debt Commissioners were to utilise this for the purchase of stock from the public. The interest receipts from the stock they held were to be used for further purchases. Provided that there was no further borrowing, ultimately the whole Debt would pass into the hands of the Commissioners and be cancelled. By 1793, the Debt had been reduced by £10 million and Pitt was enabled to reduce some of his direct taxes.

11. The wars with France. In proportion to national income, the French Revolutionary wars and the Napoleonic wars were as costly as the two world wars of the next century. The price was paid in increased taxation and borrowing.

(a) *Taxation.* Reluctant to retard trade with increased taxes, Pitt at first relied upon borrowing. Belatedly, in 1797, he accepted the necessity of taxes and introduced the triple assessment, a grouping of his earlier direct taxes at an increased level.

The yield was disappointing, and in 1799, as a temporary wartime measure, he resorted to an income tax (levied on all incomes above £200 per annum).

(b) *The National Debt.* Pitt's failure to meet war costs with adequate taxation was less blameworthy than his unsound borrowing methods. Instead of offering a £100 stock at par (i.e. £100) and at a sufficiently attractive interest rate of 5 per cent or 6 per cent, he preferred to encourage investors with 3 per cent stocks at a substantial discount. During the 1790s, the average price of £100 stock was only £57 and in the 1800s, £60. The effect was to make the future national liability greater than the amount actually borrowed, e.g.:

Face value added to debt	*Sum realised*	*Interest charge*
£1,000 stocks	£600 (10 × £60)	at 3% £30 p.a.
Less sound than £600 stocks	£600 (6 × £100)	at 5% £30 p.a.

The position was made still worse by his maintenance of the sinking fund. The Debt continued to be redeemed, now with money borrowed at higher interest rates.

The structure of taxation and borrowing remained unchanged until 1816, when the total funded debt amounted to £819 million.

NINETEENTH-CENTURY LIBERAL INFLUENCES

12. Repeal of income tax. In 1816, income tax was withdrawn. Revenue had to be made good in order to meet a budget which now ran to £66 million by comparison with the £18 million of 1792. This was accomplished with a host of duties on every conceivable item of trade.

13. Huskisson and greater freedom of trade. While not completely abandoning mercantilist theories of trade, Huskisson, as President of the Board of Trade in 1823, perceived that an industrial Britain required a less restrictive system of taxes.

Britain's industry and commerce had provided the wealth which made victory possible. He planned to relieve them of the disabilities which restrained them and reduced a wide range of duties. Simultaneously, export subsidies were abolished.

It remained clear, however, that drastic revision of the whole tax structure was necessary. This was not attempted until Peel's second ministry (*see* **14**).

14. Peel's second ministry, 1841–6. Although Peel had not accepted the doctrine of unrestrained free trade, he saw that financial order could only be restored by the following.

(*a*) *Removal of restrictive taxes.* A vast number of duties on raw materials, manufacturers and exports were reduced or abolished.

(*b*) *Balancing the budget.* Since reduction of duties meant an immediate loss of revenue, a compensating income tax of 7*d.* (about 3p) in the £ was imposed on incomes above £150 per annum.

Peel was convinced that increased trade turnover would soon produce sufficient revenue at the lower rates of duty to make the income tax unnecessary.

By 1844, Peel had achieved a budget surplus. Encouraged by this success, instead of repealing the income tax, he abolished still more duties.

(*c*) *The National Debt.* In 1844, the first really big conversion was achieved, £250 million of 3½ per cent stock being reduced to 3¼ per cent then to 3 per cent.

15. Gladstone, 1853.

(a) *Income tax.* The desirability of income tax was hotly disputed and Gladstone, who as Chancellor had inherited it in 1853, willingly agreed that it should be finally remitted in 1860.

Meanwhile, he lowered the exemption limit from £200 to £150 but made the concession of a rebate up to one-seventh of annual income, provided that the savings were invested in life assurance of deferred annuities.

Both Gladstone and his successor, Lewis, found it necessary to raise income tax to meet the costs of the Crimean War (1854) and the Indian Mutiny (1857). The prospect of war with France in 1858 caused another rise to 9d. (about 4p).

(b) *Indirect taxes.* Like Peel, Gladstone planned to devote budget surpluses to the reduction of duties. Progress was made at first but then retarded by war.

(c) *National Debt.* Gladstone intended to finance the Crimean War from revenue, but this proved impossible and £42 million was added to the Debt.

16. Gladstone, 1860. Once again Chancellor in 1860, Gladstone made further reforms.

(a) *Indirect taxes.* The early 1860s were years of prosperity, aided by his elimination of many more customs duties. By 1865, the transition to free trade was almost accomplished.

(b) *Income tax.* A temporary rise of 1d. to 10d. in 1860 was followed by a gradual reduction to 4d. in 1865. It then fluctuated slightly but by 1874 had fallen to 2d. (2.4d. = 1p).

(c) *The Finance Bill.* In 1861, Gladstone adopted the practice of embodying all the financial proposals for the year in a single finance Bill.

17. Disraeli, 1874–80.

(a) *Income tax.* Rising public expenditure was met by an increase in income tax to 3d. (just over 1p) in 1876 and 5d. (2p) in 1878.

(b) *National Debt.* The Debt had remained almost static throughout the 1860s. In 1875, Disraeli initiated a new sinking fund of £20 million per annum, out of which the Debt would be serviced and repaid.

18. Character of national finance. In the 1860s and early 1870s, financial policies indicate that even while opposing forces were

gathering momentum, certain features of *laissez-faire* philosophy were only just coming to fulfilment.

(*a*) *Free trade.* While unrestrained freedom in industry had long been accepted and was now in the course of rejection, only in mid-century was freedom of trade accomplished.

(*b*) *Financial individualism.* Liberals and Tories were united in their desire to minimise the burden of taxation and public borrowing. They shared the view that Government activity should be restricted to matters of national security and that financial and commercial affairs were most successfully conducted by the individual.

Income tax was strictly a temporary measure to facilitate the liberalisation of trade. With this accomplished, a more prosperous nation would easily bear whatever indirect taxes remained.

FINANCING SOCIAL CHANGE SINCE THE 1880s

19. A new conception of society, 1880s. The earlier view of society as a collection of independent individuals bound to each other only by "enlightened self-interest" was being slowly replaced by the concept of a single living body whose health depended upon the well-being of all its members. In safeguarding this health, the State had certain duties. A changing philosophy was reinforced by political pressure (*see* **20**).

20. Political pressure for social expenditure. The extension of the franchise in 1867 increased the power of the working classes and gave a solid political reason for ameliorative social expenditure.

From the 1830s, reforms in health, education and welfare had been financed almost entirely from local sources, but now central Government began to make a greater contribution.

No longer was national finance a matter of minimising or eliminating the evil of taxation. Rather was it a question of balancing a slowly expanding budget, e.g. Disraeli's increased income tax in 1876 and 1878.

An increasing proportion of revenue was devoted to social purposes, but there was no radical change in the methods of financing it until the 1890s.

21. The principle of progressive taxation, 1890s. The orthodox nineteenth-century view was that justice in taxation could only be achieved through a proportional levy, e.g. a flat rate of 10 per cent on all incomes, while taking absolutely more from the rich than the poor, left everyone in the same relative financial position. The natural equilibrium had not been disturbed. In the 1890s, there grew the realisation that:

(*a*) a fixed percentage cut in incomes made greater inroads into the living standards of the poor than the rich;

(*b*) the great increase in national wealth of the nineteenth century had been ill-distributed;

(*c*) existing indirect taxes were insufficient for the growing needs of the State.

The remedy for social injustice and inadequate revenue lay in progressive direct taxation, graduated in accordance with ability to pay. The new principle was first applied in 1894.

22. Harcourt's budget, 1894. This break with the principle of proportionality marked the beginning of the modern financial era. Sir William Harcourt levied a new estate duty (death duty) on a scale graduated from 1 per cent to 8 per cent according to the total value of the deceased person's property.

The budget implied some redistribution of national income, and this aim was furthered in 1906.

23. The reforming Liberal Government, 1906.

(*a*) *Asquith, 1907.* For the first time, there was discrimination in the levying of income tax. The rate was lowered from 1*s.* (5p) to 9*d.* (about 4p) on earned incomes below £2,000 per annum while the tax burden of the rich was increased by still higher death duties.

(*b*) *Lloyd George, 1909.* Fresh revenue was required to finance Lloyd George's programme of social reform (*see* XVI, **15–19**).

(*i*) Income tax: a modified form of progression was applied through a super-tax of 6*d.* (2½p) on all incomes in excess of £5,000 p.a.

(*ii*) Estate duty: a further steepening of the scale.

(*iii*) Land taxes: revolutionary proposals which recommended a 20 per cent levy on capital gains accruing from the sale of land; ½*d* (2.4*d.* = 1p) in the £ annual tax on the site value of undeveloped land; 1*s.* (5p) in the £ duty on mining royalties.

The Lords rejected the budget, but in 1910 the Liberals were able to force many of their proposals through Parliament.

24. The National Debt, 1888–1945. Concern to reduce the burden of the Debt remained. In 1888, Lord Salisbury's Chancellor,

George Goschen, converted the 3 per cent stock to 2¾ per cent, with a further fall to 2½ per cent in 1903.

(*a*) *The South African war* (1899–1902) added about £160 million to the Debt but, by utilising budget surpluses and increasing the sinking fund, by 1914 it had been reduced to £650 million.

(*b*) *The 1914–18 war*. Vast expenditure and loans to allies expanded the Debt to £8,000 million.

(*c*) *The 1939–45 war*. War expenditure trebled the Debt to £24,000 million, although mostly at low interest rates.

25. Taxation and expenditure, 1914–45. There were few innovations. The costs of the First World War caused a great increase in income tax to 6*s*. (30p), subject to a system of reliefs. In addition, super-tax was raised to 6*s*. (30p) and an excess profits tax of 80 per cent instituted. In 1919, there were gradual reductions, but taxation remained high on account of increasing social expenditure.

The Second World War raised income tax to 10*s*. (50p). With sur-tax (super-tax was renamed in 1929) at 9*s*. 6*d*. (47½p), large incomes paid a total of 19*s*. 6*d*. (97½p) in the £.

An important change was made in the institution of *Pay As You Earn*, without which collection of the very high rate of taxes would have probably proved impossible.

26. A revolution in fiscal thinking since 1945. In a nation committed to social reconstruction, taxation and expenditure have of necessity remained high. Not only has there been a vast expansion of expenditure on the social services but with the continuing growth of the public sector there has also been massive expenditure on capital account, e.g. the investment programmes of the nationalised industries. This is an aspect of the public finances which barely existed before 1939.

Beyond this the whole concept of public finance has undergone a radical change. Before 1939 the purpose of taxation was to raise sufficient revenue to meet Government expenditure and a balanced budget was thought to be entirely necessary. After 1945 a primary purpose has been to serve as the major tool with which to manage the economy and a deliberate budgeting for a surplus or a deficit has become standard practice. (For an analysis of this policy, *see* Appendix I.)

27. Taxation and expenditure, 1938–77. Making allowance for the depreciation in the purchasing power of the £, the following figures reflect the massive expansion of current account expenditure after 1945.

Total supply service expenditure (£ million)

1939	1945	1950	1955	1960
695	5,625	2,836	3,639	4,988

1965	1970	1972	1974	1977
6,479	12,016	14,817	18,624	37,066

Defence expenditure having reached a record level in 1945, total supply expenditure then declined until 1948 when it began to accelerate. The bulk of this expenditure has been on the development of the social services, defence expenditure accounting for a relatively small proportion, e.g. by 1972, the defence estimates amounted to £2,786 million while the education bill alone amounted to £3,141 million.

While tax rates have never returned to their record war-time levels, they have nevertheless remained extremely high. Taken in conjunction with an expanding national income the revenue has grown to proportions which would seem astronomical by comparison with 1939.

Total revenue from taxation (£ million)

1939	1945	1950	1955	1960
927	3,238	3,924	4,737	5,630

1965	1970	1974	1976	1977
7,431	12,016	17,431	28,116	32,455

Source: Annual Abstract of Statistics.

28. Growth of the National Debt after 1945. For the first time in years of peace the National Debt continued to rise. This reflected the Keynesian view that the best way to stimulate an economy which was underemployed was for Government to spend in excess of its income. It also reflected Government's heavy capital account expenditure. In essence, Government borrowed in order

Net Total National Debt (£ million)

1939	1946	1950	1955	1960
7,130	23,636	25,802	26,933	27,732

1965	1970	1975	1976	
30,440	33,079	46,404	56,584	

Source: Annual Abstract of Statistics.

to relend to the nationalised industries and local authorities for the purpose of their investment programmes.

29. Deficit finance and the post-war problem of inflation. In the continued growth of the National Debt and the methods by which it has been financed lies the root of the post-war problem of inflation. Borrowing which is financed by the sale of securities to the general public is not necessarily inflationary since there results only a transfer of purchasing power from the private to the public sector. The total pressure of demand is unaffected. However, when the public is unwilling to provide the funds which the Government requires, borrowing has been financed by what in principle amounts to the manufacture of new money. This represents fresh purchasing power and is inflationary (*see* XII, 1–6).

PROGRESS TEST 21

1. In what principal respect has the purpose of public finance been broadened since 1945? **(1)**

2. Distinguish between the funded and the unfunded debt. **(1)**

3. What was the principal source of seventeenth-century Government revenue? **(3)**

4. In the eighteenth century there was little that could be described as a social service, yet Government expenditure grew. Explain. **(4)**

5. How might Walpole be described as a man in advance of his times? **(5)**

6. In what way were eighteenth-century tax precepts open to criticism? **(9)**

7. Assess the merits and the weaknesses of Pitt's financial methods. **(10, 11)**

8. In what way did Huskisson attempt to remedy a commercially dangerous situation? **(12, 13)**

9. Estimate the importance of Peel and Gladstone to the cause of free trade. **(14–16)**

10. Why might mid-nineteenth-century concepts of public finance be described as both progressive and yet behind the times? **(17)**

11. Why did public expenditure increase in the last quarter of the century? **(19, 20)**

12. How did changing tax methods in the 1890s and 1900s exemplify the new conception of society? **(19, 21–23)**

13. What major change in fiscal thinking occurred after 1945? **(26)**

14. What were the implications of this change for the National Debt and for inflation? **(28, 29)**

PART SEVEN

THE DECLINE OF LAISSEZ-FAIRE

CHAPTER XXII

The Road to a Mixed Capitalist Society

NOTE: The intention of the following two chapters is to integrate the various trends already described in detail. The many references to earlier material are not specified but, when necessary, clarification should be sought under the appropriate chapter or section headings.

ASCENDANCY OF LAISSEZ-FAIRE

1. Summary of the rise of laissez-faire. As was shown in I, for many centuries economic affairs were regulated by the local authorities. When their power waned in the face of the rising spirit of individualism, the Crown assumed control.

When the nation states of Europe were created, the doctrine of mercantilism was widely accepted, but the authoritarianism which this implied conflicted with the expanding sphere of the individual's self-interest. After 1688, the absolute power of the Crown was broken and it became increasingly accepted that in economic affairs the State had no part to play.

Society's interests were viewed as the sum total of individual interests and they would therefore be maximised if every man were permitted complete freedom of self-development. The enlightened self-interest which, at the end of the eighteenth century, Adam Smith prescribed as essential to the "wealth of nations" had already been accepted as the mainspring of economic action a century earlier.

NOTE: Adam Smith was the father of the classical school of economists. In his *Inquiry into the nature and the causes of the wealth of nations*, 1776, he made the first comprehensive analysis of economics as an independent subject for study.

2. The by-products of laissez-faire. The spirit of individualism bore fruit in the spectacular progress of the Industrial Revolution and, thus encouraged, was led to excesses which ultimately provoked a reaction.

The factory system was the necessary concomitant of mechanisation, but in the hands of a society which had rejected all controls it gave rise to intolerable working conditions. The evils were recognised but it was believed that the natural economic forces of supply and demand would rectify them. The working man had the remedy in his own hands. By restricting his numbers, he could increase his scarcity value.

Any attempt by the State artificially to regulate wages or restrict working hours would raise costs and price Britain out of world markets.

3. The condition of early nineteenth-century Britain. From 1793 to 1815 Britain was almost continuously at war with France. The period nevertheless proved to be one of great expansion and prosperity. The pressure of demand from a growing population kept corn prices high and encouraged the extension of the margin of cultivation. The farmer prospered even though rents were high.

In industry, power was being more widely applied to machinery. The output of cheap manufactures, particularly textiles, therefore grew rapidly.

Despite Napoleon's blockade, overseas trade expanded. Denied European markets, Britain developed them in the colonies and the Americas.

In the midst of this great prosperity was found the direst poverty. The agricultural labourer, uprooted from the land by the enclosure movement, could not earn a living wage and was dependent upon the degrading "allowance system".

The industrial worker suffered long hours, low wages, abysmal working conditions and lived in squalid towns without proper water supply or sanitation. His expectation of life was correspondingly low.

4. Post-war depression and recovery, 1820–50. The restoration of the banknote's convertibility in 1821, the more careful maintenance of the private banks' liquidity after the failures of 1825, together with the reduced supply of new gold from the Spanish

American colonies, all served to diminish the supply of new money. In a time of expanding output, prices therefore fell. Moreover, there was no immediate recovery of markets in Europe, where the effects of war had been far more devastating than in Britain.

Declining profitability in industry led to wage reductions, factory closures and heavy unemployment. The situation was aggravated by the heavy taxation required to service an expanded National Debt. The great increase in indirect taxes, now substituted for income tax, tended further to cripple trade.

In agriculture, prices fell from their high wartime levels despite the protection of the corn law, while costs remained high. The farmer carried the burden of high rents and high rates made necessary by the "allowance system".

In the 1840s a slow recovery was staged. It was aided by a gradual increase in domestic purchasing power, the result of fresh supplies of gold from Russia and the increasing use of cheques. Overseas trade was supported by low export prices, made possible by low labour costs and the use of machinery. Despite some social unrest, general political stability also made a major contribution.

5. The culmination of laissez-faire. The condition of the working class had reached a low ebb in the 1820s and 1830s. The greater prosperity which followed brought no relief. The capitalist system, which was accomplishing so much in solving the problems of production, did nothing to secure a more equitable distribution of the national income.

Even the protagonists of the working-class cause were deterred by contemporary economic thinking from an advocacy of State intervention. (Writers such as Malthus and Ricardo were dismally predicting that wages would always be bound to subsistence level until such time as the workers voluntarily restricted their numbers. John Stuart Mill claimed that at any time there was only a limited fund of capital available for the employment of labour. An increase in the wage of one worker therefore implied a decrease in that of another.)

If these arguments were accepted, the solution to the dilemma appeared to lie in the more efficient operation of *laissez-faire* rather than its limitation. In this spirit, the combination laws were relaxed in 1824. There developed the great free trade movement, which, it was believed, would result in prosperity for the whole nation, while in agriculture the debilitating "allowance system" was abandoned in 1834.

6. Humanitarian reaction. Parallel with the extension of *laissez-faire* philosophy, another line of thought was developing. An increasing number of writers, amongst them the influential political scientist, Jeremy Bentham, were expressing the view that the criterion of economic action should not be "self-interest" but "the greatest good of the greatest number".

Society was still seen as a loose collection of individuals whose liberty of action should not be impeded, but in certain fields, such as education and public health, private enterprise had no interest. There was therefore scope for the State to provide the "collateral aids" which would create an environment in which everyone would have the opportunity of self-development.

In Parliament, the Earl of Shaftesbury led a movement which began to implement this thinking. Between 1833 and 1850 were passed a series of Factory Acts designed to protect women and children, the weakest members of society, who were in no position to strike a fair wage bargain with the employer. This, it was argued, was no infringement of *laissez-faire*. Although applicable only to the textile trades, they provided the basis for the subsequent regulation of all industry.

Education, before 1833 the exclusive concern of private enterprise, was now assisted by increasing Government grants. An educated working man, it was thought, would have a greater sense of responsibility and would be better able to discharge his social duty to maintain himself and his dependants.

The efforts of Chadwick drew public attention to the need for a healthy environment if the nation were to prosper. In 1848 was set up a Central Board of Health to encourage the development of water supply and main drainage. This was followed by a number of measures which produced a steady decline in the death rate.

7. The "Golden Age", 1849–73. In mid-century began a period in which industry, trade and agriculture all prospered. Improved transport and a rising price level (the result of the greater supply of money provided by new gold discoveries) encouraged expansion.

Britain's position as the "workshop of the world" was undisputed. Mechanisation of her industry was virtually completed while her potential rivals were still held back by political upheaval (in the U.S.A., the Civil War; in Germany and Italy, the struggles for unification; in Russia, agrarian reform).

Middle-class opposition to social reform weakened when experience showed that the nation's prosperity continued to grow apace, despite ameliorative legislation.

Simultaneously, economic thinking took a new direction. The early nineteenth-century classical economists had viewed the subject as an abstract, deductive science. Their "economic man" made only rational decisions and was motivated only by economic considerations. For them, human action and its consequences were always predictable.

By mid-century was expressed the opinion that since the subject was concerned with human behaviour, it was an art whose method should be historical and empirical. Following this method, economists perceived that there might be economy in high wages; that costs depend not on wage rates but upon labour's efficiency. In this way, the intellectual opposition to reform was also weakened.

THE ORGANIC CONCEPT OF SOCIETY

8. The Great Depression, 1873–96. A diminution of purchasing power resulted from the reduced supply of gold. This followed France and Germany's adoption of monometallist currencies and America's decision to make the dollar note convertible once more. On the other hand, world production was expanding rapidly and improved transport was intensifying competition. The general price level fell, with consequences which were more severe for agriculture than industry, where the increasing scale of production permitted lower costs.

However, even in industry, anxiety was felt. Technical change in iron and steel (the Gilchrist-Thomas process) conferred advantages on Britain's rivals. World shipping tonnage was excessive, since iron steamships had greater carrying capacity. Freight rates fell and Britain's invisible exports therefore declined. Many traditional British markets were shrinking as foreign industry grew in the lee of rising tariff barriers. The latter were especially notable in the case of the U.S.A., and of Germany, where Bismarck was actively assisting industrial and commercial growth.

9. A positive role for Government. Many remedies for depression were suggested, but increasingly there was advanced the view that the State should emulate Germany and the U.S.A. This did not imply any desire to abandon the interests of the individual in order to re-create a mercantilist state. What was required was positive Government assistance for the individual.

By 1903 this belief had grown, so that Chamberlain could advocate a policy of protectionist tariffs. In the event, the Conservatives were soundly defeated in the 1906 general election and, for the time being, free trade survived.

However, from the 1880s, even the concept of the individual's relationship to society was undergoing change. The *laissez-faire* view of the State as a loose collection of competing members, each in isolation pursuing his own self-interest, was being supplanted by the idea of a living organism. No single limb could function efficiently unless the whole body enjoyed good health, i.e. the well-being of every individual would vary directly with the total well-being of society. There was a growing realisation that Britain could not prosper in an increasingly competitive world unless her population was well-fed, better educated and enjoying some sense of economic security. The reforming Liberal Government of 1906 accepted this view and gave impetus to the new trends.

10. Relief of sweated labour. Factory legislation which had given protection in respect of hours and conditions was now extended to the regulation of wages. In the "sweated trades" where wage bargaining power was weak through lack of union organisation, minimum wages were fixed by trade boards appointed by the Board of Trade. (This was provided for by the Trade Boards Act 1909; ready-made clothing, chain, box and lace making were listed in 1910 and six other trades added in 1913. The Trade Boards Act 1918 authorised the establishment of trade boards to regulate hours and wages wherever a trade lacked union organisation.)

11. Workmen's compensation. The health of the body politic was also promoted by the protection of injured workmen. Previously they had been discarded as of no further economic use, to care for themselves as best they might. The first remedial measure had been the Employer's Liability Act 1880 which granted compensation when the employer's negligence was proven. The Workmen's Compensation Act 1906 took the next logical step and made compensation payable irrespective of negligence.

12. Conciliation. No society could be healthy when it suffered from constant industrial disputes. Strikes and lock-outs harmed not only the two participating parties but also the public at large. The Conciliation Act 1896 provided the channels through which Board of Trade mediation could be invited.

The exigencies of the First World War brought compulsory arbitration to industrial disputes, but the Industrial Courts Act 1919 attempted to encourage co-operation in place of conflict. Joint Industrial Councils (Whitley Councils, after the 1917 Whitley parliamentary committee which recommended their creation), representative of employer and employees, were established in several industries with the object of avoiding disputes before they arose.

13. Unemployment. The socially debilitating disease of unemployment was tackled with the Unemployed Workmen Act 1905 which provided relief through public works. This was followed by a more constructive measure, the establishment of labour exchanges in 1909.

14. Education. Both Germany and America had demonstrated that education, particularly in an industrial age, promoted a vigorous and healthy nation. The Education Act 1870 for the first time provided a national system of elementary education which a few years later was made compulsory. It was followed by the 1902 Act, which made some provision for secondary education, and the 1918 "Fisher Act", which raised the school-leaving age to fourteen.

15. Social security. In the field of social security, as in education, the example of German schemes influenced thinking in this country. If Britain was to compete successfully, her people had to enjoy the same advantages as their rivals.

In 1911, the Liberal Government instituted national unemployment and health insurance. This was no socialist scheme of benefits provided freely from taxation. It was a system of insurance in which the Government's primary role was, in a positive way, to assist the individual—and, moreover, to insist that he should be in a position to take care of himself. It did not therefore represent any sudden break with nineteenth-century Liberal traditions. The moral imperative remained that the individual should accept full responsibility for himself and his dependants. It was, however, a development from the earlier view that the

State, having guaranteed an adequate environment, then left the individual to sink or swim.

INADEQUATE SOCIAL SECURITY, 1920–39

16. Dislocation of world trade. With the return of peace in 1918, it was at first assumed that business would quickly pick up from the 1913 position. After the interruption of war, normal progress could now be resumed. There was no real understanding of the complexities of a global economy in which interdependent nations practised a high degree of specialisation. Failure of demand in any major trading nation would have repercussions throughout the world. It was scarcely appreciated that the non-belligerents had not stood still during the war, and that now the whole pattern of world trade had changed.

Old-established industries, particularly the British mainstays of textiles, coal, iron and steel and steam engineering, found that their traditional markets had been invaded by lower-priced competitors or that demand was evaporating in the face of technological advance in new industries.

17. Economic nationalism. The situation was aggravated in Britain by an inflated currency which was effectively pricing her out of world markets. International credit facilities, moreover, were insufficient to sustain world demand and, after a short post-war boom, in 1920 markets everywhere collapsed. The world then retired into the shell of economic nationalism.

Tariffs were raised almost everywhere, save in Britain, and the volume of international trade shrank. The consequences were particularly serious for Britain, whose dependence upon foreign trade was exceptionally high.

18. Deflation and unemployment. Britain sought to remedy her competitive weakness by currency deflation, and this served to accelerate the fall in price which was accompanying the loss of demand. In these circumstances, business contracted and unemployment increased, particularly in the coalfields of the north, which were entirely dependent on the traditional heavy industries.

The strain on unemployment insurance proved too great. The scheme had not operated long enough to accumulate adequate reserves. In any case, it had not been designed to cope with the chronic unemployment which now appeared for the first time.

In the nineteenth century, the unemployed had always tended to be reabsorbed at lower wage levels. In the 1920s, the trade unions resisted such tendencies, with the result that, while wage rates were largely supported, many workers remained permanently unemployed.

19. Government intervention. The 1929 crisis almost brought the economy to a standstill and there was an outcry for action by the State. In 1931, the pretence of a gold standard was abandoned and the ruinous deflationary policy of the 1920s was halted. The note issue (and therefore domestic purchasing power), as well as international exchange rates, now had a measure of elasticity and were no longer tied arbitrarily to the size of the gold reserves.

In 1931, the demand grew for protection from the unfair competition of cheap foregin imports "dumped" at prices below cost. Free trade was abandoned. The Government raised a general import duty and the home market, at least, was safeguarded.

Agriculture, like industry, benefited from State assistance. The Wheat Quota Act 1932 guaranteed prices to the wheat farmer, while the Agricultural Marketing Acts of 1931 and 1933 assisted the small mixed farmer with the problems of distribution and regulated prices in order to give them some stability.

The magnitude of the problem of unemployment now compelled the State to intervene. Unemployment insurance benefit was extended into a "dole" financed by the Treasury. For the first time, therefore, central Government accepted a measure of responsibility for the relief of the unemployed. This was also expressed in the 1936 Special Areas Act, which aimed to relieve the parts of the country where unemployment was especially accute.

20. Continuing movement away from laissez-faire. The period between the wars therefore saw a continuing movement away from the principles of *laissez-faire* in trade, industry, agriculture and social thinking. Free enterprise was clearly ill-equipped to meet the problems which resulted from structural change in a world economy infinitely more complex than that of the nineteenth century. The responsibilities of Government grew accordingly, but neither public opinion nor technical economic knowledge were yet prepared for large-scale Government supervision of business affairs.

CHAPTER XXIII

The Management of the Economy Since 1945

THE SOCIAL AND ECONOMIC IMPACT OF WAR

1. Wartime mobilisation of the economy. The war began in September 1939 and ended in Europe in May 1945 and in the Far East in August. From a fairly slow start in 1939–40, the economy was rapidly geared up to a wartime basis and by 1943 some $8\frac{1}{2}$ million people were mobilised, either in the armed forces or in the armaments industries. Of these, nearly 5 million were drawn from occupations which were now accorded a lower priority, $2\frac{1}{2}$ million from groups normally outside the field of employment, e.g. housewives, and 1 million from the unemployed.

Since this was a struggle which commanded infinitely more popular support than had the First World War there was unreserved agreement in directing all of the nation's resources of manpower and capital to the attainment of victory. The resulting transformation was to have far-reaching social and economic effects (*see* **2–5** below).

2. Creation of the machinery of economic planning. The direction of the economy required the creation of a planning apparatus which could assess the available resources and decide upon their allocation between competing priorities. To this end it was necessary to develop means for collating and processing a mass of statistical information. Central planning also called for new macro-economic concepts and these were available in the Keynesian economic theories which had hitherto been rejected.

The post-war significance of these developments was that the machinery of economic management already existed, had been proved to work in practice and was therefore much more readily acceptable.

3. Social attitudes. For other reasons too, public opinion was now much more willing to accept a large measure of Government intervention in social and economic affairs. The war was fought under a coalition Government, all parties sharing the same common objectives. Behind them, the people were united by the same goals and by shared experiences which promoted mutual sympathy and understanding. In this climate flourished a much greater disposition towards ideas of social justice.

The immediate result of these changing attitudes was a landslide Labour victory in 1945. Despite universal acknowledgment of Churchill's greatness as a war leader it was clearly the view of the electorate that their social aspirations were more likely to be realised under a Labour Government.

When in due course a Conservative Government was returned in 1951, it was seen that social and economic objectives together with the means of achieving them remained fundamentally the same. The coalition of the early 1940s was in a sense continued by the "Butskellism" of the 1950s. In the 1960s, this approach remained with the "consensus politics" of Harold Wilson. Arguably, post-war politics have become a matter of comparative administrative efficiency rather than any deep-rooted clash of conflicting ideologies.

4. The basis of consensus. The first expression of a growing social conscience was the publication in 1942 of the Beveridge Report. This was to be the blueprint for the post-war Welfare State. Its proposals covered financial provisions for sickness, unemployment, maternity, old age and burial, Family Allowances and the creation of a National Health Service.

Beveridge saw that the success of his proposals depended ultimately upon the guarantee of full employment. As the pre-war years had demonstrated, no scheme of social insurance could otherwise be successful. With the war still in progress, the Government accepted this proposition with its publication in 1944 of a White Paper, "Employment Policy". Henceforth, a primary responsibility of any Government was agreed to be the level of economic activity.

Finally, in the pursuit of social justice, equality of opportunity was universally accepted to be of paramount importance. A step in this direction was taken with the Education Act of 1944 which raised the school-leaving age to fifteen and planned to extend the facilities available in further education.

5. The effects of the war on Britain's external trading position. While the war industries were built up, the export industries declined. Imports on the other hand continued to rise and there consequently developed a serious deficit in the balance of payments on current account. Although North American grants helped to bridge this gap it still proved necessary to sell off a substantial part of British overseas investments, worth about £1.2 billion, and to run down the gold reserves.

Britain therefore emerged from the war in a much weaker trading position. Not only had the export industries to be restored to their former capacity, it was also necessary to expand them sufficiently to compensate for the loss of overseas investment income. During the 1930s, this income had paid for about one-third of the import bill. Another major source of invisible exports had been the shipping industry but with the merchant fleet much depleted these earnings too were adversely affected.

This basic external weakness was repeatedly to prove the major constraint upon post-war economic policies.

THE COURSE OF EVENTS, 1945–76

6. Secular trends. Economic policy aims to achieve full employment with growth at stable prices. In practice, the simultaneous attainment of the three goals eluded all Governments and the course of events from 1945 to 1973 suggests that broadly speaking priority was therefore given to each in turn. The most striking success was achieved in maintaining very high levels of employment, the policy goal which seemed in the light of Britain's pre-war experience to be most desirable. Compared with unemployment of over 10 per cent between the wars, between 1945 and 1973 there were only two occasions when the figure of 3 per cent was exceeded, in 1947 and 1971, and for much of the time it was well below 2 per cent.

By the 1960s, with the shadow of the 1930s less ominous and full employment now taken for granted, attention was directed to a growth rate which seemed sluggish when compared to that of our major industrial competitors. Although there had been only one occasion, in 1958, when the gross domestic product of any one year had not been greater than that of the preceding year the annual average growth rate was only of the order of $2\frac{1}{2}$ per cent. Moreover, growth had been spasmodic, the economy progressing in fits and starts in response to what came to be labelled "stop-go" economic policies. No sooner had a period of expansion begun than inflationary pressures induced a balance of payments crisis which caused the brakes to be applied.

During a brief spell from 1962–6 more rapid economic growth

became a policy priority. However, such were the inflationary pressures that in 1966 price stability was viewed as a pre-condition for continuing full employment and further economic growth.

Prolonged inflation is therefore the third major trend which can be observed after 1945. It is a phenomenon without parallel, at least in the modern economic history of Britain. The nineteenth century witnessed alternating inflation and deflation but the price level in 1913 was still somewhat lower than it had been in 1815. Prices trebled during the First World War but in 1939 were half the level of 1918.

The attempt to achieve a satisfactory short-term compromise between the three policy goals has resulted in spasmodic economic progress (*see* 7–14 below).

7. The sterling crisis of 1947.

It has been observed that balance in overseas payments on current account was only achieved during the war with American assistance. With the war in Europe over, it was estimated that victory in the Far East was still eighteen months away. The atomic bomb in fact brought this war and American aid to a conclusion within three months.

The economic effects were disruptive and loans had to be hastily negotiated. The U.S.A. advanced $3,750 million at 2 per cent to be repaid over fifty years to which Canada added a further $1,250 million. This assistance was less generous than it appears at first sight. Britain's financial plight arose because, of all the allies, she had been most totally committed to the war effort and grants spread over a period of years rather than a single lump sum loan might have been more appropriate.

In the event, within the year the loans were almost exhausted for three reasons. Firstly, in a period of reconstruction, the volume of imports far exceeded the volume of exports. Secondly, an especially severe winter in 1947 had a disastrous effect upon industrial output. Thirdly, and most significantly, a condition of the U.S. loan had been ratification by Britain of the Bretton Woods agreement, implying amongst other things immediate convertibility for sterling. Very reluctantly Britain followed this course in 1947 at a time when nearly all other currencies with the exception of the dollar were inconvertible. The result was a rapid and almost complete exhaustion of the reserves. Foreign holders of sterling immediately switched to dollars in order to settle their accounts in the U.S.A., virtually the only source of the goods which the rest of the world so badly needed.

However, in retrospect, some criticism may also be levelled at the management of the domestic economy. As Chancellor of the Exchequer, Hugh Dalton had continued the wartime policy of cheap money in the belief that this was appropriate both to reconstruction and to full employment. With interest rates at rock bottom a high level of internal demand drew in imports and diverted to home consumption.

In the resulting crisis, sterling convertibility was suspended and an autumn Budget was for the first time addressed to the task of restraining domestic demand.

By 1947, it will be seen, there had already emerged two features of the British economy which were to remain until 1972. It was the external situation which caused the brake to be applied to the economy and this was accomplished by means of fiscal restraints.

8. Austerity, 1947–51. The progressive scrapping of wartime controls after 1947 led to increasing reliance upon fiscal measures as the principal means of managing the economy. Together with the gradual abandonment of a cheap money policy, the draconian tax measures of Sir Stafford Cripps did result in some reduction of inflationary pressure. Even so, it seemed impossible to escape the problem of external deficits, particularly with the U.S.A. This dollar shortage was, however, the experience of all European countries and finally in April 1948, relief arrived with the passage through the U.S. Congress of the Foreign Assistance Act.

This Act implemented the "Marshall Plan" which through the instrument of the simultaneously formed Organisation for European Economic Co-operation afforded massive "extraordinary assistance" for the purpose of European reconstruction.

Despite American aid and restrictive domestic economic policies, Britain's external position remained precarious and in the first half of 1949 the dollar gap widened. The U.S. economy was experiencing a mild recession with a resulting reduction of imports of both British manufactures and Commonwealth commodities. As banker to the Sterling Area Britain consequently experienced a drain upon the reserves, not only because of her own trade imbalance but also because of the sharp deterioration in the Commonwealth/U.S. balance. The crisis came to a head in September 1949 and resulted in a sterling devaluation of 30 per cent.

Devaluation in conjunction with continued disinflationary policies and the recovery of the U.S. economy improved the reserve position during the following twelve months. However, the outbreak of the Korean War in June 1950 began to generate fresh strains upon the economy. The decision to rearm in an economy which was already fully employed diverted productive effort away from the export industries. At the same time the position was aggravated by a rise in world commodity prices and a corresponding deterioration in Britain's terms of trade. In the resulting crisis the Labour Government was swept out of office and there began a thirteen year period of Conservative administration.

9. Expansion, 1951–4. A change of Government did not bring any fundamental change in social and economic policies. There remained a commitment to full employment and to the ideals of the Welfare State. There was no large-scale contraction of the public sector and with the exception of steel and a section of the transport industry the nationalised industries remained intact. There was, however, some variation in the technique of economic management. After twenty years' disuse an active monetary policy was revived in support of fiscal measures and the "package deal" became the means by which the level of demand was controlled.

Although the immediate causes of the 1951 crisis had in fact waned, there was still little optimism at the time of Butler's 1952 "neutral" Budget which many thought to be insufficiently stringent. However, a healthy balance of payments emerged by the end of the year which facilitated a positively expansionary Budget in 1953, a course which was held through to 1955.

10. Restraint, 1955–9. In 1955, with unemployment down to 1.1 per cent, domestic consumption and investment running at very high levels and a rising volume of imports converting the external balance to deficit, a give-away pre-election Budget was a recipe for crisis. By July, a credit squeeze had been implemented and substantial cuts in public expenditure announced. An autumn Budget then reinforced these restraints which were to remain until the middle of 1958. The need for their continuance was underlined by the Suez crisis at the end of 1956.

The immediate economic effect of the Suez invasion was a wave of speculation against sterling. The drain on the reserves necessitated the exercise of Britain's drawing rights at the I.M.F.

and the negotiation of an additional loan from the U.S.A. Despite a standfast Budget in 1957, speculation on the possibility of a sterling devaluation continued and the subsequent drain upon the reserves was only checked after further tightening of monetary policy convinced the world of the Government's determination to defend the sterling parity.

Paradoxically, the 1957 balance of payments on current account was favourable and the continuance of this trend in 1958 in conjunction with a rising unemployment figure brought a very gradual relaxation of monetary restraints. These developments heralded a pre-election Budget in which a substantial stimulus was given to what was by now an accelerating upswing in the economy.

11. Spasmodic growth, 1960–4. The expansion generated in 1959 rapidly converted a balance of payments surplus in that year of some £140 million into a deficit in 1960 of over £260 million.

Warning signals appeared in April 1960, when hire-purchase restrictions were applied and for the first time calls for special deposits made from the commercial banks. It appeared at first that these measures would be sufficient since by mid-1961 the current external balance had moved into surplus with the level of domestic demand checked and the economy slowing down.

Despite these internal trends, foreign speculation against sterling produced an outflow of reserves which in turn inspired further monetary restrictions and curbs in public expenditure. The hypersensitivity of the economy to external factors was once more made evident.

Restraint was still observed in the Budget of 1962 but by now the economy stood in danger of a major recession. It was not, however, until the 1963 Budget that an expansionary stimulus was given which ultimately proved to have been an over-reaction. Some attempt was therefore made to damp down the pace of economic growth in 1964. The curbs might well have been more severe but for an approaching general election. Their lack of stringency might also be taken as evidence of a desire to break away from "stop-go" policies by making the attempt to accelerate out of economic crisis. The result however, was a massive £400 million deficit on current account made infinitely worse by a further £400 million deficit on capital account.

12. An attempt to continue growth policies, 1964–6. A new Labour Government took office in October 1964 and was immediately confronted with a major crisis. At the root of the problem lay the balance of payments deficit which was emerging for the year and with which much play was made for internal political purposes. This reaction served only to increase the anxieties of overseas sterling holders when it was coupled with a November Budget which, far from taking the restrictive action which they expected, was largely neutral. Moreover, the fact of an inexperienced Labour Government in office was in itself suspect.

The crisis was temporarily overcome by large-scale overseas borrowing but the formulation of a more lasting solution was delayed, largely because of strongly conflicting views within the Government. A new Department of Economic Affairs under George Brown was totally committed to growth even at the expense of devaluation. This view was consistent with a party in office which could scarcely choose the alternative course of deflation and un-employment. At the Treasury, however, the more traditional view prevailed and here there was a commitment to the preservation of the sterling exchange rate.

Until 1966 the D.E.A. had its way, basically continuing the attempt of the preceding Government to accelerate out of crisis.

The 1965 Budget was very mildly restrictive but domestic demand continued to run at very high levels. The trade balance consequently worsened and there was further speculation against sterling. This prompted some tightening of credit and minor cuts in public expenditure.

During a pause in the external pressures, a snap election returned the Labour Government with a substantially increased majority. Then, in the first half of 1966, the external position continued to worsen and by July it was clear that the Treasury view was to prevail. A powerful disinflationary package of measures was introduced which raised purchase tax, tightened hire-purchase restrictions, cut back public expenditure and imposed severe controls on prices and incomes.

13. Stagnation, 1967–71. The restrictions imposed in 1966 brought some improvement in the trade figures but a rise in un-employment. This inspired a very mildly reflationary Budget in 1967 followed in mid-summer by a less understandable relaxation of hire-purchase controls and the announcement of increases in social security payments.

This stimulus to domestic demand was accompanied by a deterioration in the trade figures and heavy speculation against sterling. Britain's continuing difficulties throughout the 1960s had convinced many that sterling was over-valued, whatever internal remedies she might adopt and that a devaluation could not therefore be long delayed.

The defence of sterling was continued throughout October and into November at very heavy cost to the reserves. Then, after international consultation, a 14.3 per cent devaluation was effected on the 18th November. There was, however, to be no respite for the economy. In order to ensure that the advantage of devaluation to Britain's international price competitiveness was not eroded by continuing inflation, consumer demand had to be severely curtailed. There followed an immediate tightening of credit controls and a strongly deflationary 1968 Budget.

The second half of 1968 saw an encouraging expansion of exports and an equally discouraging refusal of imports to respond. Accordingly the beneficial results of devaluation upon the trade figures was not fully seen until the second half of 1969 when the current account moved into surplus. In the following year this position was greatly strengthened and there was some very cautious relaxation of monetary policy. There was, however, little over-all confidence in Britain's ability to sustain this position. Since 1967, the economy had experienced a new phenomenon, rising unemployment accompanied by escalating inflation.

The incoming Conservative Government of 1970 made it clear that the control of inflation was of paramount importance but was a problem to be dealt with by resistance to individual wage claims rather than by a prices and incomes policy or any attempt to curtail demand.

Meanwhile unemployment was approaching record post-war levels and a mildly reflationary 1971 Budget was followed in midsummer by purchase tax reductions and the complete removal of hire-purchase restrictions. Despite these measures, the unemployment figures continued to rise and by 1972 were clearly of greater concern to Government than the rate of inflation.

14. Expansion, inflation, currency depreciation, 1972–6. Backed by a very strong 1971 current account surplus, the Government addressed itself to the problem of unemployment in a 1972 Budget which projected a substantial Exchequer borrowing requirement. By the autumn, there was a strong upsurge in consumption expenditure and the unemployment figures were beginning to respond. Investment however, remained disappointingly sluggish.

It was also apparent that such a powerful stimulus to domestic expenditure would have adverse effects upon the balance of payments and this could in due course lead to yet another sterling crisis. In anticipation of this problem, in the summer of 1972 the sterling exchange rate was floated. For the first time since 1945 a period of economic growth was not to be cut short by the need to preserve a fixed rate of exchange.

By mid-1973, the unemployment figures had been almost halved and a 5 per cent per annum growth rate achieved. This, however, was at the expense of a rate of inflation trending in excess of 10 per cent per annum, an increasing deficit in the current account and a rapidly depreciating foreign exchange rate.

Observing the mounting inflationary pressures resulting from unbridled monetary growth, the Conservative Government began to retrench in December 1973 with some minor public expenditure cuts. These were reversed by the incoming Labour Government of 1974 and public spending proliferated. There was a determination to resist by compensatory Government action the effects of a world recession induced by the 1973–4 rise in oil prices.

A COMMENT ON 1976 AND AFTER

15. Retrenchment, unemployment, currency stabilisation 1976–?
During 1976, production stagnated, unemployment climbed and inflation continued at rates far in excess of Britain's industrial competitors with catastrophic results for the rate of exchange. With the rate falling towards $1.50, Britain was obliged to seek a short-term loan from the U.S.A. It was repayable at the year's end. This backing revived world confidence in sterling and the decline was checked.

In December 1976, in order to repay the U.S. loan, Britain approached the International Monetary Fund. A further loan was negotiated subject to very stringent conditions. In effect, throughout 1977 the broad outlines of Britain's macro-economic policies were dictated by the I.M.F. Of greatest significance was the insistence upon a substantial reduction in the rate of growth of the money supply with consequential real cuts in the growth of public spending. (At the root of monetary growth lies the extent to which public expenditure exceeds tax revenues and borrowing from the private sector.)

These policies were rewarded in 1978 with a substantial reduc-

tion in the rate of inflation. However, this still remained in excess
of Britain's principal competitors. Unemployment, moreover,
continued to increase and although oil revenues had made a significant impact upon the balance of payments deficit, imports of
foreign manufactures continued at an embarassingly high level.

16. Long-term trends. By the late 1970s many economic com-
mentators were beginning to question the viability of the British
version of a mixed economy. Stagnant output, large-scale unemployment and an accepted rate of inflation which a generation
previously would have been thought intolerable were all witness
to the failure of demand management techniques (*see* Appendix
I). Direct Government intervention to offset this failure had led
to substantial portions of the private sector being taken into
public ownership where they continued to operate on public
subventions. Other heavily subsidised public industries showed
resistance to modernisation wherever vested interests were
at stake. Productivity throughout the economy lagged far
behind that of the country's major competitors. This was evidenced by the low return on capital invested and by overmanning.

Taxation was universally recognised as having reached levels at
which there were powerful disincentives to work and enterprise
not only for the upper income groups but also for the low-paid
whose wage was little greater than their benefit entitlements if
unemployed. Incentives were further diminished by the erosive
effect on earnings of inflation coupled with continuing incomes
policies. The annual public sector borrowing requirement remained at an astronomical level and was financed all too frequently by resort to the banking system, i.e. "printing the
money".

Economic failure was reflected in a faltering of the Welfare
State. Despite absorbing an ever increasing quantity of the
nation's resources the National Health Service was afflicted with
shortages and riven with dissension, while in education complaints of lowered standards grew. The crime rate was also increasing. There was a housing shortage, yet in every city munici-
pally built blocks crumbled, untenanted, into disrepair and private housing remained unlet in fear of the Rent Acts. Minority
groups of all persuasions voiced their discontents, frequently
assisted by newly appointed State agencies. Bureaucracy proliferated as "the compassionate society" receded.

The collectivisation of society over 100 years had produced an insatiable desire for individual rights with an inadequate collective apparatus and an individual unwillingness to bear the responsibilities. Some analysts viewed this impasse as a critical juncture in the nation's history. On the one hand the transition to a fully collectivised, centrally planned society could be completed with all speed. The social disciplines implicit in this choice would require the exercise of political power in a way quite different from the practices of liberal democracies. On the other hand the State could retreat from the many areas of social and economic life where it had proved ineffective. New forms of organisation, ownership and control would evolve in a way which restored to the individual a greater independence of action coupled with greater personal responsibility. The choice remained to be made.

The Keynesian Monetarist Controversy

1. The unemployment problem between the world wars.
World experience in the 1930s confirmed that private enterprise
economies were ill-fitted to achieve the objective of full employment. Between 1921 and 1938, only once did the proportion of
insured persons unemployed fall below 10 per cent. In two years,
it was above 20 per cent and the over-all average was in excess of
14 per cent.

In material terms, it was estimated that this waste of productive resources was costing the country about £400–£500 million per
annum. In human terms, a great deal of hardship was experienced and a great strain placed upon the social structure of the
country.

2. A sphere for Government action. During the war, unemployment virtually disappeared and post-war inflationary pressures
maintained the position until 1948, when world reconversion to
peacetime production was almost complete and consumer goods
were arriving on the market in increasing quantities.

By 1949, it was evident in most countries that the immediate
post-war boom was over. Production was beginning to level off
and unemployment figures were rising to 2–3 per cent of the insured population.

The conclusion which emerges and which is stressed by the
employment pledge of the U.N. charter is that this is a sphere for
positive Government action, and also one for international co-
operation, since no national policy can succeed if it conflicts with
the national policies of other countries.

From this point, we can begin to analyse the problem but we
must first start by understanding what the economist means by
full employment.

3. Full employment. Not all unemployment is of the same nature
and in some cases it is impossible to eliminate it entirely.

(a) *Shortage of capital.* The first type of unemployment is that which results from insufficient capital resources and which is characteristic of the underdeveloped countries.

(b) *Seasonal unemployment.* This results from seasonal variations in the demand for particular types of labour, e.g. the building and catering trades.

(c) *Structural unemployment.* This will occur when productive resources are redeployed to meet new demands while old demands are declining, e.g. engineering on the one hand and cotton on the other.

(d) *Deficiency of effective demand.* In industrial countries, a major cause of large-scale chronic unemployment has been a deficiency and instability of effective demand.

4. The Keynesian explanation. In his *General Theory of Employment, Interest and Money* (1936), John Maynard Keynes seeks to explain the long observed fluctuations in economic activity referred to as the trade or business cycle. The focal point of his analysis is the concept of aggregate demand, i.e. the sum of all expenditures. One man's expenditure is another man's income and employment and when in total this is deficient, national income and employment will decline. Equally, once full employment has been achieved, any increase in expenditure unaccompanied by an increase in output will result in inflation.

The implication is that the Government should attempt to manage the level of aggregate demand, primarily through regulating taxation and public expenditure but with monetary policy in support. In avoiding the complete central planning of totalitarian regimes these methods seemed consistent with free enterprise and liberal democracy.

5. The inflation/unemployment trade-off. This thinking was furthered with the publication in 1958 of an essay by Professor A. W. Phillips, "The Relation between Unemployment and the Rate of Change of Money Wages in the United Kingdom, 1861–1957". He sought to show a regular inverse relationship in which wages rose more rapidly in periods of high employment. Since wages constitute a major element of total costs, when they rose rapidly so would prices.

It followed that if the rate of inflation was considered unacceptable it could be reduced by increasing the rate of unemployment. Keynesian demand management techniques, it was thought, could stabilise unemployment at any desired level. The new economic orthodoxy therefore sought to steer a middle course between too much unemployment and too much inflation.

By the late 1960s and increasingly into the 1970s it became apparent that the steering mechanism no longer worked. This failure had always been predicted by Keynes's critics.

6. The modern monetarists. The new monetary economists, associated particularly with Professor Milton Friedman of the University of Chicago, denied that fiscal manipulation achieved anything other than a reallocation of resources from the private to the public sector. There was no first order effect upon the level of economic activity and employment. This was determined by real factors such as the state of technology, the resourcefulness and enterprise of the people and the institutional framework of the economy. If the latter impeded the operation of markets and the movement of productive resources in the direction where demand lay, then unemployment (overt and in the form of overmanning) would be accompanied by inflation. This appeared increasingly to have been the case in Britain.

7. The fallacy of the inflation/unemployment trade-off. The success of Keynesian techniques in securing high levels of employment in the post-war world was illusory. In the short term the impact of stimulating monetary demand was primarily on income and employment and only marginally on prices. In the longer term of decades, monetary expansion was absorbed almost wholly in higher prices. It did not increase income, output and employment.

Consequently, although *nominal* wages might rise, inflation ensured that *real* wages fell. Only through the acceptance of lower *real* wages could the higher levels of employment be maintained. When labour insisted on sufficiently higher money wages to offset the decline in living standards it succeeded only in pricing itself out of the market.

If the Government wished now to restore the higher employment levels it had two choices. It could continue to stimulate monetary demand, accelerating inflation at a rate greater than could be anticipated by the wage demands of labour. In this way, real wages would remain depressed below a level which labour would willingly have accepted. Or it could achieve the same result politically through a statutory or voluntary incomes policy.

From this point of view incomes policies are to be seen as employment policies, work being shared at lower real wages between a larger number of workers. They have no bearing whatever upon inflation which is induced only by excessive monetary expansion by governments.

APPENDIX II

Bibliography

The following short bibliography is intended as a general guide for further reading.

Aldcroft, D. H. and Richardson, H. W. *The British Economy 1870–1939* (Macmillan, 1969)

Ashworth, W. *An Economic History of England 1870–1939* (Methuen, 1972)

Ashton, T. S. *The Industrial Revolution 1760–1830* (O.U.P., 1969)

Beckerman, W. *The Labour Government's Economic Record, 1964–1970* (Cambridge, 1972)

Beckerman, W. and Associates *The British Economy in 1975* (Cambridge, 1965)

Carus-Wilson, E. M. (ed.) *Essays in Economic History, Vols II and III* (Arnold, 1962)

Chambers, J. D. and Mingay, G. E. *The Agricultural Revolution 1750–1880* (Batsford, 1969)

Cole, G. D. H. and Postgage, R. *The Common People 1746–1946* (Methuen, 1965)

Court, W. H. B. *A Concise Economic History of Britain* (Cambridge, 1954)

Deane, P. and Cole, W. A. *British Economic Growth 1688–1959* (Cambridge, 1969)

Dow, J. C. R. *The Management of the British Economy, 1945–60* (Cambridge, 1970)

Flinn, M. W. *An Economic and Social History of Britain since 1700* (Macmillan, 1963)

Hobsbawm, E. J. *Industry and Empire* (Penguin, 1968)

Lewis, W. A. *Economic Survey 1919–1939* (Allen & Unwin, 1949)

Lipson, E. *The Growth of English Society* (Black, 1959)

Perkin, H. *The Origins of Modern English Society* (Routledge & Kegan Paul, 1972)

Pollard, S. *The Development of the British Economy 1914–1967* (Arnold, 1969)

Sayers, R. S. *A History of Economic Change in England* (O.U.P., 1967)

Worswick, G. D. N. and Ady, P. H. (ed.) *The British Economy 1945–1950* (O.U.P., 1952)

Worswick, G. D. N. and Ady, P. H. (ed.) *The British Economy in the 1950s* (O.U.P., 1962)

Youngson, A. J. *Britain's Economic Growth, 1920–1966* (Unwin, 1967)

The student is also referred to the following series. Economic History Society, *Studies in Economic History* (Macmillan); *Debates in Economic History* (Methuen); *Sources of History Series* (Macmillan); *Fontana Economic History of Europe.*

Useful statistical series are *Abstract of British Historical Statistics*, Mitchell, B. R. and Deane, P. (Cambridge, 1962) and the *Annual Abstract of Statistics* (H.M.S.O.).

Examination Technique

The examination candidate will profit from the following advice.

(1) Read the whole paper, *including any special instructions*, carefully and unhurriedly and make a selection of the questions to be answered.

(2) Apportion the time allowed so that the *required number* of questions are attempted. Failure to complete the paper automatically lowers the maximum possible marks which can be scored. (Remember that the first 5 per cent for any one questions is relatively easy to earn and the last 5 per cent extremely difficult.)

(3) Before attempting a question, read it carefully and be confident that you fully understand what is required. *Then answer to the point and without irrelevancies*.

(4) Treat your answer as an argument in which you are providing the examiner with evidence of the truth of what you write. Plan this argument systematically and give it a logical progression so that you arrive at a natural conclusion. *Avoid making a series of disconnected points which don't lead anywhere*.

(5) Pay attention to the tidy presentation of your work. A carelessly composed paper immediately creates an unfavourable impression.

APPENDIX IV

Examination Questions

Part 1. The rise of laissez-faire

1. What do you understand by the term *laissez-faire*? Why did this theory become so powerful in England in the late eighteenth and early nineteenth centuries, and with what results? (G.C.E. (O), J.M.B.)

2. How far had Britain's economy been prepared for the Industrial Revolution by the middle of the eighteenth century? (G.C.E.(A), J.M.B.)

3. How far is it appropriate to apply the term "revolution" to the industrial and commercial changes of the eighteenth and nineteenth centuries? (G.C.E.(A), J.M.B.)

4. "At one extreme we have Professor Nef tracing the beginnings of the Industrial Revolution back to the middle of the sixteenth century ...; at the other extreme we have Professor Rostow's dramatic compression of the essential transformation into a couple of decades at the end of the eighteenth century." Discuss the problems of defining and dating the Industrial Revolution and indicate where you believe its beginning should be dated. (G.C.E.(A), J.M.B.)

5. "The characteristic of any country before its industrial revolution is poverty." Comment, with reference to Britain in the early eighteenth century. (G.C.E.(A), J.M.B.)

6. "The inadequacy of the word 'industrial' and the overtones of the word 'revolution' make the term 'industrial revolution' a not very useful one for the economic historian." Discuss. (B.Sc.(Econ.) Part 2, London External)

Part 2. Agriculture

7. Were enclosures beneficial or harmful? (G.C.E.(O), J.M.B.)

8. Why was British agriculture prosperous in the third quarter of the nineteenth century, but depressed in the last quarter? (G.C.E.(O), J.M.B.)

9. What were the causes of agricultural prosperity in the third quarter of the nineteenth century? (G.C.E.(O), J.M.B.)

10. Discuss the factors that hastened the pace of agricultural

349

improvement in the late eighteenth century. (G.C.E.(A), J.M.B.)

11. With what justification is the term "Great Depression" applied to the period 1873–96? (G.C.E.(A), J.M.B.)

12. Does the condition of British farming after 1875 prove that the repeal of the Corn Laws was a mistake? (G.C.E.(A), J.M.B.)

13. In what ways did methods of farming change in the eighteenth and early nineteenth centuries, and with what results? (G.C.E.(O), J.M.B.)

14. How was it that English agriculture was able to produce substantial surpluses of grain for export during the first half of the eighteenth century? (G.C.E.(A), J.M.B.)

15. "It was precisely because enclosure released men from the land that it is to be counted among the processes that led to the Industrial Revolution with the higher standards of consumption that this brought with it." Discuss this statement. (G.C.E.(A), J.M.B.)

16. How far can it be said that the Corn Law of 1815 initiated the great debate on free trade? (B.Sc.(Econ.) Part 2, London External)

Part 3. Industry

17. Write briefly about any *four* of the following. (*a*) iron puddling, (*b*) Henry Maudslay, (*c*) the Combination Laws, (*d*) the Limited Liability Acts, (*e*) Henry Bessemer, (*f*) the Local Government Boards, (*g*) Cecil Rhodes, (*h*) the National Insurance Act 1911. (G.C.E.(O), J.M.B.)

18. Outline the main developments in steelmaking in the second half of the nineteenth century, and show their importance to industry generally. (G.C.E.(O), J.M.B.)

19. It is sometimes said that Britain was tending to stagnate economically in the late nineteenth and early twentieth centuries. What may be said for and against this view? (G.C.E.(O), J.M.B.)

20. Explain the importance of the engineering industry to general industrial expansion in the first half of the nineteenth century. (G.C.E.(O), J.M.B.)

21. Describe the changes in the cotton industry before about 1820. (G.C.E.(O), J.M.B.)

22. Discuss the importance of the steam engine in industrial advance before the railway era. (G.C.E.(A), J.M.B.)

23. Why has the cotton industry been regarded as the one most typical of the "Industrial Revolution"? (G.C.E.(A), J.M.B.)

24. Trace and account for the changes in the prosperity of the cotton industry since 1914. (G.C.E.(A), J.M.B.)

25. "The British coal industry in 1914 was already infected with ills which became apparent later." Discuss this view. (G.C.E.(A), J.M.B.)

26. Discuss the consequences for the British iron and steel industry of the technical changes it experienced between 1850 and 1914. (G.C.E.(A), J.M.B.)

27. "Once an economy is on the move, innovations become cumulative." Discuss this statement with reference to technical developments in British industry before 1850. (G.C.E.(A), J.M.B.)

28. "A full knowledge of the position and problems of the coal industry is essential to a real understanding of the economic and social history of the 1920s." Discuss this statement. (G.C.E.(A), J.M.B.)

29. Examine the factors which helped to determine the location of industry during the second half of the eighteenth century. (B.Sc.(Econ.), Part 2, London External)

30. Analyse the reasons for industrial unrest between 1914 and 1926. (B.Sc.(Econ.), Part 2, London External)

Part 4. Commerce

31. What reforms were made in currency and banking between 1819 and 1844? (G.C.E.(O), J.M.B.)

32. What were the effects of foreign competition upon British trade and industry between the two world wars? (G.C.E.(O), J.M.B.)

33. What factors brought about economic recovery in Britain between 1932 and 1939? (G.C.E.(O), J.M.B.)

34. Explain the nature, and discuss the consequences, of the "South Sea Bubble". (G.C.E.(A), J.M.B.)

35. Illustrate and account for the spread of joint stock organisation between 1850 and 1914. (G.C.E.(A), J.M.B.)

36. Why, and by what steps, did Britain abandon free trade? (G.C.E.(A), J.M.B.)

37. Why did the country banks increase between 1750 and 1815? What were their advantages and defects? (G.C.E.(A), J.M.B.)

38. In what respects were the economic circumstances of Britain less favourable after the First World War than they had been before it? (G.C.E.(A), J.M.B.)

39. What measures were taken by the Government to encourage recovery from the slump of the early 1930s? How successful were they? (G.C.E.(A), J.M.B.)

40. Examine the role of overseas trade in promoting economic growth in Britain during the eighteenth century. (G.C.E.(A), J.M.B.)

41. Consider whether the structure of the banking system was a significant cause of economic instability during the first half of the nineteenth century. (G.C.E.(A), J.M.B.)

42. "Between 1870 and 1914 Britain's balance of payments and indeed the whole pattern of her overseas economic relations were becoming dependent on earnings from overseas investment, banking, shipping and other 'invisibles'". Discuss this statement. (G.C.E.(A), J.M.B.)

43. Analyse the structure of the English banking system at the end of the eighteenth century. (B.Sc.(Econ.) Part 2, London External)

44. Why did the growth of real income per head of the population become markedly slower between 1896 and 1914? (B.Sc.(Econ.) Part 2, London External)

45. Analyse the structure of the English capital market between 1830 and 1855. (B.Sc.(Econ.) Part 2, London External)

46. Compare and contrast the major features of British foreign trade in 1760–93 with those of 1875–1914. (B.Sc.(Econ.) Part 2, London External)

Part 5. Transport

47. Trace the development of railways to the middle of the nineteenth century, and describe their effects upon trade and industry. (G.C.E.(O), J.M.B.)

48. What changes occurred in the shipping and shipbuilding industries during the second half of the nineteenth century? (G.C.E.(O), J.M.B.)

49. Show how transport developments aided Britain's economic expansion between 1750 and 1825. (G.C.E.(O), J.M.B.)

50. Why were improvements needed in road, river and canal transport in the eighteenth century? What improvements had been made by about 1820? (G.C.E.(O), J.M.B.)

51. Discuss the economic and social effects of the British railways between 1850 and 1900. (G.C.E.(A), J.M.B.)

52. Show the importance of Brindley and the Duke of Bridgewater in the development of inland transport. (G.C.E.(A), J.M.B.)

53. Show how steam navigation developed as compared with sail in the second half of the nineteenth century. (G.C.E.(A), J.M.B.)

54. Examine the growth of shipping shown in the following statistics. Why did sail stay so important for so long?

Total shipping tonnage registered in the U.K.

Annual Average	Sailing ships ('000 tons)	Steam ships ('000 tons)
1790–9	1,443	—
1800–9	2,003	—
1810–19	2,379	1
1820–9	2,291	17
1830–9	2,278	52
1840–9	3,009	123
1850–9	3,867	319
1860–9	4,590	724
1870–9	4,240	1,847

(From P. Mathias, *The First Industrial Nation*) (G.C.E.(A), J.M.B.)

55. Assess the economic and social importance of the creation of the railway network between 1830 and 1850. (G.C.E.(A), J.M.B.)

56. Compare the difficulties facing the transport system in 1820 with those facing the system in 1920. (B.Sc.(Econ.) Part 2, London External)

57. Consider the policy of the British Government towards the transport industry during the inter-war years of the present century. (B.Sc.(Econ.) Part 2, London External)

58. What was the significance of the amalgamation movement in the history of English railways between 1839 and 1876? (B.Sc.(Econ.) Part 2, London External)

Part 6. Social developments (with reference to Appendix I)

59. Why was the poor law in need of reform in the early 1830s

and what remedies were prescribed by the Poor Law Amendment Act of 1834? (G.C.E.(O), J.M.B.)

60. Describe the developments in elementary and secondary education in England between 1833 and 1914. (G.C.E.(O), J.M.B.)

61. In what ways did Liberal governments lay the foundations of the Welfare State between 1906 and 1914? (G.C.E.(O), J.M.B.)

62. Did the Industrial Revolution raise or lower the general standard of living before the middle of the nineteenth century? (G.C.E.(O), J.M.B.)

63. Compare the aims and organisation of the "New Model" unions of the 1850s and 1860s with the "New Unionism" of the 1880s and 1890s. (G.C.E.(O), J.M.B.)

64. In what ways were urban living conditions improved in the second half of the nineteenth century? (G.C.E.(O), J.M.B.)

65. How and with what success did trade unions deal with the problems facing them in the first half of the nineteenth century? (G.C.E.(O), J.M.B.)

66. What were the chief causes of poverty in the eighteenth century? How were the poor relieved? (G.C.E.(O), J.M.B.)

67. What were the chief economic and social problems facing Britain after the Second World War? (G.C.E.(O), J.M.B.)

68. Why was there serious unemployment from 1918 to 1939 and what steps were taken to deal with it? (G.C.E.(O), J.M.B.)

69. Describe and discuss the fiscal policy of Sir Robert Walpole. (G.C.E.(A), J.M.B.)

70. Examine the connection between land enclosures and pauperism in the eighteenth and early nineteenth centuries. (G.C.E.(A), J.M.B.)

71. With what justice has Malthus been called an "economic pessimist"? (G.C.E.(A), J.M.B.)

72. "Hitherto it is questionable if all the mechanical inventions yet made have lightened the day's toil of any human being." Explain and discuss this view of J. S. Mill. (G.C.E.(A), J.M.B.)

73. Why did Gladstone want to abolish the income tax and why could he not do so? (G.C.E.(A), J.M.B.)

74. Why was a national system of education delayed until 1870? (G.C.E.(A), J.M.B.)

75. Examine the aims and achievements of "new model" unionism. (G.C.E.(A), J.M.B.)

76. How far did the working classes have social security before 1914? (G.C.E.(A), J.M.B.)

77. Discuss the social problems created by town growth to 1850. (G.C.E.(A), J.M.B.)

78. Show how and why the Combination Laws came to be imposed and discuss their effect on the early trade union movement. (G.C.E.(A), J.M.B.)

79. Account for the rise of the factory reform movement and for its concentration on conditions in cotton factories. (G.C.E.(A), J.M.B.)

80. In what ways can the 1870s be regarded as a turning-point in British economic history? (G.C.E.(A), J.M.B.)

81. Explain the factors influencing the growth of trade union membership as indicated in the following figures.

Trade Union Membership in the United Kingdom
(*thousands*)

1895	1,504	1925	5,506
1900	2,022	1930	4,842
1905	1,997	1935	4,867
1910	2,565	1940	6,613
1915	4,359	1945	7,875
1920	8,348	1950	9,289

(From Judith Ryder and H. Silver, *Modern English Society*.) (G.C.E.(A), J.M.B.)

82. On what grounds can the Education Act of 1902 be regarded as a landmark in the development of the State system of education? (B.Sc.(Econ.) Part 2, London External)

83. How do you account for the slow growth of trade unionism between 1760 and 1825? (B.Sc.(Econ.) Part 2, London External)

84. Account for the decline of the rate of population growth after 1881. (B.Sc.(Econ.) Part 2, London External)

85. Why did the State promote education schemes before it promoted insurance schemes? (B.Sc.(Econ.) Part 2, London External)

86. The partial revival of trade in 1843 marked the beginning of a new era in trade union policy. How far was this true? (B.Sc.(Econ.) Part 2, London External)

87. Consider the statement that "the poor law problem with which the Act of 1834 attempted to deal was essentially rural". (B.Sc.(Econ.) Part 2, London External)

Index

Details of some other Macdonald & Evans
publications on related subjects can be found
on the following pages.

For a full list of titles and prices write for the
FREE Macdonald & Evans Educational Studies
catalogue and/or complete M & E Handbook
list, available from Department BP1,
Macdonald & Evans Ltd., Estover Road,
Plymouth PL6 7PZ

British Economic and Social History 1700—1977
J. WALKER, *revised by* C. W. MUNN

This book describes some of the more important social and economic consequences of the industrialisation of British society since 1700. Topics dealt with include developments in industry and agriculture, means of communication, overseas commerce, banking and finance, social reforms and working-class movements. For this latest edition, the text has been updated and a chapter has been added which details developments since the mid-1960s.

British Political History 1784—1939
S. T. MILLER

This HANDBOOK has been produced for all those who are beginning a study of nineteenth-century British and Imperial history leading to the G.C.E. "O" and "A" Level examinations and their equivalents. Covering most of the developments in government up to the Second World War, it will also be of value to students of British Government and Politics in both schools and colleges.

Economic Geography
H. ROBINSON

This HANDBOOK is invaluable for professional students taking Economic Geography at intermediate level and for students on higher level BEC courses. For this new edition the text has been fully revised and the statistical matter has been updated, using the most recent figures available.
Illustrated

Economics for "O" Level
L. B. CURZON

This HANDBOOK is based on the "O" Level syllabus and will be most useful to students preparing for this examination and its equivalents. The latest edition has been prepared to take account of the changing economic scene. The statistics have been updated and further material has been included on the commercial banks.
Illustrated

European History 1789–1914
C. A. LEEDS
This HANDBOOK is intended for the student who wishes to examine in detail the political history of Europe in the nineteenth century, and should be especially useful as an introduction for those studying for "A" Level or beginning a degree course. Special attention is paid throughout to constitutional, diplomatic and military factors, and four chapters consider the activities of European powers in Africa and Asia. For the latest edition, the text has been thoroughly revised.
Illustrated

Europe Since the Second World War
J. R. THACKRAH
This HANDBOOK sets out in detail the political and diplomatic events of the last thirty years, and examines the unique contribution of Europe to world affairs. It places particular emphasis on the last decade, about which little has been written. The book is intended for students preparing for examinations at "A" and "S" Level, and students on courses leading to a degree or professional qualification, including those with a legal content.

Twentieth-Century History 1900–45
C. A. LEEDS
This HANDBOOK approaches an important period of world history from two points of view: firstly covering certain problems and issues in world affairs which affected all countries, and secondly focusing on special regions and their significance in international relations. It is aimed primarily at C.S.E. or "O" Level students but will also be most useful as an introductory or revision text for "A" Level. The text is fully supported with detailed maps.
Illustrated

Twentieth-Century History: Since 1945
C. A. LEEDS

This is a companion volume to *Twentieth-Century History 1900—45* and brings the discussion of world history up to the present day. It is aimed primarily at C.S.E. or "O" Level students, but will also be most useful as an introductory or revision text for "A" Level.

Illustrated